*The Cape Fear*

# BOOKS IN THE RIVERS OF AMERICA SERIES

*Rivers of America*

*Edited by Carl Carmer*

*As planned and started by*
*Constance Lindsay Skinner*

*Associate Editor Jean Crawford*

*Art Editor Ben Feder*

# *The* CAPE FEAR

## *by Malcolm Ross*

### *Holt, Rinehart and Winston*

*New York : Chicago : San Francisco*

*To three along the Cape Fear:*
Malcolm Fowler
Jack Crane
Paul Green

# Contents

## II

### THE NINETEENTH CENTURY: REVOLUTIONISTS INTO REBELS

## III

### THE TWENTIETH CENTURY: LONGINGS FOR LOST INNOCENCE

•

*The Cape Fear*

VIRGINIA
NORTH
Tar
Bennett's House
HILLSBORO
DURHAM
RALEIGH
New Hope R.
CHAPEL HILL
QUAKERS
BURLINGTON
Battle of Guilford Courthouse
GREENSBORO
Haw R.
Mermaid Point
Buckhorn Falls
Smilie's Falls
Battle of Alamance
WINSTON-SALEM
MORAVIANS
HIGH POINT
LILLINGTON
HIGHLAND SCOTS
Little R.
FT. BRAGG
Deep R.
Naomi Falls
Lower
FAYETTEVILLE (CROSS CREEK)
PIEDMONT
CORNWALLIS 1781
Pinehurst
Rockfish
FALL-LINE (approx. 900')
SHERMAN 1865
CHARLOTTE
Kings Mountain
SOUTH
CAR
Pee Dee R.

# CAPE FEAR RIVER

Area of Detail Map

# I : The Eighteenth Century

*Europeans into Americans*

# 1 : The "Cape of Feare"

A naked, bleak elbow of sand jutting far out into the ocean. Immediately in its front are the Frying Pan Shoals pushing out still farther twenty miles to the south. Together they stand for warning and for woe . . . the kingdom of silence and awe, disturbed by no sound save the seagull's shriek and the breakers' roar . . . Imagination cannot adorn it. Romance cannot hallow it. Local pride cannot soften it. There it stands today, bleak and threatening and pitiless . . . And as its nature, so its name, is now, always has been, and always will be the Cape of Fear.

> ——George Davis, Attorney General,
> Confederate States of America

The rivers of the southeastern Atlantic coast change character three times during descent from their highland origins to their tidewater merger with the sea. They begin either as mountain springs in the Great Smokies and Blue Ridge or as meadow rills on the slopes of the piedmont. In their swift-water youth they cascade from the heights until they reach a physical feature common to them all, the fall-line, a granite ridge extending southwesterly from Virginia into Georgia. With their tumble over this ridge they are on gently shelving land over which they meander a hundred miles or more to the sea. In their final phase they become wide tidewater streams, with the trees on their banks replaced by tall marsh grasses and gulls announcing the near presence of the sea.

The Cape Fear River shares these characteristics with its sister rivers, the Neuse and the Tar to the north, the Pee Dee and the Savannah to the south. The force of gravity and the nature of the terrain account readily enough for these river changes. But there are other aspects-in-common which require explanation by the geologist.

From the fall-line on, over the coastal plain, each river swings in a southeasterly parabola, an inverted comma with its tail in the mountains and its head in the sea. Had the Savannah taken an expectedly due east course to the sea, its mouth would be at Wilmington, where the Cape Fear empties. The mouth of the Cape Fear would have been north of Hatteras. The explanation of the southward bend in each river begins with the cataclysmic changes in climate during the ice ages.

The last warm interglacial period—say twenty-five thousand years ago—raised the ocean level up to the fall-line. When a global freeze again drew on the ocean waters to form the polar ice-caps, the receding sea left behind a sand overburden through which the rainfalls of the eastern Appalachian slopes would have to churn their paths to the sea. In the same way that rivulets from an ebbing tide leave runnels on a seashore beach, the mountain-bred waters cut channels in the interglacial sand which at long last became the Tar, the Neuse, the Cape Fear, the Pee Dee, and the Savannah.

The parabolic curve which they own in common was imposed during their sand-cutting era by the force of the earth's rotation acting upon the force of their flow. The effect was first defined in 1859 by a mathematician, Professor W. Ferrell, who held: "In whatever direction a body moves on the surface of the earth [a river on land, a hurricane at sea], there is a force arising from the earth's rotation which deflects it to the right in the northern hemisphere but to the left in the southern."

In 1870 the first State Geologist of North Carolina, W. C. Kerr, applied Ferrell's law to show how the Cape Fear dug its parabolic course to the sea. The flow of the river's piedmont tributaries was not affected, since the sea's sand deposits had not reached the uplands. But at the fall-line where the river must begin to force its way seaward through the overburden, the component forces of water flow and earth rotation began to nudge the channel southward.

Two other facets of the river's sand-carving would be of im-

mense importance to the first European settlers. W]
had eroded away most of the overburden, the earth-rotation
halted and the senescent river stopped gnawing at its west bank.
The land over which it had swept would be low and marshy, only
in parts fit for farming. The high ground on the west bank would
be the pioneers' timber-and cropland.

The places where the river deposited its sand would also shape
a people's future. The great bulk of the overburden went out to
sea to form the Atlantic shelf. Along the north-south Atlantic
coastline some surplus sand was left as the barrier now known as
the Outer Banks. Behind these were formed shallow sounds—Albemarle, Pamlico, Core, and Bogue—into which the Roanoke, the
Tar, and the Neuse rivers emptied. The only North Carolina river
to break through the barrier to the open sea was the Cape Fear.
But in terms of the convenience of sailormen, the waning strength
of the sand-sculptor could not force its way boldly into deep water. The carrier stream, the fresh-water Upper Cape Fear, petered
out into a salt estuary thirty miles long, protected on its seaward
side by a long sandspit. In disgorging the last of the movable upcountry sand, the river laid down a dragon's tail of submerged
shoals running twenty miles due south from the point of land
forming the seaward side of the estuary.

Early European adventurers named the hidden sandspit the
Frying Pan Shoals. From dread experience they called the exposed landfall the Cape of Feare.

•

Two sixteenth century navigators contrived to thread the channel
past the Shoals into the salt-water estuary. Giovanni de Verraz-
zano, a Florentine, in 1524 explored the Lower Cape Fear and
returned to describe to his employer, Francis I of France, a region
of huge trees and odoriferous flowers, inhabited by natives
charmed with their first sight of white men. Francis, occupied
with European politics, failed to act on the report.

In 1526 Lucas Vasquéz de Ayllón, in attempting to plant a

Spanish colony there, lost to the Frying Pan its first European ship. Ayllón stayed on the Cape Fear only long enough to build a new ship.

The early English colonizers never solved the riddle of the hidden shoals. In 1585 Sir Richard Grenville, leading Sir Walter Raleigh's first expedition, fell "in great danger of a wracke on a beach called the Cape of Feare." Two years later the same siren shoals almost ended Governor John White's journey up the coast to Roanoke Island. For more than a century there were no attempts at colonization south of the Virginia Capes.

England had a claim to the territory based on John Cabot's 1497 discoveries, and in 1629 Charles I moved to assert it by granting his attorney general, Sir Robert Heath, a patent to the vacant coastline from Virginia to Spanish Florida and extending west to the "South Seas." In the monarch's honor it was first called Carolana. Sir Robert did little to exploit his title to a territory into which the empire of Alexander the Great would have fitted snugly. When its absentee owner finally did begin negotiations with some French associates, Charles frowned on foreign participation. Sir Robert's title, except for some rear-guard legal action, was made extinct. During the eleven years of Oliver Cromwell's Roundhead regime, the Indians held their natural title without ever learning that their hunting grounds had been honored with the name of a King whose own subjects had chopped off his head.

In 1660 Charles II regained the Throne. As reward to the generals, admirals and statesmen who had aided his restoration, Charles handed over Carolina to eight Lords Proprietors, retaining a one-quarter right to the gold which it was supposed the Indians were hoarding.

The name Clarendon County, after Edward Hyde, Earl of Clarendon, was given to a vaguely defined region running south from Albemarle Sound to Florida. It included the Cape Fear country, to which various groups now made their bid for land patents.

The first settlers were Plymouth Colony Puritans seeking a

warmer climate and a less hardscrabble soil. They sent one of their sea captains, William Hilton, on an exploratory voyage. Upon his report of good grazing lands along the Cape Fear, a ship was sent there with a cargo of hogs and cattle. The livestock survived to feed other mouths. The Puritans themselves returned to New England, leaving a lugubrious message on a post. Two years later, Captain Hilton—now in the employ of a Barbados company —found the message.

It remains a teasing question what fearful mishaps made the New Englanders abandon the place. The Indians were peaceful. There was no sign of catastrophe. Had, perhaps, the canny New Englanders invented a slander which would add further terror to a region already named the Cape of Feare? Were they hoping to keep others away in expectation of their own return?

Captain Hilton, in a report to the Lords Proprietors on his second voyage, denies the slander without saying what it was:

> Whereas there was a writing left on a Post at the Point of Cape Fair River, by these New-England men that left cattel with the Indians there, the Contents thereof tended not only to the disparagement of the land about the said River, but also to the discouragement of all those that should hereafter come into these parts to settle; In answer to that scandalous Writing, we whose names are underwritten do affirm, That we have seen facing on both sides of the River, and branches of Cape-Fair aforesaid, as good Land, and as well timbered, as any we have seen in any other part of the world, sufficient to accommodate thousands of our English Nation, lyeing commodiously by the said River.
>
> Arthur Long<br>William Hilton<br>Peter Fabrian

The inventive Hilton's change of the river's name to "Cape Fair" did not stick, but his favorable report stimulated potential settlement. His was the first written report on the Cape Fear.

Dropping anchor in the estuary on October 12, 1663, Hilton

spent two months probing its fresh-water tributaries. He found oaks rising sixty feet to the first branches, "innumerable Pines, tall and good for masts and boards . . . good pasture land . . . the woods stor'd with abundance of Deer and Turkies everywhere. . . . Ducks, Tiels, Widgeon and in the woods great flocks of Parakeeto's."

He reported a visit to an Indian town where the chief man "made a large speech with great signs of Love and Friendship." A hostile incident had occurred the day before when an Indian had shot an arrow at the longboat. Hilton showed the chief the arrow stuck in the boat's side. So stricken was the chief that "when he heard of the affront we had received, it caused him to cry."

As if this sentimental display were not enough to atone for the rudeness of his tribesmen, the chief now presented Hilton with "two very handsome proper young Indian women." The Elizabethan connotation of "proper" must have undergone change, for these handsome maidens "crowded in and were hardly persuaded to go out again."

A citation for gallantry goes to Hilton. His happy relationships might have remained between the white colonists and these gentle Indians, easily given to tears and gifts of Indian maidens. But within four years the first settlers were sending Indian children away, ostensibly to be Christianized, actually to be sold into slavery.

•

On December 1, 1663, Hilton bought "the River and the land of Cape Fair of Wattacoosa." A celebration feast followed to which the Indians "brought aboard a very good and fat Beef, also fat and very large Swine . . . they may thank their friends of New England who brought their hogs to so fair a market." In addition to English beef, one larder-filling hunt provided: "4 swans, ten geese, 29 Cranes, forty Duck and Mallard, three dozen of Parakeeto's and seven dozen of other small Fowls as Curlues, and

Plovers." In the shallow waters there was abundance of "Shel-fish called Horse-feet," more familiar on modern menus as cherrystone clams.

Hilton made this voyage on behalf of the "Corporation of the Barbadian Adventurers." The Island of Barbados was rich from sugar but overcrowded. The islanders had commissioned Hilton to discover whether the mainland was suitable to supply the wine, silk, olive oil, and almonds which England needs must import from Mediterranean countries. So, after viewing the Cape Fear, Hilton sailed to the harbors and tidal rivers of what is now South Carolina. His report on that region's climate persuaded the Barbadian Adventurers that their destiny lay there. The Lords Proprietors, reading the same report, agreed with the Barbadians and had one of their members, John Yeamans, created knight baronet with authority to colonize this promising fount of riches.

There ensued a period of confusion on who had proprietory rights to colonize. The Plymouth Colony gave some color to the theory that their message on a post had been a stalking horse by now sending agents to London demanding rights to a Cape Fear charter. One unsanctioned Barbadian group impatiently set out to take lands on the Cape Fear whether their expedition was blest or unblest by the Lords Proprietors.

Henry Vassall, with his son John as his lieutenant, sailed from Barbados with a company of settlers and established them on the west bank of the Lower Cape Fear estuary. Others joined them from Virginia and New England. From the first all went well. In two years there were frame houses as far as sixty miles up the fresh-water river. Cattle fattened in the meadows, swine on the forest mast. They were fortunate in "a rich fatt soil, black mould on the topp and under mixt with a soft redd marles."

An Indian trading post was built at the mouth of Old Town Creek. This became Charles Town, not to be confused with the later Charleston, South Carolina. Carolus Rex must have been pleased with the names of Charles Town on what they now called the Charles River in the Province of Carolina. The Lords Proprietors gave the settlement a semblance of legitimacy by appointing John Vassall surveyor and Robert Sandford secretary.

Sir John Yeamans as governor of Clarendon County held authority in both the Cape Fear and southward regions. He now sailed from Barbados to explore his demesne, bound first for the Cape Fear and leading the flotilla on his flyboat, the *Sir John*. A gale discouraged his first try at navigating the channel through the Frying Pan. The second run of the *Sir John* into the maelstrom was described by Robert Sandford in a confusion of words and syntax which somehow captured the confusion of wind, tide, and scudding spray which sent the flyboat to its doom:

> . . . for returning with a formable wind in a second viewe of the entrance, but, destituted of all pilates, save their own eyes (which the flattering gale that conducted them did also delude by covering the rough visage of their objected dangers with a thick veile of smooth waters) they stranded their vessel on the Middle Ground of the Harbour's mouth, where the Ebbe tide presently left her, and the wind with its own multiplyed forces and the auxiliaries of the tide of flood beat her to peeces.

Sir John and the crew escaped. A ship under Captain Stanyon was dispatched to Barbados for replenishments. Although these eventually arrived, the Frying Pan put up stout resistance. Captain Stanyon went mad and threw himself overboard. His second in command "Yett assisted by a miraculous Providence after many wanderings, brought her safe to Charles River in Clarendon, her desired Port and Haven."

It must have been about this time that the name Charles River was dropped as no longer worthy of the sovereign's name. Cape Fear it again became and stayed.

Sir John Yeamans sailed southward to tidal rivers not guarded by a Cerberus of sand, spume, and waterspouts.

The Vassalls' settlement on the Cape Fear might have survived without the aid of Sir John Yeamans, except for the whimsical application of the land policies of the Lords Proprietors. Their broad charter, the "Declarations and Proposals," applied to all of Clarendon County. Under it a typical settler, let us say on the Upper Cape Fear, had acquired 350 acres, 100 each for himself, his wife and child, and 50 acres of rich black soil, 150 acres of pasture, a 100-acre wood lot and 50 acres of marshland. In two years of labor the family had converted this into a balanced and self-sustaining farm. Now came the application of a second proprietary document, the "Concessions and Agreement." This edict, decreed a uniform system of land distribution, a sensible scheme had the land been uniformly forest or arable, but disastrous when it carved up the settlers' variegated holdings. The upper Cape Fear family discovered that its new allotment excluded their house and the garden, leaving them with an equal acreage of marsh. The quitrent applied to all acreage, good or worthless. The absentee landlords had cut the heart out of the settlers' incentive.

John Vassall drew up a petition for redress. Governor Yeamans declined to sign it. In London Henry Vassall appealed to the now deaf ears of the Lords Proprietors. The Barbados Adventurers were too wrapped up in their southern venture even to answer a request for a ship to take the Cape Fear colonists away. John Vassall had better luck with Massachusetts, from which supplies were sent.

By that time (1667) the sufferers from negligence in high places became trapped by their own neglect of the feelings of the Indians. On the pretext of sending them to be Christianized, the settlers had sold Indian children as slaves. The Indians declared war. If arrows were not effective against guns, they could at least kill the settlers' cattle.

John Vassall tried to hold the disintegrating structure together. Would twenty men remain with him? Would ten? No. So Vassall found a ship to transport the sick and weak. The others made their way with Vassall overland to Virginia.

The logs of the Charles Town cabins rotted into the forest floor. The river that had been the Jordan to the Spanish in 1526, the Cape of Feare to the victims of the Frying Pan, the Cape Fair to those who tried to conjure away the curse put on it by the New England cattle raisers, and the Charles for the cozening of a distant monarch, now reverted to being the Waccamaw. Over the next half century the Indians held their oyster feasts undisturbed. When armed white men crossed the valley, the Indians took forest cover. In revenge for their lost children, they massacred crews and passengers when ships were wrecked on the Shoals.

# 2 : *Setting the Stage*
# *for Settlement*

*In 1660's*

All Atlantic coast colonies except the Cape Fear were prospering during the years of the failure of Vassall's settlement. At Massachusetts Bay Colony, Harvard College was entering its fourth decade. In 1664 England took over the Hudson from the Dutch and the Delaware from the Swedes. Virginia was building in brick out of tobacco profits. The Albemarle settlement, 150 miles north of the Cape Fear, had a governor appointed by the Lords Proprietors. At a like distance to the south Sir John Yeamans was laying out a town on a point where the Ashley and Cooper rivers meet. The Cape Fear was at the center of three hundred miles of wilderness.

An interplay between the Albemarle and Charleston settlements began in the second decade of the eighteenth century when South Carolinians marched to avenge a Tuscarora massacre of Albemarle people. Two years later an Albemarle expedition went to the rescue of Charleston from attacking Yemassee Indians. In crossing and recrossing the Cape Fear on these expeditions, the Indian fighters took note of an empty salt-water harbor bordered by thousands of acres of longleaf pines. When the times became out of joint in their own communities, they would converge on the Cape Fear, claim plantation grants from the Frying Pan to the forks of the fresh waters, and make the estuary their private lake.

The men who began this occupation of the Lower Cape Fear in 1725 were of the same ilk, Irish and English adventurers with the money to acquire land and with black slaves to work it. They were trained as soldiers, lawyers, merchants. By blood and intermarriage, and the charm to win like-minded men to their side, they became known as The Family. Their role in the half century before the opening of the American Revolution would be to support their own interests against proprietary and royal governors.

It required six years for the Lords Proprietors to produce the "Fundamental Constitutions for the Government of the Carolinas." This was not through indifference. They knew what they had. Every one of them in England owned his thousands of acres of deer park and income-producing farms. Overseas—if each eighty-mile grant on the Atlantic coast were merely extended three hundred miles back toward its "South Seas" western boundary—each now owned a million and a half acres and the right to establish laws concerning its settlement.

Catastrophe intervened. In the England of 1665 the plague killed ninety thousand people. A year later the Great Fire of London destroyed in four days thirteen thousand two hundred houses and eighty-nine churches. When the City began to rebuild, the Lords Proprietors were ready to inform the English public on what terms they might acquire land in Carolina. Here are the main tenets of the Lords Proprietors' "Grand Model" for a New World civilization:

> Establishment of the Anglican Church in America, with the Bishop of London to hold the power to make all appointments of vicars.
>
> Creation of a New World aristocracy, a Palatine to correspond to a Duke, a Landgrave to an Earl, a Cassique to a knight baronet.
>
> The new nobility, through a Grand Council, to have complete judicial authority and control of legislation.

Two fifths of Carolina land to go to the new nobility: 72,000 acres to a Landgrave, 24,000 acres to a Cassique.

One fifth of the land to be the personal property of the Lords Proprietors; two fifths to be open to settlers at an annual quitrent of ha'penny the acre.

The white workers on the nobles' estates to be "perpetual leetmen," bound for all time, and their descendants, to their lord's land and service.

Black slavery to be legal. (The settlers would interpret this clause as freedom to make slaves of Indian women, children, and the braves captured in battle.)

A concession to liberal opinion appeared in a clause granting Carolina settlers the same rights as enjoyed by citizens in England. The document's over-all intention was to "avoid creating a numerous Democracy."

This potpourri of feudal and liberal thinking was declared to be "forever unalterable." It was amended four times before the attempt to make it permanent was defeated by the New World settlers. Still, the notion of milking the colonial cow for England's benefit lingered long after the disillusioned Lords Proprietors sold their grants to George II in 1729.

In hindsight the Proprietors' Fundamental Constitutions have been called "a strange admixture of unmitigated folly and theoretical wisdom." Certainly it was folly for the best minds of Restoration England to suppose that a Carolina "leetman" would scrape the knee to milord Landgrave in a wilderness three thousand miles from Berkeley Square. Nevertheless the thinking of the Lords Proprietors was in sound support of their own stakes in England. Since their folly and their hopes alike came to grief among the adventurer-planters of the Lower Cape Fear, and since opposition to the Proprietors molded the character of that region, it is pertinent to see just what the great men of the Restoration had in mind.

They hated the Presbyterian fanatics who had put the flowing curls of Charles the First on the block in 1649. Now it was essential that America would have an Established Church with its livings controlled by London.

During the Protectorate, these men had been reviled, driven into exile, and their estates confiscated by the Roundheads. In America, they realized, they must not permit any extension of Roundhead democracy. Whatever feudal loyalty to the King could be salvaged from unruly mobs must in Carolina be attached to the person and image of the Landgrave, and he in gratitude and self-interest must see to it that there should be no uprisings of the "numerous Democracy." This was the "Grand Model's" central intent, reflecting many centuries of Europe's struggles to bring order out of the collapse of Rome.

Funds for the salaries of proprietary governors, judges, surveyors, and rent collectors were to come from the settlers' quitrents—fixed amounts which relieved the payer from feudal service. The modest ha'penny per acre became a substantial sum when multiplied by millions. As rewards to themselves the Proprietors would take quitrents on the one fifth of the land they had reserved in the Grand Model.

The clause granting to Americans the same rights as citizens in England reflects the private philosophy of the two men assigned to produce a workable charter for Carolina, Lord Proprietor Anthony Ashley Cooper and his secretary John Locke. Living under Lord Ashley's roof, Locke the philosopher must have considered how far he and his patron could go in inserting a rights clause in the Grand Model without at the same time encouraging an abominated democracy.

The other seven Proprietors were not disturbed by these quibbles. All rights were lodged in themselves to bestow or deny, this by dint of restoring Charles Stuart to the line of succession. George Monck, Duke of Albemarle, had convened the Parliament which invited Charles to return as King. Sir John Colleton had spent £140,000 in Charles's cause, with William Earl of Craven not far behind in generosity. Sir George Carteret, ablest seaman

of his time, had defended the Isle of Jersey against the Roundheads. Edward Hyde, Earl of Clarendon, in 1660 had secretly married his daughter Anne to Charles's brother James, and so was to
have two Queens, Mary and Anne, as grandchildren.

Their names are on our maps. Albemarle Sound, Craven
County, Carteret County, Granville County, the Ashley and the
Cooper rivers, and Charleston remain in the Carolinas as reminders of the puissant Lords Proprietors and their Merrie Monarch.
Compared to these the homely American name of Goose Creek
lacks grandeur; yet it was the "Goose Creek Faction" which first
upset proprietary government in South Carolina and then migrated to the Lower Cape Fear to become "The Family," gadfly to
proprietary and royal governors alike.

Leaders in the Goose Creek Faction were the Moores. Their
line stems from Roger Moore, descendant of Irish kings and
leader of an Irish rebellion during the Roundhead wars. The first
Moore in Carolina was his son James, who joined the Charleston
colony and married Sir John Yeamans' stepdaughter, Margaret
Berringer. She bore him nine children, of whom James, Maurice,
Roger, and Nathaniel were to be the Cape Fear pioneers.

As the sparks fly upward, the Moores were born to trouble,
most of it of their own contriving; and when the sparks flickered
and died, there sat a Moore on a few thousand additional acres
and a weapon in hand to defend them.

James Moore the first became Proprietary Governor of South
Carolina in 1701. Since he was the last of the Moores to pretend
any loyalty to the Lords Proprietors, he stands on a dividing line
between Old World obeisance to rank and a cocky New World
liking to run its own affairs.

The hatreds left by the English Civil War were still in the
hearts of James Moore's generation. He would have heard from
his father's lips the story of war between brothers—kinfolk killed,
scorched earth, and confiscations. So James Moore served the Proprietors who had saved the Throne for Charles. Yet in the next
generation a Goose Creek planter revolt would oust South Caroli-

na's last proprietary government and elect James Moore the son to
be their governor.

Perhaps along Goose Creek there was some miasmic exhalation
which made people on its banks contentious and bold in support
of their fortunes. Indian trading and Indian fighting inspired in
them an equal fervor. In 1712 James the son was of an age to lead
an expedition northward against the Tuscaroras. The New Bern
colony on the Neuse River had cheated the Indians in trade and
had taken game, ammunition, and arms away from them. The
Indians had saved up their resentments until one September
morning in 1711 when five hundred braves in small bands drifted
into New Bern, pretending friendly errands. Within two hours of
the signal for attack they slaughtered 130 settlers. Infants they
swung against trees. Stakes were driven through women's bodies.
In one account, the pillage is so unlike Indian warfare as to sug-
gest a renegade white among them. Says Samuel A'Court Ashe:

> Bodies were fancifully arrayed by the savages in their wild and
> merry glee. Mr. Nevill, an old gentleman, was laid on his floor with a
> clean pillow beneath his head, which was ornamented with his
> wife's headdress, while Mrs. Nevill was set upon her knees in the
> chimney corner, her hands lifted up as though in prayer; and a
> son was laid out in the yard with a pillow under his head and a
> bunch of rosemary at his nose.

At New Bern's first call on South Carolina for help, "Tuscarora
Jack" Barnwell marched a mixed force of whites and friendly Indians three hundred miles north to the stricken Neuse. He defeated the Tuscaroras but left an uneasy truce, many of his men
having hurried away to sell Indian captives at the going rate of
£10 per head. Next year James Moore headed the second punitive expedition with thirty-three whites and one thousand Indians.
At Fort Nohoroco on Contentia Creek, March 25, 1712, Moore
broke the power and spirit of the Tuscaroras. His score: "Prisoners 392, Scolps 193 . . . at least 200 Kill'd & Burnt in ye fort." A

remnant of the Tuscaroras slunk north to become the Sixth Nation of the Iroquois Confederation in New York Province.

Soon after Fort Nohoroco, brother Maurice arrived with another body of whites and Indians, too late for action. James returned to Goose Creek. Maurice remained in the Albemarle for two years. Then word came that his own Goose Creek was being harassed by the Yemassees. On his trip south Maurice made the Lower Cape Fear crossing to the west bank at the spot where he would eventually found the town of Brunswick.

•

Maurice Moore had to nurture his plan for a Cape Fear settlement for the next dozen years. The hard times at Goose Creek had to become even worse before the planters there were willing to migrate northward. And in the interim the whole flotilla of Caribbean pirates took over the Lower Cape Fear estuary.

The victorious conclusion of Queen Anne's War in 1713 allowed the British to spare a Navy force to clean out the pirate base at New Providence Island. Captain Woodes Rogers added to his laurels as rescuer of Alexander Selkirk, the original of Robinson Crusoe, by defeating the buccaneers at New Providence and extending the King's pardon to those who promised to abandon their trade. The pious ex-pirates took the oath for what it was, a confession that the British were still too occupied in home waters to police the Spanish Main. The Lower Cape Fear became their rendezvous for rest and refitting after sallies against Charleston and Virginia Capes shipping. Governor Johnston of South Carolina and Governor Spotswood of Virginia took up the pirate chase where Captain Rogers had left off.

But while they were fitting out ships to run down the buccaneers, Governor Eden of North Carolina lent himself as a receiver of pirate plunder. The waters behind the Outer Banks provided safe channels for occasional pirate trading and social visits to Eden at Albemarle. The cloak for this remarkable compatibility between provincial governor and freebooter was the easily shed

King's oath. Edward Teach, alias Blackbeard, absolved and re-formed by the oath, could now innocently appear in Eden's company. If he backslid and brought in good trading booty, the news of a scuttled ship might never arrive, and the Governor was reticent.

Blackbeard on his quarterdeck was a horrendous figure, hung about with pistols and a cutlass, lighted tapers entwined in his long black hair and beard. Far less calculated to inspire terror was his lieutenant and sometimes rival, Stede Bonnet.

A former British Army major, retired in affluence at Barbados, the bored Bonnet decided to go a-pirating, and built what was probably the only ship ever designed explicitly for sailing under the Jolly Roger. Common pirates stole small ships and used them to capture big ones. Stede, as befitting an English gentleman, must have the best at once. In this custom-built ship he sailed to apprentice himself to the professional and experienced Blackbeard, who took the ship away from him, but gave the amateur a berth as observer on his own flagship.

Bonnet learned quickly. In time he recovered his ship, rescued twenty-five pirate seamen whom Blackbeard had marooned on the Outer Banks, and, without the aid of his insufferable tutor, himself captured a dozen merchantmen. But the Virginia-South Carolina pincers were now closing.

Rich with booty, a real pirate at last, Stede Bonnet was surprised in his Cape Fear haven by an avenging expedition under Colonel William Rhett of Charleston. The pirate was no Captain of the *Pinafore*. He gave Rhett five hours of battle before he and his crew (some of them had slipped ashore) were overpowered. Stede Bonnet was hanged at Charleston December 10, 1718, along with twenty-nine other pirates.

Blackbeard was still at large, a quasi-respectable dinner guest of Governor Eden's at Albemarle. Then the itch to be back at his old trade seduced him into capturing a French vessel laden with oranges, sugar, and spices. Such fancy goods, when smuggled in duty-free, made pirates seem decent chaps after all. Blackbeard brought the delectable cargo back to the Albemarle and stored it in the barn of Tobias Knight, secretary of the colony by appointment of Governor Eden. Word of this now reached Governor Spotswood of Virginia who sent the sloop *Adventure*, Lieutenant Maynard in command, on secret search for the most wanted pirate. Maynard came upon Blackbeard at Ocracoke, killed him in personal battle, and found in his blood-drenched coat a "Dear Friend" note from Tobias Knight. Again secretly, for many Virginians also were not averse to pirate-supplied goods, Spotswood sent agents to the Albemarle. They found sugar and spices in Knight's barn. Governor Eden was highly indignant that Spotswood should invade Carolina privacy.

Here entered Maurice Moore and his friend Edward Moseley, young, yet the leading lawyer of the colony. Tobias Knight kept his records in a private house. Maurice and his confederate broke in and barred the door while searching for documentary evidence of Eden's complicity with Blackbeard. For this they were arrested by Eden, and in October 1719 were tried by the Council. Maurice Moore was fined £5. Moseley, in that he had made scandalous (if true) charges against Knight and Eden, was fined £100 and forbidden to practice law for three years.

It may be supposed that Moore and Moseley, while cooling their heels in enforced idleness, discussed the Lower Cape Fear, now free of pirates and as unclaimed as when Maurice had first seen it on his Indian-fighting expedition. On the Albemarle events were shaping the future of the estuary, at the same time that brothers James, Nathaniel, and Roger were helping to make Goose Creek a good place from which to escape.

One month after Maurice Moore was fined by the Council at Albemarle, his brother James was made governor by the Faction, following the revolt which had unseated South Carolina's proprietary governor. When this news reached London, the heirs of the original Lords Proprietors washed their hands of any further attempt to govern South Carolina, and began talk of selling all of Carolina back to the Throne.

A major cause of South Carolina trouble remained under James Moore as governor. "Hot tar" was the cause of it. No wine, silk, or almonds had been produced in Charleston's warm climate to satisfy the original London hopes. But there was another British import that could be produced there, naval stores. The planters, encouraged by a London bounty on tar and pitch, had begun to work their forests, and in order to do so had bought many slaves on credit. The good times did not last long enough for them to own their black workers in fee simple. They were producing "hot tar" which London rejected. British admirals, with what horror it can scarcely be imagined, discovered their ships' ropes being burned by the very tar applied to preserve them. Parliament demanded a cleaner product. To compound the distress, London ruled that the planters must maintain a high ratio of white workers to black slaves. The knout at the end of this whip was a notice to pay quitrents in silver at London. The Goose Creek Moores were now in a mood to listen to brother Maurice's alluring accounts of the Cape Fear as a refuge from South Carolina distress.

When Eden died in 1722 he was succeeded as proprietary governor by George Burrington, as short-tempered and arrogant as his fellow Devonshire man Sir Francis Drake. Burrington listened to Moore and Moseley, and made his first act of office an expedition to survey the possibilities of the Lower Cape Fear. Here for weeks he camped in the open, observing the great stand of virgin longleaf pine and sounding the broad estuary for channels and harbors. He returned to the newly named town of Edenton as a Cape Fear convert.

Not one to quibble with proprietary rules, which forbade settlement within twenty miles of the Cape Fear and limited land grants to one hundred acres per person, Burrington set up a land office. Within the six weeks following June 3, 1725, he signed patents for thirteen thousand acres on the Cape Fear, eight thousand of them divided between Maurice Moore and Eleazar Allen of Goose Creek. Ten thousand river-front acres were assigned by Burrington to himself. This openhanded policy resulted in his recall by London. But Burrington would return as North Carolina's first royal governor. And he had broken the silence of the Lower Cape Fear forever.

# 3 : *"The Family"*

The physical formation of a country is the key to the history of its early settlement.

————George Macaulay Trevelyan

The tidal basin of the Lower Cape Fear as Governor Burrington found it was a sheltered harbor thirty miles long and nearly two miles wide at mid-point, with a depth to accommodate vessels up to 100-tons burden. The horrific face of the Frying Pan had concealed from Europeans the mild and opulent nature behind it. December winds might whip the Shoals to fury, but the soft air of February opened the buds of the wild azaleas.

At its northern end the estuary tapered to a point where two fresh-water rivers poured in the red silt and black swampwater of a vast drainage area. The low-lying east shore of the estuary was forested and fit for river-front plantations, not running very far back since the forest strip died out in the encroaching sands of the Atlantic beaches. The dunes, the gray skeletons of sand-drowned cedars, and the surf—much admired by today's picnickers— would be left to the seabirds by an eighteenth century people who had seen enough of Atlantic rollers from the decks of small sailing vessels.

The choice plantation sites were on the west bank. The ground here was high. A man could feel tall, and scan the river for his inbound ships. No ocean would put a limit to his back holdings, which reached westward into uncharted country. Streams navigable for small boats reached inland from the west bank. Marshes and fresh-water ponds were breeding grounds and migrating resting places for wildfowl. The forest offered the choice of bear steak, haunch of venison, or breast of wild turkey. In the river guileless fish awaited the hook. Oysters, crowded by their underwater mates, climbed tree trunks to high-tide limit.

Aside from this easy provender for master and workers, the controlling physical feature of the Lower Cape Fear was the stand of longleaf pine. This would determine the size of the plantations, the kind of people who would settle there, and, through their quarrels with proprietary and royal governors, would greatly influence the course of the American Revolution.

The resinous heart of the longleaf was essential to the mother country's destiny. During the first half of the eighteenth century, England was to engage successively in Queen Anne's War, the War of Jenkins' Ear, and King George's War. The titles are misleading. Parliament did not really blanch when Jenkins fished a dried ear out of his pocket as evidence of a Spanish sea captain's barbarity. What England wanted was favorable bloodlines on European thrones and a free sweep of the seas for her men-of-war and mercantile fleet. That meant vasty supplies of tar, pitch, and resin. The supply was uncertain in the nearby Baltic but boundless in her own Carolina. The Town of Brunswick on the Lower Cape Fear would become the British Empire's greatest source of naval stores.

The nature of naval stores production required plantations of a thousand acres and upwards. Great holdings in pinelands, black slaves to work the woods and run the kilns, 100-ton ships to carry the stores to England, and enough money to finance the period between the pine and London bank—all this was eighteenth century big business, and could be accomplished only by adventurers with swords in hand and gold in pouches. The Moores and their allies were such people. Naval stores had been hurt at Goose

Creek by the "hot tar" controversy, but now in 1725 the bounty was restored and the pines of the Cape Fear inviting.

Roger Moore led the Goose Creek contingent to the new lands. His first act was to clear the area of Indians. One Landgrave Thomas Smith of Charleston had wangled a 40,000-acre grant reaching from the Cape of Fear to the Hauleover. This he had used for trading with the Indians, a peaceful tribe albeit descendants of those who had slaughtered mariners shipwrecked on the Frying Pan. Now they were repentant. A stranded crew and passengers, expecting to lose their scalps, the Indians rescued with every sign of affection. This change of heart had been wrought by their need of protection by the English from raiding bands of Senecas. But to Roger Moore no Indian was a tolerable neighbor. He turned his hundred black slaves into a private constabulary and crossed to the Hauleover. The Indians were defeated there in a battle whose details were understandingly not bruited about. It was a ha'penny-tuppenny affair compared to the ferocious descent of brother James on the Tuscaroras. But it sufficed. The Indians fled to South Carolina where, happily for them, Moores were decreasing in number.

This was during the summer when Governor Burrington was enjoying his six weeks' distribution of Cape Fear acreage and in consequence was called back to England. His successor, Sir Richard Everard, continued a free hand with land grants. By 1728 these patents were on the books: Maurice Moore, 9,210 acres; Roger Moore, 12,780 acres; Eleazar Allen, 1,280 acres; Samuel Swann, 3,280 acres; John Porter, 640 acres.

Sir Richard even improved on Burrington's technique by signing blank patents which could be filled in for acreage and location. Since the land records were carelessly filed, the same acreage might be claimed by two patentees. James Murray, a Cape Fear merchant, wrote home to England: "People that are acquaint with ye country and know where ye vacant land is, get a warrant survey and patent, and then screw as much as they can from a stranger."

The squabbles of the captious Carolinians, the rapid turnover of proprietary governors, and the inadequate sums coming from quitrents had discouraged the heirs of the first Lords Proprietors. "Being sensible of the great disorders the inhabitants of Carolina are in," they requested the Crown to buy back their grants. In 1729 George II paid £22,500 for the shares and back quitrents of seven Proprietors. The Carteret interest decided to keep their one eighth. The others had sold out too soon. It would not be long before a single Cape Fear holding would be worth what they had jointly received for a generous portion of North America.

When Burrington came back in 1731 to succeed Sir Richard, The Family by blood and marriage held 83,000 of the 105,000 acres patented on the Cape Fear. Governor Burrington at once began to quarrel with Edward Moseley, but by now Moseley was Maurice Moore's brother-in-law and Burrington was taking on the entire transplanted Goose Creek complex. Burrington found himself contending with Roger Moore for the same 640 acres, with armed retainers ready to do battle for them. Roger, for once, gave in; which did not prevent the Governor from writing to the British Board of Trade that ". . . a noted family whose name is Moore, of the sett known as the Goose Creek Faction . . . were always troublesome in the Government and will without doubt be so in this." Mild words, these, from a master of invective who proclaimed Sir Richard Everard "an ape, a noodle, and no more fitt to be a governor than Sancho Panza."

The record of marriages in The Family's Bibles began to duplicate the filings of patents in the land office. Maurice Moore's first wife, Elizabeth, was the daughter of Major Alexander Lillington and the widow of Colonel Samuel Swann. Swann's daughter married John Porter. Maurice took a Porter as second wife. Roger Moore and Eleazar Allen were brothers-in-law, both having married daughters of the Colonel William Rhett who captured Stede Bonnet.

•

The first of the dreamer-warriors had been Maurice, and it was his 1,500-acre patent on the high west bank opposite the Hauleover which became the hearthstone of The Family life. In June 1726 he laid out a gridwork plan for a town and called it Brunswick. He sold one of the first lots to Cornelius Harnett who had proven his Family compatibility by an enforced flight from Edenton after having assaulted Sir Richard Everard. Harnett set up as tavern-keeper and operator of a ferry across to the Hauleover. His son Cornelius Junior would one day be the "Sam Adams of North Carolina," chief organizer of resistance to the Crown, as the third James Moore, Maurice's son, would be military leader of the province in the Revolution.

Timber, naval stores, and rice were to bring in the money to buy bricks for slaves to fashion into Georgian plantation houses. Orton was built by Roger Moore north of Brunswick Town, leaving space for Russellboro where two royal governors would live. Eleazar Allen raised Lilliput beyond Orton. Still farther on was Town Creek with space for a dozen plantations and dynasties along its black water. Pleasant Oaks, Belvidere, Clarendon . . . the great grants would extend along the west shore from the Frying Pan to the Forks, each in testament to their builders' resolve to establish estates rivaling the baronial manors of England. They lacked the velvet of two-hundred-year-old turf, yet their wildflowers were shaded by live oaks already two centuries old. Instead of swans, cottonmouth moccasins rippled the surface of their garden pools. Their deer ran unfenced. Bears afrighted the saddle horses. Their workers were slaves, their butlers Africans. Their river, knowing no gentle course through university towns, led to wild and unknown upper reaches.

Orton was a working plantation, for cash or political advantage. The Moores, however, knew how to manage the civilities, as the account written by a young Englishman of Quality demonstrates. He left Charleston on June 10, 1734, with a party on horseback bound for Brunswick Town. Arrived there: "Mr. Roger Moore hearing we were come, was so kind as to send fresh horses for us to come up to his house, which we did, and were kindly received by him, he being the chief gentleman in all Cape Fear. His house is built of brick and exceedingly pleasant . . . a creek comes close up to the door, between two beautiful meadows, about three miles length. He has a prospect of the Town of Brunswick, and of another beautiful brick home belonging to Eleazar Allen, Esq., late Speaker of the Commons House of Assembly in the Province of South Carolina . . ."

The young Englishman's journal presents the region as it was ten years after George Burrington first fell in love with it. Deer gazed in calm innocence at the horseback party. Plantation houses already had two-mile driveways flanked with saplings proposed someday to rival the arched-over avenues of ducal parks. Nathaniel Moore had taken him in hand at Orton. They traveled by easy stages with overnight stays at plantation houses until they reached Nathaniel's own home on the Upper Cape Fear, "at least sixty miles from the bar, whence came a sloop of 100 tons and upward, to be laden with corn. . . ."

Game was abundant. They made a hearty dinner on a brace of deer, shot a she-bear and two cubs, and downed enough wild turkeys, geese and ducks "to serve forty men, though there were but six of us." He visited Colonel Maurice Moore and others. His farewell was from Orton where Roger offered a horse and a servant to accompany him. The most pleasing touch of hospitality occurred on the ride south from Orton:

"I intended to stop at the next spring and take a tiff of punch; but by some unfortunate accident, I know not how, when I came within sight of the spring, my bottle unluckily broke, and I lost every drop of my shrub; by examining my bags, I accidentally found a bottle of cherry brandy, with some ginger-bread and cheese, which I believe good Mrs. Moore ordered to be put up unknown to me. I drank two drams of that, not willing it should all be lost in case it should break, and mounting my horse, took some ginger-bread and cheese in my hand and pursued my journey."

•

Orton Plantation stands today, unscathed by a 1748 Spanish invasion of Brunswick Town, the 1776 raids of British landing parties, or the 1865 Federal bombardment of a Confederate fort built over Brunswick's ruins. A short walk from its portico, and also facing the river, are the brick burial vaults of the first family. The center one bears the name: KING ROGER MOORE—simply that, without quotation marks to mar the dignity of Roger's self-bestowed royal title.

# 4 : *Short Life of Brunswick Town*

The Lower Cape Fear quickly supplanted Albemarle Sound and the Neuse as a place to do business and play politics. When George Burrington took the oath as royal governor in 1731 he did so at Edenton, but forthwith returned to the place of his enthusiasm, the Cape Fear. Around its estuary were now twelve hundred people, two thirds of them black slaves.

Except for a few, the Cape Fear mansions could not compare with Westover, Lower Brandon, and Carter's Grove on the James. Yet there was this interesting and overlooked aspect: the great Virginia houses were miles apart, each with its wide expanse on the James; the Cape Fear plantations had narrow river frontage, so that houses were within sight of each other. It made for sociability and a sense of solidarity of fortune. Virginia governors resided grandly remote in their Palace at Williamsburg. North Carolina governors lived at or near Brunswick Town in houses of less pretension than those of their neighbors. It was difficult to maintain the aura of the Throne in this nest of fractious and irreverent subjects. Those with whom you shared the bridle path would harry you next day in Assembly. The tempers of all the royal governors of North Carolina, save one, were testy.

George Burrington was the bridge between proprietary and royal North Carolina. As proprietary governor in the 1720s he had pioneered the Cape Fear, enduring as he said: "all the hardships that could happen to a man destitute of a home to live in . . . four times I sounded the inlets, bars and rivers, discovered the chanel of the Cape Fear River . . . ran the risk of drowning and starving. . . ."

This good deed done, his generous hand with blank land patents created a snarl which the British Board of Trade was twenty years in disentangling. His rule as proprietary governor had ended when the Chowan County court indicted him for riotous conduct in the streets with rowdy companions. Burrington sailed secretly to London where he mortgaged and lost 10,000 of the Cape Fear acres he had patented for himself.

His 1731 return in the role of royal governor did something, not much, for Burrington's split personality. He became the champion of the small landowner, encouraging Welsh, English, Scotch, and Swiss to patent modest tracts up the rivers, while he acquired 50,-000 acres personally.

He was a quarrelsome neighbor. When his servants branded two mares claimed by John Baptista Ashe, Burrington as governor met Ashe's action against him by arresting the wronged man for "scurrulous libel." In a letter to London, Burrington described his Cape Fear neighbors as men "subtle and crafty to administer, who always behaved insolently to their Governors, who maintained that their money could not be taken from them save by appropriations made by their own House of Assembly . . . All the Governors that ever lived in this Province lived in fear of the People (except myself) and Dreaded their Assemblys."

Edward Moseley was his Speaker of the House, which Burrington three times convened and three times prorogued without passage of a single law. When he put in for a salary of £700, the Assembly refused it. One of his lost measures was a bill which

Burrington, in pique at his neighbors, proposed for the establishment of a town on the Cape Fear, as though Brunswick did not
exist. Moseley pulled enough votes out of his pocket to defeat this
willful affront to The Family's own town. William Byrd II of Virginia wrote to Burrington: "I wish you all success in the world in
bringing the chaos into form and reducing that Assembly into a
Republican Government. In doing so you will deserve to have
your statue erected, or, which is perhaps better, to have your salary doubled."

Neither of Byrd's kind wishes eventuated. The British Board of
Trade in 1734 called Burrington back to London. There is "impious and disgraceful death" was supposed to have followed an all-
night party in London's Bird Cage Walk.

•

Burrington's successor as royal governor was Gabriel Johnston, an
able Scot whose eighteen-year term would see the settlement of
the Cape Fear hinterland. He was as much the angry man as Burrington, and perhaps by reason of that same choice of either forwarding The Family's interests or obeying his instructions from
London. He chose to oppose The Family. Roger Moore and Moseley he characterized as "base tools to work Burrington's arbitrary
will on deserving gentlemen who had the manhood to disagree
with him." He accused the Moores of burning over the King's
pinelands for the sake of feeding their kilns with the lightwood
centers, and so ruining the soil for farming and depriving the King
of quitrents. He fought The Family on land patents, asserting the
Crown's position that no one man should have more land than he
could cultivate. This came with no more grace from Johnston than
it had from Burrington, for Johnston too acquired his broad acres.

There were, in fact, no more lands to be had on the banks of the
estuary. Yet Johnston, for all his hypocrisy about personal holdings, served well in making small farms available up the fresh-
water rivers. By 1740 there were Scots living on the Upper Cape
Fear a hundred miles from the Frying Pan.

Land, by royal grant, by blank patent or legally acquired; held
in fee simple or on quitrent; land to make an adventurer into a
great squire; land of his own to warm the heart of a Highlander
crofter—land was the dream of every passenger on every sailing
ship, and the New World treasure trove in every London counting
house. Being so distant and in extent so unimaginable, wilderness
areas greater than any dukedom passed in London as counters in
the game of favors done for favors received.

Governor Johnston appointed his kinsman Henry McCulloh as
his agent in London. McCulloh first acquired 60,000 acres for
himself on the Black River, a tributary of the Upper Cape Fear,
and next 100,000 acres on the latter river's headwaters. His was
only one of twelve 100,000-acre grants, with a ten-year exemption
on quitrents, awarded its friends by the British Board of Trade.

While Johnston lost many small encounters with The Family,
he won the big battle. The Assembly had turned down Burrington's bill to create a town on the river, upon the firm ground that
it already had one in Brunswick. Now Johnston revived this jibe
at the Moores by himself buying property at the Forks. It was the
first of many moves which in thirty years would turn Brunswick
Town back to the greenbriers and the Cherokee roses.

Actually Burrington had started it in 1733 by granting one John
Watson 640 acres at the Forks, these in turn being platted into lots
and sold to such people as Higgins the tavernkeeper and Winkle
the mariner—not names to be entered as vital statistics in The
Family's Bible. The first few shacks went by the name of New
Liverpool, then New Town and Newton under which last name
Gabriel Johnston in 1735 ruled that it should become a town as
soon as six brick houses, forty by thirty feet each, should adorn
the strips designated as principal streets.

A "town" was not simply a cluster of houses and facilities. It
was a political entity stemming from the King's grant of representation to English towns in exchange for support in Parliament.
This was a threat to Brunswick, already a town with an Assembly

member and already taxed for a jail and courthouse as yet unbuilt.

On May 13, 1735, Johnston opened a land office in Newton and decreed that the Court of Exchequer should meet there. The next canny (and dubiously legal) move was to bring the customs and naval officials to Newton, in effect setting it up as a port of entry. "By reason of the depth of water, safety of its roads, and the secure and easy access," Newton officially became the town of Wilmington, named for Johnston's patron, Spencer Compton, Earl of Wilmington. Now every tenant of a habitable house, twenty feet long and sixteen feet wide, was entitled to a vote in the election of a General Assembly member. The courthouse partially paid for by Brunswick taxes was now ordered built in Wilmington.

In the Council meeting which decided on the incorporation of Wilmington The Family had four votes and Johnston's clique four. The tie was broken when Chief Justice William Smith, who had already voted in favor of Johnston, ruled that he as first magistrate was entitled to a second vote, and being a man of consistent nature he again voted for Wilmington's charter.

Geography in fact favored a townsite at the Forks. Brunswick stood open to winds of gale to hurricane force, and its position near the Frying Pan made it tempting to Spanish marauders. Wilmington was thirty miles in from the Atlantic and at the juncture with the Upper Cape Fear whose boatmen were beginning to float farm produce downstream on equally marketable log rafts. Brunswick would have to be content with its pre-eminence in naval stores and the social distinction of being the residence of two more royal governors.

Johnston now thought to make Wilmington the capital of the province. The Albemarle laid claim to more Assembly votes, so in the winter of 1741 Johnston summoned the Assembly to Wilmington for the crucial vote, hoping "to keep at home the northern members." The strategy failed to bring any decision. An appeal to the King languished among Whitehall's state papers, leaving

North Carolina's legislators to continue in saddlebag transit from Wilmington to New Bern to Edenton according to the governor's pleasure in summoning his Assembly.

Perhaps it was a relief for Johnston to take action for once against opponents who controlled no Assembly votes. Bears were scooping potatoes out of the ground, parakeets stripping the apple trees, wild turkeys getting "plump on Pease, Wheat and Indian Corn"; eagles were carrying off young lambs. The Governor's request for a bounty on these vermin met with the Assembly's approval.

But when Governor Johnston scolded them for failure to build a single schoolhouse, the Assembly remained its passive self. Education was a private affair. The first Alexander Lillington's 1697 will directed his executors to "Carry on my son, John, in his learning as I have begun." That John's son, a second Alexander Lillington, now pleaded with the Assembly: "In all civilized Societys of men it has always been looked upon as a matter of the greatest consequence to their Peace and Happiness, to polish the minds of young persons with some degree of learning." Since this Lillington was the father of Mrs. Roger Moore, the lady who secreted cherry brandy, gingerbread and cheese in the saddlebags of the Young Gentleman of Quality, it may be assumed that she was cultured as well as kind.

The wills of the estuary planters mention from twenty to fifty books in their estates. Moseley, a liberal who was even a proponent of Quakers, had a library of four hundred volumes, including Greek and Latin classics, Shakespeare, Milton, Bacon, Locke, Voltaire, and Swift.

It would have well served Parker Quince of Rose Hill if his learning had comprehended an ability to spell. His order on London for a dozen cheeses and several gross of black tacks brought back a dozen English chaises battened to the decks and in the hold several cases of black jacks, a japanned drinking mug, with the merchant's apology that he had exhausted the London supply of black jacks without quite being able to fill Mr. Quince's esteemed order.

•

If formal religion fared little better than formal schooling, the fault lay in the Anglican Church ruling that the Bishop of London must ordain all Carolina clergymen and license all schoolteachers. Colonial divinity students lacked funds for London voyages to be ordained in person by the Bishop. The religious climate in England was not such as to produce learned young clerics with a passion to immolate themselves in the wilderness. Perhaps the word got back to London that those clergymen whom the Bishop did send to the Cape Fear lost many bouts to the devil of indifference and nearly starved to boot.

The Reverend John Lampierre arrived to serve the Lower Cape Fear in 1728. For four years he went without compensation, working in the fields to stay alive. When he set himself up as a merchant, the Council investigated this unworthy secular activity. Lampierre went to London seeking a vestry in Carolina having a fixed living attached. The Bishop would not see him.

The next Anglican incumbent, Reverend Richard Marsden, failed for some years to make any report to London. Services at his Prince George's Creek plantation were attended for the most part by his dinner guests. The Society for the Propagation of the Gospel in Foreign Parts, the missionary branch of the Established Church, placed Marsden on its list, then removed him for financial misconduct.

The Reverend James Moir chose to live in Wilmington, which frowned so sternly on the occasional services he held in Brunswick that he moved to that town. There he was required to live in the tavern, "the very worst upon the face of the earth in more ways than one." His complaints won him a sixteen by twenty-four foot shack, abandoned in turn when Brunswick resented the occasional services he held in Wilmington.

Perhaps the most cavalierly treated was the Reverend John Mc-
Dowell. Upon the death of his wife in childbirth, his stipend was
reduced on the ground that there was one less mouth to feed.

These were the clergymen who served during the administration of Governor Johnston. His liberal land policies had brought
hundreds of settlers of modest means into the countryside inland
from the Lower River, and to these small farmers the clergymen
tracked afoot and on horseback, up to the saddle in swamps,
through cottonmouth moccasin waters and wolf ranges and, if
lucky, in small boats manned by slaves. They accepted ill health
and hunger. They baptized, joined in marriage, and buried the
country folk. Even the Reverend Mr. Marsden was said to have
baptized 1,300 babies, including Negroes. For their devotion the
clergy were paid in neglect and penury. It was not until Arthur
Dobbs became governor in 1754 that a brick church, St. Philips,
began to rise at Brunswick.

•

The War of Jenkins' Ear brought the first armed invasion of the
Cape Fear. The real issue was Caribbean trade. Spain claimed a
monopoly there, allowing the exception that England's Royal African Company might supply the Spanish Main with "merchant-
able Negroes at moderate rates." The British slave traders, however, succumbed to the temptation of a side line in merchant
goods. Spain in reprisal harassed English ships. A war was brewing and poor Jenkins' mummified ear touched it off. Not everyone
approved. Horace Walpole prophesied: "You are ringing the joy
bells now, but before this war is over you will be wringing your
hands."

The tragic British siege of Cartagena justified Walpole. Wilmington contributed to it a hundred men under Captain James
Innes. Only a handful returned from Cartagena where twenty
thousand British sailors died, nine out of ten from fever. But the
war continued and brought Spanish raiders to Carolina's Outer
Banks where they carried off Ocracoke cattle. The Assembly took

notice that ". . . such parts of this Province which are situated most commodious for shipping to enter may be invaded by the enemy . . . the entrance of the Cape Fear River may tempt them to such an enterprise while it remains so naked and defenceless as it is now." To thwart the Dons it was decided to construct Fort Johnston, south of Brunswick, and the usual committee members of Moores, Swann, Moseley, and Innes were appointed to carry out the project. A tax on powder entering the port was to finance it.

In fact the Spaniards did arrive on plunder bent. In September 1748 the Spanish ship *Fortune,* 130 tons and 24 guns, Captain Vincent Lopez, and the *Loretta,* captained by Joseph Leon Muños, captured the American *Nancy* off the coast and compelled her pilot to steer them through the Frying Pan Shoals. They landed downriver from Brunswick, whose inhabitants had fled, and spent two days in pillage.

The militia of the countryside gathered to the defense of Brunswick, Captain John Swann in command of nearly one thousand men. In a landward encirclement of the town the colonists surprised the Spanish looters and killed many. The others fled to their ships, which now brought their 24-pounders to bear on Brunswick. A brisk exchange of cannon ball and musketry ended when the powder magazine of the *Fortune* exploded. The invaders now became the hunted. Swimmers from the sunken *Fortune* were killed or captured. Captain Muños under flag of truce offered a cease-fire if his *Loretta* were allowed to depart with the captured *Nancy.* With or without permission, off Captain Muños sailed, leaving Brunswick to bury Spanish dead and to sell captives as slaves.

To the participants these were legitimate acts of war, they not yet having learned that a treaty of peace had been signed between England and Spain. To Brunswick it was a windfall. The hull of the *Fortune* contained considerable treasure. It was held in trust and finally given in aid of the estuary's two Anglican churches, St. Philips in Brunswick and St. James in Wilmington. A painting, *Ecce Homo,* from His Catholic Majesty's ship *Fortune* still hangs in the vestry room at St. James.

The near disaster to Brunswick moved the Assembly to vote £2,000 for the proper armament of Fort Johnston. The violence of nature and the assininity of man were to frustrate this monument to Gabriel Johnston's foresight. A 1760 hurricane forced a navigable channel, New Inlet, through the beach, establishing a bypass to both the Frying Pan and Fort Johnston. The builders of the eventually completed fort had put too much sand in with their oyster-shell binder so that every time a gun was fired a part of the "tabby-work" parapet fell down. Fort Johnston never fired a shot at a foreign foe.

•

Gabriel Johnston died in 1752. Since the Assembly held the purse strings, and had been at odds both with him and with many of the rulings made in London for his guidance, his salary as governor was fourteen years in arrears; yet his eighteen years as governor had advanced the Cape Fear community to first place among Carolina settlements. The merchants of Brunswick and Wilmington now had back-country inhabitants with whom they might profitably trade goods for longleaf pine logs and farm produce.

While the prospering merchants and planters of the Lower Cape Fear were disputatious and downright arrogant toward their royal governors, they never challenged the authority of the Crown itself. Their own privileges were too closely linked to His Majesty's. Money, great houses, titles, and protection all flowed from royalty down the descending levels of society. A Moore of Carolina might be a rude colonial in the eyes of a belted earl, yet he had a place on the staircase. Below him was the tenant farmer, the tradesman, the indentured servant, and that new manpower contrivance, the African.

The governors acknowledged the social level (it was their own) whence came the Council, the Assembly, judges and pewholders at St. James. In his tussles with them the royal governor was his own referee. He could convene or prorogue the Assembly; conceal orders from London; line his own pockets or promote the colony's welfare, sometimes both. In the lives and prospects of the people it mattered very much what kind of royal governor they had. The critical decade from 1755 to 1765, which included the costly French and Indian War and ended with the Stamp Act, cried out for a governor of ability and a light hand on the reins of government. Instead, George II appointed Arthur Dobbs, a peevish, self-willed man who was seventy years old when he assumed his duties and eighty when he gave up clinging to office and to life.

Governor Dobbs took over Russellboro as his residence. Whatever private neighborliness came of this proximity to Brunswick and Orton, it failed to carry over into Assembly sessions. Dobbs brought with him instructions to cancel all charters of counties and towns (including their rights to Assembly representation) and to lay out new geographic units according to the King's wishes. This was the same arbitrary cancellation of units-in-being which the Lords Proprietors had applied to the ruin of the Vassall settlement. But a century had hardened the sinews of colonial resistance. What with the Governor's right to dismiss the Assembly, and that body's power to refuse to allocate funds, the seesaw invariably found the balance of a compromise.

In politics, the second generation of The Family were as bright as otter pups learning how to follow their parents down a mud slide. Sam Swann, Speaker of the Assembly since 1743, gave way to his nephew John Ashe. He with another Swann nephew, George Moore, and one non-Family member, comprised the Committee of Correspondence, an official line from the Assembly to the British Board of Trade. Governor Dobbs dubbed the committee a junto bent on lessening the power of the Crown and aggrandizing its own.

This Dobbs decade was Last Chance for peace on the Cape Fear. There was joyous firing of cannon in the spring day in 1761 when news came that George III had succeeded to the Throne. Here was a monarch who proposed to shake off the torpor of his predecessors and to be actively King. The celebration was heart-felt. There had been a mellowing of feelings toward the Crown since the brawling days of proprietary forebears. No one questioned the common good to be derived from close ties to the mother country. England had taken over from France the entire continent from Labrador to Florida. No more Indians would murder the western province settlers; no pirates or Spaniards infest the river. Rice culture flourished. Forty sawmills produced thirty million feet of lumber annually. Naval stores exports were at their peak.

There were men of stature on the Cape Fear as well as in English politics. At this juncture, where politics was the arena for the great decisions, the Crown and the colony could have found a compromise position to assure peace.

In October 1763 Henry McCulloh, Gabriel Johnston's kin and the owner of huge Carolina acreage, proposed a Stamp Act "for protecting, securing and defending" the Colonies. Arthur Dobbs four months later seconded this recommendation in a letter suggesting the Board of Trade impose import duties as a means of "saving our great acquisitions on this continent." At the same time Dobbs, being ill and nearly eighty years old, asked to be relieved as governor. In October of the next autumn William Tryon, British Army lieutenant colonel, arrived at Brunswick expecting to become governor at once. Dobbs held on until his death a few months later. As there was no Anglican clergyman on the Cape Fear, it became the duty of a justice of the peace to close his eyes.

Upon William Tryon fell the obligation of making the colonists accept the revenue tax set by Parliament, a stunning change of policy from the self-imposed Assembly levies to which they were accustomed. The British Army officer, a scholar of the Age of Enlightenment, personable and courteous, set his breast to a storm long a-brewing. As his residence Tryon in turn bought Russellboro, which nine years later would go up in flames with the rest of Brunswick Town.

# 5 : *Bagpipes up the River*

In 1734 when Gabriel Johnston became royal governor of North
Carolina there were millions of acres of well-watered forest land
in the Upper Cape Fear Valley, free of hostile Indians and open
to settlers for the asking. In the Highlands of Scotland there was
hunger in the thatched crofts and an unease among lairds, tacksmen, tenants, and ghillies. The opportunity in America and the
distress in Scotland conjoined during the next half century to
make the fresh-water Upper Cape Fear a Highland Scot community. Their descendants still hold the land.

Governor Johnston, himself a Scot, stood godfather to this
greatest of Highland settlements in the New World. During his
term, from 1734 to 1752, the sailing vessels began picking up the
first adventurers from Argyll and the Hebrides, in time transport-
ing whole shiploads, a floating countryside of McNeills, MacDonalds and McAllisters, with pain in their hearts for what they were
leaving and a great hope ahead.

Johnston was the man to spread the word. His energies increased by being divided. Against the Moores, the Moseleys, and
the Ashes he fought to diminish their town of Brunswick and

scolded the slaveowning gentry for pre-empting the entire pleasant lagoon of the Lower River to the exclusion of small farmers. But when it came to promoting the settlement of the Upper River lands in workable family tracts, Johnston was equipped to win.

The Crown land policy, superceding the blank patents and nepotism of the Proprietors, limited each settler to a grant of fifty acres, with a like amount to each of his family and his indentured servants. Such a group of a dozen persons might have a square mile on the Upper River, or on a feeder stream deep enough for rafts and longboats.

News of this great free land fell on Highlander ears attuned to misery at home. Their hardscrabble hillsides and grazing moorlands were wasted away under the ancient tenantry habits of the clans. The laird assigned portions of his desmesne to tacksmen who in turn sublet to crofters. Each season the crofter had a new strip of land upon which to grow his oats, and of what use was it then to guard the soil for another's use next season? Arable earth over the centuries had leached to a thinness where starvation waited on a crop failure. The small Highland cattle roamed unfenced, scrawny critters made weaker by the practice of drawing off their blood to mix with oatmeal that the family might survive.

Gabriel Johnston began the hegira to the Cape Fear by importing Scottish adventurers whose reports back home confirmed that free land in America was no hoax. Scotus Americanus, pseudonym of a man of the Isle of Islay, passed the news that in North Carolina "poverty is almost an entire stranger . . . The Highlander should seek for refuge where freedom reigns, and where, unmolested by Egyptian task-masters, they may reap the produce of their own labour." No forty days a year obligatory working for the laird. No fealty due. And Governor Johnston had persuaded the Assembly to grant "foreign Protestants exemption from Publick or County taxes" for a period of ten years.

The first Highlanders to patent lands on the Upper Cape Fear were James Innes, Hugh Campbell, and William Forbes. Their longboats bucked the tawny current for many miles above the farthest-up farms which had been settled and abandoned by Vassall's people sixty-five years before. Hugh Campbell's land lay halfway between Rockfish Creek and Cross Creek (now Fayetteville). Forbes and Innes pushed on another twenty miles to the alluvial soil where the Lower Little River comes down from the hills to join the Upper Cape Fear. Since their grants were each in the hundreds of acres, it is likely that they were family groups with indentured servants. Their instincts had led them to what would become the heart of the Highlander Scot country.

It required a few years of clan consultation and tavern talk before the first full shipload, 350 of them, left a Scottish port for the Cape Fear. They brought along their tools, and, valuing oak for its high cost at home, they carried ax-handle staves to the land where a giant oak or hickory would be something to cut down to let sun into the vegetable garden.

They sailed the Atlantic for six weeks, £5 for fair accommodations or £3 for miserable food and a below-decks space only a few inches in excess of the body's bulk. In the channel of the Frying Pan they breathed soft air off the Gulf Stream, and from the port rail saw palmettos dotting the sandy shore. Once they were safe inside, the salt breeze blended with the scent of pines standing tall on the bank above the deepwater stretch to Brunswick Town. Their ship tacked to avoid the Flats beyond Brunswick and followed the channel along the east bank to Newton, a poor substitute, as human dwellings were then valued, for the gray-stone towns they had left behind. Yet it was their cherished goal, the taking-off place to lands of their own upriver. If the Newton people laughed at their Gaelic tongue and the kilts, it would be only a two weeks' longboat trip to Cross Creek and the new life.

•

Overland and faster than the immigrants could travel up the river went a sailor from their ship, Red Neill McNeill, weary of long voyages and liking the idea of an inland trek into the unknown. Once he had put a hundred miles between himself and salt water, he found that he was crossing the trails of other restless men. The sailor turned woodsman became their leader and naturally enough, for he was six feet six, with a fist that could stun a steer, and a flaming beard and poll which to his brother Gaels made him An Ruadh Mor—the Big Red One. His intimate was bowlegged Archie Buie the piper, small shadow and mighty friend to the giant.

Neill's Creek and Buie's Creek run parallel and empty into the Cape Fear five miles apart. Fifteen miles to the west is Barbecue Creek, named by the Red One because the stream's early morning mists reminded him of smoke rising from the barbecue pits of the West Indies. A Barbecue Church, successively in a presbyter's log cabin, in colonial frame and plank, and now of brick, has stood above the misty creek for two hundred years.

The Red One's memory of the pungent West Indies smoke brought its more secular benefits. A barbecue pit proper for charcoal broiling a whole beef needs a settled sort of place, with a split poplar log table, a keg of brandy, pewter mugs in readiness, and a weatherproof cabin to be used as recovery room in the dawn of the day after. Red Neill McNeill bought his own acres, dug his pit, and let the word of an upcoming barbecue drift along the trails. With the dark at their backs and the circle of faces picked out in the last glow of the embers, with the meat washed down by mugs of ale and the brandy broached, his guests let the drone, bubble, and shriek of Archie Buie's pipes evoke the Highland nights, lost to them now except for a wildness still in the blood and in their Gaelic songs.

•

The basin of the Cape Fear has 397 named streams. They begin in frog ponds in the upland meadows, as springs bubbling from under the ledges of ravines and joining rill to rivulet to form streams up to a cow's belly. Then somehow they have homes on their banks and later pine log rafts are assembled on them for a trip down the big river, the Cape Fear.

During the ninety-mile course of the semicircular Deep and Haw rivers the descent in white water and dark pool is nearly nine hundred feet. Below Buckhorn Falls the Cape Fear's wild youth settles down to its sedate meanderings through the coastal plain, navigable now for longboat and rafting journeys to tidewater.

The Highlanders pushed on to the tributary streams—Rockfish, Cross Creek, and Lower Little River. The first arrivals staked claims on the high west bank of the Cape Fear itself. The next wave moved up the tributaries and the feeder creeks, the families afoot now and searching the land for a spring. The great longleaf pines were everywhere. Their lowest branches were a dozen feet above a man's head. Their taproots went deep for water. They offered a century's supply of timber for cabin sidings and barrel staves, and their lightwood hearts could go to the kiln and be cash in hand at Wilmington.

In the abundance of their new country the islanders of Skye, Jura, Barra, and Benbecula tempered their grief at loss of the familiar and dear. The laird back home had his grouse. The trees of his former tenants bent under the weight of plum-breasted passenger pigeons. In place of the few gathered twigs of the old country they had great logs to burn on their own hearths. They named some of their creeks McLeod, Skibo, McDuffie, Patchet, and Robeson; but for others they found native names—Buffalo, Crane, Cypress, Juniper, Bear, Pokeberry, and (in memory of the carcasses of skinned buffalo) Stinking Quarter Creek.

These "100-acre men" spread west from the valley of the Cape Fear to the Yadkin. Some went north across the fall-line into the piedmont where the land begins its ascent to the Blue Ridge, not more than a week's trek beyond. There they would have come on six-thousand-foot peaks reminiscent of their own Grampians. Assuredly they would have settled there, become clans again, the creeks their burns, the hollows their glens. The nostalgia for high ground is written on a small tombstone in a graveyard on Cameron's Hill, near Barbecue. It is not much of a hill, but a Highlander family living on the coastal plain sent their twelve-year-old son there on horseback with the body of his infant brother behind the saddle, for burial on Cameron's high and holy ground.

That which stopped the Highlander hegira above the fall-line, and persuaded those already there to return, was the extension of Lord Granville's property in an east-west line across the Haw and the Deep. The Highlanders remembered the rents in the old country and would have naught to do with Granville agents.

•

Red Neill McNeill lived through the brief period of the blazing of the Cape Fear Trail and the settling of the valley by the 100-acre men. After death his remains would span another century into the last days of the War Between the States.

In 1759 the fever came up the river. The Big Red One tended his neighbors, buried the dead, and himself came down with the fever. This was not the swift ravager that kills in a few hours. The Big Red One lived long enough to watch Archie Buie shape and hollow a ten-foot gum log coffin, with auger holes and pegs at the ready. He died on the east shore, with Archie's pipes sounding the lament. The river being in flood, his neighbors buried him in a temporary grave, awaiting the chance to fulfill his wish that he be buried on the slope of Smilie's Hill across the river. It took a far greater force than Archie's to move the log.

A century later, in the early spring of 1865, the river was again in flood, this time such a frog-strangler that it deserved a name, and the fitting one for its destructive wrath was "Sherman's Fresh" since the General and his bummers were at the time down-river at Fayetteville burning the Arsenal.

On the west bank where the receding flood left it, a Buie descendant came upon the gum log and prised it open. What he saw recalled the family tale of the restless one with a red beard, and the dying request for a place on Smilie's Hill. Belatedly they buried Red Neill there under four feet of clay and gravel, facing west.

# 6 : *Backwoods Saints and Sinners*

The earliest settlers of North Carolina came to the Province not for religious but mainly from economic motives. From 1701 to the Revolution there was an Established Church; there was positive persecution; there was not religious freedom, and we must acknowledge the facts.

———Stephen Beauregard Weeks

The Scots Highlanders came to the Cape Fear because the breakup of the clans had resulted in the ruin of farming and cattle raising. The people of North Carolina who became Quakers originally left England to escape the poverty of cities. The Scotch-Irish had been lured by James I to fill the lands of two exiled earls of Ulster, then had tarried a century in Ireland until an English tariff cut off their linen industry and sent them overseas to Philadelphia and overland to Carolina. If religion had a share in the immigration of French Huguenots, Swiss, and Germans to the Cape Fear, the wide advertisement in Europe of that river's goodly lands was also in the reckoning.

There was religious motivation, but the distinction was between religion as an adjunct to worldly power and religion as hope and comfort to an individual. Most of the Cape Fear immigrants were dissidents against power-vested religion, and so broke the stout beam of church authority into the abhorred splinter groups.

The first minister of Christ in North Carolina was William Edmundson, a Quaker convert of rude eloquence and earnest piety. He had gone with Cromwell to Scotland in 1650, become a

Quaker, and by 1661 was the leader of the Friends in Ireland. By canoe down the Chowan from Virginia he made his first missionary journey into the then very new Albemarle community. The pioneer families were isolated and without any religious leaders. Edmundson found "they had little or no religion, for they came and sat down in meeting smoking their pipes." But they came, and heard with receptive hearts that the godhead resided in every man and woman, and that veneration for others was thus implicit. Religion needed no physical adornments, nor any preachers. In Meeting each might speak when the spirit moved within. George Fox himself, the Founder, came in 1672 for eighteen days of meetings in scattered cabins, confiding to his journal the holding of "a sound, precious meeting, the people being generally tender and open."

It was not by Quakers fleeing the wrath of New England Puritans, but by the adoption by native people that Quakerism came to North Carolina. As in New England, however, hostility soon rose against them. The plantation crossroads along Albemarle Sound at once put them under the interdict of the Established Church of England. Governor Henderson Walker wrote to the Bishop of London in 1703:

> We have been settled near fifty years in this place, and I may justly say most part of twenty-one years, on my own knowledge, without priest or altar, and before that time, according to all that appears to me, much worse. George Fox, some years ago, came into these parts, and, by strange infatuation, did infuse the Quakers' principles into some small number of the people . . . it hath continued to grow ever since very numerous . . . sending in men to exhort them in their wicked principles.

Quakers were not the only thorns in the Governor's side. The vacuum left by the absence of any Anglican church was being filled by Scotch Presbyterians, Dutch Lutherans, French Calvinists, and Irish Catholics. Together they comprised the Dissenters, and together they rose in revolt when the Assembly levied a poll tax which everyone in the colony must pay in support of the Established Church.

A roster of tho battle forces was made up by the Reverend John Blair, visiting official of the Association for the Propagation of the Gospel in Foreign Parts. There were, he reported:

1. Quakers.
2. Those who had no religion but would be Quakers if it did not demand greater purity of life.
3. Something like Presbyterians, upheld by some idle fellows who preach and baptize without any manner of orders from any pretended church.
4. Zealous Churchmen, fewest in numbers but the better sort of people.

Quaker ways were repellent to the better sort of people. They refused to take off their hats to anyone, however highly placed. There was the outrageous custom of letting women speak up in so-called religious meeting. When accosted with St. Paul's views in this matter, the mild and infuriating reply came back: "Thee knows St. Paul was not partial to females."

The use of "thee" and "thou" also rubbed raw the better sort of people. In the amused words of Penn: "Thou *me*, thou my dog! If thou thou'st me I'll thou thy teeth down thy throat!"

A kindlier view of the Dissenters of Albemarle than Governor Walker's was presented by John Lawson, surveyor-general of the Province. Their women he describes as "the most industrious Sex in that Place . . . they are often fair, and have very brisk, charming eyes which sets them off to Advantage. They marry very young; some at Thirteen or Fourteen; and she who stays till Twenty is reckoned a stale Maid." The women were fruitful, most houses being filled with Little Ones. Sterile wives "have removed to Carolina and become joyful Mothers."

Lawson praises their making of clothing, their handling of canoes, their helping in the fields at harvest, "pride seldom banishing good Housewifery." The children were docile; the young men of a bashful, sober behavior.

This gentle-minded observer's solution of the Indian problem was intermarriage, in place of the casual taking of Indian maidens he had seen on the trails.

John Lawson's warmth toward the Dissenters appears to advantage over Governor Walker's chilly disapproval of their "wicked principles." Yet the Governor was being officially correct, for the times held that the welfare of the kingdom depended on all its subjects being under discipline of the one Church.

Only forty years had passed since the warrior aristocrats had won back the Throne for Charles II from Cromwell's Covenanters. Lord Shaftesbury and John Locke in drafting the Fundamental Constitutions for Carolina had thought to make certain once and for all that the intermingled authority of the Crown and the Established Church should stand supreme in the New World.

Proprietary Governor Walker was right in scolding London for not supplying the funds and clergy necessary to create strong parishes. The one small brick Anglican church built at Bath could not serve all the better sort of people, let alone the new hundreds of Quakers and other Dissenters. These, finding themselves a majority, took to politics and captured the Assembly. The Governor fought back by denying seats to elected Quaker Assemblymen who would *affirm* loyalty to the King but not *swear* it. In retaliation the Dissenters unseated one governor and wound up caught between two claimant governors. When one faction attempted to capture the rival governor with an armed brigantine, Governor Spotswood of Virginia intervened. This was "a numerous Democracy" run riot.

•

From its first settlement in 1725, the Lower Cape Fear became the inheritor of these politico-religious quarrels. John Porter and

Edward Moseley, another friend of the Friends, both moved to the Lower Cape Fear and both intermarried with and became stalwarts of The Family. They remained Anglicans in good standing, as did those who came up from Goose Creek. But the treatment they were to accord the Established Church was by London standards little better than dissidence itself. Of all the peoples eventually occupying the Lower and Upper Cape Fear, the tidewater planters had the least of formal piety.

The concept of a nearness to God in the wilderness implies communion in an undisturbed cathedral of trees, rocks, and sea. The Moores, Allens, Moseleys, Ashes, and others of the Lower Cape Fear were vigorously active in taking nature's cathedral apart to turn the pieces into barrels or turpentine and the shore lines into rice paddies. They were happily content in reshaping disorderly nature into orderly plantations. This was not to foreclose the qualities of kindness, gallantry, a standard of ethics, and a respect for the development of the mind. Good books were brought in from England along with good furniture. But of devotion to religion there was little to show.

It required thirty years to raise the structure of St. Philips Church at Brunswick. The Assembly created St. Philips Parish in 1735 and levied a poll tax to build the church. Planters permitted their slaves to work on it during off-crop seasons. Two lotteries were held in aid of the building fund. By 1754 the walls had risen above window level. In that year Arthur Dobbs, a devout Anglican, took over as royal governor and made his residence at Brunswick. The rising church edifice lay on the west edge of the town where the Governor must have kept an eye on its rather painfully slow progress. He proposed St. Philips should be the King's Chapel of North Carolina. But when, in 1760, it was finally finished, a summer storm launched a thunderbolt at St. Philips' new roof and collapsed it. Repairs were made under Dobbs's successor, William Tryon, who contributed forty guineas to import windows from England, and persuaded King George to donate a silver altar service. Yet the church rolls in this period showed only fifteen communicants, three of them Negroes.

•

In North Carolina's colonial period, viable religion was more the possession of the Dissenter groups who settled the Upper Cape Fear.

On a map the river's entire system takes the shape of a lopsided goblet. Its base is the thirty-mile salt estuary which The Family pre-empted in 1725. Its 150-mile stem rises from Wilmington into the high piedmont. Scots Highlanders took the land west of the stem. East of it the lowland plain was occupied by Scotch-Irish from Pennsylvania, English from Virginia, and some pockets of Swiss, French, and Germans. The bowl of the goblet, outlined by the Haw and Deep rivers, remained a hunting ground for Cherokee and white buckskin boys until 1750. Then the Quakers settled on a Haw tributary, Cane Creek. Two years later the Moravians bought 98,985 acres of Granville land lying northwest of the goblet's rim.

All of the Upper Cape Fear settlements were made between 1732 and the Revolution. Since no other racial or religious invasion occurred, the original groups remained their own selves. In Harnett County you were a Scot, in Guilford a Quaker, in Forsyth a Moravian. Isolation and poor roads for generations preserved the special group qualities—clan loyalty, or Quaker love of peace, or Moravian simplicity. Religion, too, bound each group together and made strangers of other sects.

The osmosis of land hunger drew varied peoples up other Atlantic coast rivers. On the Hudson the Dutch and the English, on the Delaware the Swedes and the English, intermingled and intermarried and became the new race of Americans. Uniquely, the Cape Fear valley was a patchwork of peoples who held hard to their own prejudices. It would require violence and bloodshed to meld them.

•

John Lawson influenced Quakers in their choice of the Cane
Creek settlement. At Albemarle, he was their friend and must
have related his 1708 trek across the Deep and the Haw. Lawson
was their kind of man, an advocate of peace with the Indians, an
observant traveler who had spent his trail nights with the chiefs in
feasting and good-natured talk.

The Cane Creek country was along Lawson's piedmont route.
This was his description of it:

> All the pine trees have vanished . . . We passed through a deli-
> cate rich Soil this day; no great Hills, but pretty Risings and Levels,
> which made a beautiful Country. We likewise passed three Rivers
> this day . . . not the least question but we had passed over the
> North West Branch of the Cape Fair [it was the Deep River] . . .
> We were much taken with the Fertility and Pleasantness of the
> Neck of Land between these two Branches . . . At last there ap-
> peared to us such another delicious, rapid stream as that of the
> Sapona . . . we stripped, and with great difficulty (by God's As-
> sistance) got safe to the North side of the famous Hau-River (so-
> called) from the Sissipahau Indians, who dwell upon this Stream,
> which is one of the main branches of the Cape Fair, there being
> rich land enough to contain some Thousands of Families; for which
> Reason I hope in a short time it will be planted . . . the Land is
> extraordinary Rich, no Man that will be content within the Bounds
> of Reason, can have any grounds to dislike it.

Forty more years passed while the oaks grew bigger and the
passenger pigeon flights darkened the skies. Then the oxcarts
came in slow streams, carrying the girls with very brisk, charming
eyes and a propensity to fill the houses with Little Ones.

The Quakers became backwoodsmen, remote alike from the an-
tagonisms, politics, and culture of the tidewater. Their farmhouses
would be slab shacks with dirt floors, their household goods
homemade. Between them and the Lower Cape Fear all communication and rapport halted. The Quakers had far better contact
with Philadelphia. They read Benjamin Franklin's homilies and

had their understanding of colonial politics from Eastern opinions.

The Quakers may be ranked as backwoods saints, yet with a worldly touch compared to the Moravian brothers and sisters who inherited the earth to their northwest.

The Unity of Brethren began in the fifteenth century among the followers of John Huss. That martyr's code of obedience only to conscience was sufficiently unpopular to harry the Brethren from Moravia into Saxony, and threaten their survival as a church. In the early eighteenth century they found a patron in Count Nikolaus Ludwig von Zinzendorf, who gave them sanctuary on his Herrnhut estate and eventually arranged for their transport to Pennsylvania. There the idea of a North Carolina colony developed. Bishop August Gottlieb Spangenberg, traveling as Brother Joseph, led a six months' exploration up the Cape Fear to the Yadkin, naming the tract Wachovia after the South Austrian home of Count Zinzendorf.

On October 7, 1753, the advance party, led by the Reverend Adam Grube, set out for their new holdings. No nine men ever were more carefully chosen to assure the success of a wilderness settlement. Among them they mustered these callings: pastor, cook, gardener, treasurer, work superintendent, surgeon, tailor, baker, and stockman. They would subsist occasionally on cornmeal mush and stewed pumpkins, but there would be no "starving time," nor lack of shelter where these craftsmen put their careful plans into execution.

When the nine reached their land, they held a love feast and Brother Grube made a song:

We hold arrival love feast here in Carolina land,
    A company of Bretheren true, a little pilgrim band
Called by the Lord to be of those who through the whole world go
    To tell of Jesus everywhere, and nought but Jesus know.

To the first town they built, Bethabara, came Anna Catharina wearing the blue ribbon of a Single Sister. Four times in her long life she was to exchange this for the wife's white ribbon, and three times for the widow's ribbon, each marriage arranged to suit the community's need, yet each marked by serenity and a devotion to the spouse of others' choosing. She kept a diary, and the music of Bethabara, the hard labor, and the days of walking in God's sight live in the simplicity of her prose.

Unitas Fratrum were not all born Morevians. They were joined by Lutherans, English, Catholics, Danes, Swiss, and Germans. In time they would be asked by Governor Dobbs to admit to their services backsliding Anglicans of the vicinity. Bethabara became a crossroads for lone hunters. The Cherokee roamed to the north of it.

The French and Indian War began during Bethabara's first years. The Moravians, exempted by Parliament from military service, thought it well to lay in a supply of arms, and stockaded their town. The Indians massacred one of their outlying families. Others living outside the stockade galloped their horses whenever bent on a visit to the town. This inspired a Cherokee to excuse his bad aim with the remark, "the Dutchers had big fat horses and rode like the devil."

Moravian products and produce went two ways, the long route to Charleston where European imports were varied and cheaper, and the shorter route to Cross Creek on the Cape Fear where flatboats could pick up the cargo to Wilmington and bring merchandise back. One Cross Creek shipment brought rosebushes, rosemary, Chickasaw plum and longleaf pine seedlings; and on one day of rejoicing a pipe organ from England was uncrated, the first in western North Carolina.

The Brethren, alone of the Upper Cape Fear pioneers, nursed no grievances against the tidewater planters and the King's government. When Governor Dobbs was nearing eighty and reported ill, two Moravians journeyed to Brunswick to comfort him. After Dobbs's death, Governor William Tryon would become their friend and honored guest.

Music marked the hours and song accompanied work in Bethabara. Once the Cherokee, creeping close to the stockade for an attack, heard the night watchman's trumpet and then the dawn bells ringing for early prayers. The Indians, supposing these were alarums to indicate that they were discovered, backed off for a better chance to catch the Dutchers napping.

Sister Anna Catharina, when the war was over, wrote in her diary: "I sometimes wonder whether different treatment in the beginning might have kept them friendly instead of making them our enemies." She was right, yet she was innocent of the trade rivalries of distant England and France.

Fever once decimated the settlement. Anna Catharina's then husband, the surveyor Christian Reuter, wrote a song about it:

> This hundred-thousand acre field
> Now truly consecrate shall be,
> Therefore the angel reapers come
> And bear the first fruits home to Me.

The fever victims were buried in God's Acre, the Sisters in their allotted half, the Brothers in theirs. At Salem, the Moravians' architectural masterpiece, the Brothers House, stands as a monument to their feeling, whether born of delicacy or hardheaded precaution, that the sexes should stand at a little distance from each other.

•

The Moravians, who owned their land and paid taxes when due, were calculated to please a royal governor harassed by all other back-country people with clamors against taxes and rebellious attempts at evasion. But however annoying were the clamor and the rebellion, they were justified. For if the Moravians and the Quakers were the saints of the backwoods, the sinners were the members of Tryon's official family.

These were the cheating tax collectors, the sheriffs who fore-closed on delinquents and sold to their own profit the property thus obtained, the county clerks and judges whose demands the sheriffs enforced. Every member of the tax-collecting system had bought his office as an investment. His living depended on how much he could collect legally or beyond set rates. Back country officialdom was on a spree of extracurricular collecting.

A boom had struck the grassy uplands and forests of the piedmont. A thousand wagons heaped with household goods, women, and children entered the territory in 1765. Orange County grew from twenty taxables to 4,000. It was worth while to bid high for the office of clerk or have Assembly friends to recommend your appointment to the bench.

Governor Tryon was chief of the Council, that Upper House political forum of the same planter families who had played ducks and drakes with proprietary governors. Tryon appointed the chief justice of the province and his two associates. The county courts were appointed by the Council; the county sheriff was drawn from a panel of three names submitted by the court. Through this line of command the Council fixed the fees and taxes to be paid in the counties, named the judges who decided penalties and, through them, the sheriffs who would do the collecting. This "courthouse ring," as Chapel Hill's historian, Hugh Talmage Lefler, puts it in modern connotation, had a practical interest in the burgeoning population of the piedmont. The clerk of pleas rented the office of county clerk to the highest bidder. Each of the thirty-four county clerks reaped fees ranging from £50 to £500 a year.

The spoils system was not considered discreditable. The governor himself was expected to profit in office. The check on abuses was personal integrity, and that William Tryon had. But it was a far piece up the river to Orange County where local quitrent, fee and tax collectors were taking what the traffic would bear. Word came out of the woods of mass meeting and rioting by farmers who called themselves Regulators. It was the misfortune of Governor Tryon to inherit a crisis long brewing under Governor Dobbs.

No British administrator had arrived in North America with better qualifications than William Tryon. He was a vigorous thirty-eight years old, with the aplomb of Eton and Cambridge and the military skills of nineteen years as a British officer. The £30,000 dowry brought to their marriage by Margaret Wake relieved him of the necessity to be more than respectably acquisitive. His descent from Queen Elizabeth's Essex could have, or should have, impressed the squires of Brunswick and Wilmington. In point of fact, they liked him and he liked them, and their mutual tragedy was the existence of arbitrary Crown power which it was Tryon's duty to assert and the Americans' choice to oppose.

During Tryon's six years as royal governor the matters of baptism, marriage permits, religious education of the young, and tenure of the clergy were in dispute between Cape Fear vestrymen and the Crown. The heat generated by this religious friction, when combined with political dissidence, would eventually mount to a flame in which St. Philips would be consumed. In 1776 a landing party from the British fleet of Lord Cornwallis would set the torch to Brunswick Town and St. Philips.

Today inside its still standing walls the oblong of ground is a venerated spot. Confederate dead were placed there after the Battle of Fort Anderson in 1865. Occasional services are held there, with song and prayer of a perhaps more heartfelt quality than any which ever rose when the St. Philips roof briefly sheltered worshipers.

Yet piety is not the quality most associated with St. Philips. The bare walls stand as a martyr's monument to a New World religious triumph, the final breaking of the bonds which held the worship of God to secular power.

The waters of the Lower Cape Fear in 1765 were bright with sails. Coastal schooners and sloops were trading with islands of the Caribbean. The larger brigantines were serving on the stormy New England run. Three-masted ships and two-masted snows were working the Atlantic crossing. Brunswick, with an annual export of 50,000 barrels of tar, pitch, and turpentine, was still the leading port for naval stores.

Wilmington had the larger part of the lumber trade. The fifty mills in the region exported a million and a half feet of lumber and as many shingles. The location of Wilmington at the Forks made it the market for upriver deerskins and farm products. Cypress canoes and periaugers brought passengers from Cross Creek.

The port of entry had become the trading center for the prosperous planters of the coast and an expanding hinterland population. Both relied on overseas imports for the staples of living and frivolities of fashion. They paid in bulk products of forest and rice paddy for West Indian sugar, spices, molasses, and slaves, and for all the English finished products which they could not make for themselves.

The shoppers at Jonathan Dunbibin's "ready money store" near the Wilmington Market alighted from post chaises driven up the Brunswick road or along the highway extending now above Wilmington all the way to Bath and Edenton. For thirty miles below Wilmington, and as many above on the banks of the fresh-water river, the plantations adjoined each other. The second generation of the founding families had come into the security of profitable trade and the pride of fine establishments.

George Moore of Moorefield was perhaps the first to arrange an annual hegira from the river to the Atlantic sand dunes. Along a fifteen mile road hacked through the forest, the first hot days of summer saw a procession of the family on horseback followed by slaves afoot and shouldering the chairs, bedsteads, and tables which would furnish the seashore retreat.

Judge Maurice Moore and his brother Colonel James Moore had their seats upriver from Orton Plantation. The second Cornelius Harnett built Hilton on a promontory beyond Wilmington. Colonel John Ashe had the family place, Grovely, at the mouth of Old Town Creek. Moses John De Rossett was Mayor of Wilmington, Alexander Lillington, the second of his name, had organized the militia of Hanover and Duplin counties. The Assembly speakers and the members of the Assembly and Council were descendants of The Family, or akin in interests.

There were a few eccentrics. Lawyer Archibald Maclaine was described as a man of "irrisistable passions . . . The slightest spark sufficed to kindle into flame his combustible nature: The explosions of his wrath were sudden and terrific, and his fiery denunciations and heated satire seethed and scorched as burning lava." The author of this incandescent characterization found it appropriate that Archibald Maclaine's body should eventually lie under the acid chamber of a guano plant built over his grave.

Across from Orton, on the less socially acceptable eastern shore of the estuary, lived Major Jack Wheeler, a military man and one who also excelled in vituperation. He was fond of personal fights, yet good-natured and never seriously injured anyone, except when he indulged his fun-loving habit of carrying a forceps with which he used to extract a tooth from a prostrate antagonist. His abilities later raised him to the rank of brevet major on the battlefield of Brandywine.

Excepting a few of brick, the plantation houses were comfortable frame structures with breezy verandas and many farm outbuildings. Most of them eventually burned by domestic accident or the torch of war. Wilmington, building now in brick, had by 1765 supplanted Brunswick as a social and trade center. The sons of the Indian-fighter founding fathers were spending more time in their libraries. James Innes of Point Pleasant left an estate for education. Edward Moseley's will listed four hundred books. Speaker Samuel Swann had edited with Moseley the *Revisal of the Laws of the Province of North Carolina*, the first book printed in the province. The laughter of the London coffeehouses re-echoed upon arrival of copies of *The Spectator* and *The Tatler*. Dr. John Eustace corresponded with Laurence Sterne. A young poet, Thomas Godfrey, earning his living as a factor at Wilmington, wrote a blank verse drama, *The Prince of Parthia*, which became the first play written by an American and performed in America by a professional company.

Godfrey died at Wilmington in 1763, four years before *The Prince of Parthia* had its premiere in Philadelphia. North Carolina remembered him 200 years later by a revival of *The Prince* in the high Blue Ridge town of Burnsville. And Tom Godfrey may have left something in the aura of Wilmington which caused it later to pioneer the American Little Theatre movement.

•

William Tryon arrived at this pleasant peak of the Lower Cape Fear's trade, social, and cultural life. Expecting to succeed Governor Dobbs at once, he was forced to wait six months while the aged and ailing Dobbs clung to office. In April of 1765 Dobbs died while preparing to sail to England. Tryon took the oath as governor before the council at Wilmington and moved his wife and small daughter into Russellboro, the house between Orton and Brunswick which Dobbs had made the governor's residence.

Tryon's training in the British Army equipped him to serve as ex-official commander of the militia of the province. But a greater asset was his learning. Latin was as basic to him as English. Pliny, Epictetus, Cicero, Horace, Virgil were in his library alongside his contemporaries of the Age of Enlightenment. Military manuals picked up in his years of service were outbalanced by treatises on religion and philosophy. That he wanted to be prepared for his colonial duties appears in his collection of Americana—Burke's *The European Settlement in America*, Captain John Smith's *Description of New England*, John Lawson's *History of North Carolina* and the accounts of the French explorers in America.

The crude problems of earlier governors—land patent grabs and personal assaults—were gone with the pioneer generation which created them. Governor Tryon, with the enthusiasm of all new administrators, at once confided to his Assembly plans for new roads and an efficient mail service. He might have saved his breath. Ten days before he took the oath of office at Wilmington, Parliament in London had passed the Stamp Act. It would not become effective until November 1, 1775, leaving eight months of trouble ahead.

•

While the Stamp Act opened the rift between England and America, a colonial resistance to overseas control had been going on for a century. Upon the Cape Fear the Lords Proprietors had imposed rules wholly unrealistic for the administration of affairs in an opening continent. Still more important than the blunders of Proprietors and Parliament was the ignorance in London of the fact that life in Carolina was roughing out a new non-European man, cocky in his self-reliance, not awed by greatness to the extent of subserving his own sense of worth. Roger Moore had

called himself King Roger out of emulation of the admired powers
of royalty. But his nephews took the titles of Judge and Colonel in
respect for both the Crown and for their fellow provincials. When
the Crown seemed to fail them, they spoke up and acted. Judge
Maurice Moore in 1765 said of the Stamp Act that the colonists
could legally "be taxed only with their own consent" and that,
lacking representation, they could not "with the least degree of
justice be taxed by Parliament."

These were familiar words, told to the House of Commons by
Benjamin Franklin two years before when Parliament first began
to think up ways by which the colonies could help defray the
mounting costs of protecting their own western boundaries. It was
the method of taxing to which Franklin objected:

> An *external* tax is a duty laid on commodities; that duty is added
> to the first cost and, when it is offered for sale, makes a part of the
> price. If the people do not like it at that price they refuse it; they
> are not obliged to pay it. But an *internal* tax is forced from the
> people without their consent, if not laid down by their own repre-
> sentatives. The Stamp Act says we shall have no commerce, make
> no exchanges of property with each other, neither purchase nor
> grant nor recover debts; we shall neither marry nor make out wills,
> unless we pay such and such sums, and this is intended to extort
> our money from us or ruin us by the consequences of refusing to
> pay it.

The French and Indian War had ended a few months before
Franklin's explanation to the House of Commons. The Treaty of
Paris had given England the French possessions from the Blue
Ridge to the Mississippi. Wolfe had won Canada six years before.
England's public debt was doubled by the war. The proceeds of
the Stamp Act were to be used exclusively in protecting the colonial western frontier and keeping the conquered French and their
Indian allies at peace. England would still have to pay twice as
much as the Stamp Act could yield in this protection of colonial
interests. From the viewpoint of the Empire—the joint holdings
of the English people in which the colonists were participating

owners—there was everything to be said for contributions by the provinces to help pay the costs of this expensive purchase, by war, of very valuable adjoining western real estate.

The stubborn Americans would neither pay as individual provinces nor acknowledge the right of Parliament to settle the problem by placing a not onerous tax on bills, legal documents, newspapers, leases, and insurance policies. No, this method was granting the right of Englishmen in England to tax the purses of Englishmen in America, and where would it end? They took comfort from weighty defenders of their principle in Parliament. Said William Pitt: "This Kingdom has no right to lay a tax upon the Colonies . . . Americans are the sons not the bastards of England."

Pitt clothed these raw assertions with supporting logic, but what clanking of tankards on Wilmington tavern tables must have resounded when the news came in that Americans were not the bastards of England!

•

The professors I listened to at a New England college (the same Yale that Edmund Fanning and Nathan Hale attended) left me with the impression that resistance to the Stamp Act began in Boston and extended as far south as Philadelphia. Sam Adams and Benjamin Franklin were the bellwethers; eventually the South tagged along. . . . This needs rereading. That the first armed resistance to the Stamp Act happened on the Cape Fear was no accident.

Cape Fear merchants and planters were in the same frame of mind as their New England counterparts. They had done their part in the French and Indian War, had sent militia against the Cherokee and voted more money for defense than the province had in circulation. But now they saw no need to import British redcoats to police the far borders of the Ohio. They had paid high import duties which, as Franklin said, merely marked up the prices of goods; but they would not pay direct taxes imposed by rulers of what they now began to consider a foreign state.

•

The attitude toward the Crown was also deteriorating. In 1761 Brunswick had staged a fine noisy demonstration upon arrival of the news that George III had ascended the Throne. The twenty-three-year-old youth, "Farmer George," honest and plodding soul, had shown no talent in selecting ministers alert to Brunswick or Wilmington needs. It has been said that George Grenville, who in 1764 succeeded Lord Bute as the King's adviser, made the Revolution certain by his innovation of reading dispatches from America. Instead of "the Island of New England," to which one of his innocent predecessors had addressed a document, Grenville's poking into colonial affairs revealed a very rich milch cow whose distended udders in all kindness should be relieved.

The inventors of Stamp Act procedures intended that an official in each community have a stock of blank documents—one for wills, one for marriage certificates, etc.—each requiring an appropriate tax. Newspapers were to reserve a space for the stamp. Dr. William Houston of Wilmington was made Stamp Act official. Ships bringing in this expensive stationery were expected about November 1, 1765. In anticipation, the wits of Wilmington, with an assist from John Barleycorn, on October 19 prepared an effigy of Lord Bute (actually Grenville should have been their model) and let it "hang by the Neck for some Time, near the Court-House." By evening five hundred people had gathered. Tar barrels were lit for a bonfire in which the effigy was consumed. The three-year-old *North Carolina Gazette* reported: "they went to every House in Town, and bro't all the Gentlemen to the Bonfire, and insisted upon their drinking LIBERTY, PROPERTY AND NO STAMP Duty, and confusion to Lord B-te and all his Adherents . . . They continued together until 12 of the Clock, and then dispersed, without doing any Mischief."

Hallowe'en being the night before the Stamp Act's effective date, the wits chose this time to prepare an effigy of LIBERTY, put it in a coffin, and march in solemn procession to St. James' churchyard: "But before they committed the Body to the Ground, they thought it advisable to feel its Pulse; and when finding Remains of Life, they returned back to a Bonfire already prepared, placed the Effigy before it in a large Two-arm'd chair, and concluded the evening with great Rejoicings, on finding that LIBERTY had still an Existence in the Colonies.—Not the least Injury was offered to any Person."

Two weeks later the resurrectors of LIBERTY discovered a living figure for their railleries in the person of Stamp Distributor Houston. Behind drums and a flag, three hundred marched to Houston's lodgings where their spokesman demanded to know whether he intended to execute his stamp duties. Houston disclaimed any purpose disagreeable to the people and regaled the crowd with "the best liquors to be had." Nevertheless, they made sure by carrying Houston to the courthouse where he signed his resignation.

This left the port without either stamps or stamp master. Since November 1 it had been illegal to move cargo or ships, to marry, or print newspapers. The *Gazette* came out with a blank space where the stamp should have been and a skull and crossbones underneath.

Tryon summoned fifty citizens from the estuary and upriver to dine with him at Russellboro on November 18. The Governor could not blink at this insubordination. He let his guests know that he had personal doubts about the wisdom of the Stamp Act, yet he was Vice Regent for the King who had signed it. Tryon expressed the hope that none was "desirous of destroying the Dependance on the Mother Country." He promised them that he would try to get North Carolina exempted. Think it over, gentlemen . . .

It would be ten days before H.M.S. *Diligence* sailed into the Cape Fear with a supply of stamped paper aboard. Then the tension would break into action. Meanwhile the Russellboro dinner guests drove back to their homes and their host sat pondering an impossible dilemma. The fact that they had sat in discussion over the Governor's port is extraordinary. Tryon had no redcoats to overawe the people—as Gage had in Boston—nor British Army officers to be amused at the crudities of the provincials. Tryon had been forthright and conciliatory; yet here he was, less than a year in office, caught between the friendships he had carefully cultivated and the hated measure he must soon impose. Nowhere else in America at this time was the situation duplicated. In Boston, New York, and Philadelphia the royal governors and their staffs lived remote from those citizens who were emerging as their fiery antagonists. On the Cape Fear, Bute's hanging, LIBERTY's remarkable return to life, and Houston's resignation had occurred "without any Mischief" and "not the least Injury offered to any Person." The numerous Democracy had decorously drunk their toasts in the best liquors available.

Now the drama was moving into the stage where one side or the other would have to give way. It would come to within the squeeze of a trigger finger; and if the finger had tensed, the lawn at Russellboro, not the streets of Boston, would have known the first blood of the Revolution. No shots were to be fired. Voices remained at conversational level. No liquor, best available or bartender's choice, was involved. What did happen was the confrontation of a royal governor and a Cape Fear citizen, each equal in education and courage, on the issue of the Stamp Tax, a concise enough dispute yet one which in retrospect grows to the proportions of a decision between the old Europe of royal prerogatives and the New World of democracy.

Tryon's confronter was to be Cornelius Harnett. Since he came to be known as "the representative man of the Cape Fear" and "the mightiest single force in North Carolina history during the Revolution," it is pertinent to recall that his father, Cornelius Senior, in company with George Burrington, had assaulted Governor Richard Everard at Edenton, for which he was indicted and forced to flee to Brunswick. Here he ran the tavern and the ferry across to the eastern shore, grew prosperous and was accepted as a member of The Family. That his friendship with the Moores caused Burrington to denounce his former friend Harnett as "fool, blackguard, puppy," is merely evidence of the lively physical and verbal donnybrooks enjoyed by all hands during the early days on the river. In contrast with his father's fisticuffs and billingsgate vis-à-vis two proprietary governors, the younger Cornelius Harnett stood eye to eye with Governor Tryon, at deadly odds but holding on to the conventions of gentlemanly discourse. It came about this way . . .

On November 28 the sloop of war *Diligence*, Captain Phipps, entered the harbor with supplies of stamps and stamped documents. The *Viper*, Captain Lobb, followed in support. There being no port stamp official, the two naval vessels rocked at anchor and the trading ships at Wilmington and Brunswick idled at their docks. Tryon, as helplessly inactive, fumed: "The stagnation of all public business must be attended with fatal consequences to this colony if it subsists but for a few months later."

The deadlock was broken when the trading vessels *Dobbs* and *Patience* arrived from Philadelphia without stamped clearance papers. Captain Lobb seized them in the name of the King. The attorney general of the province was called on to give a decision on the legality of the seizure. During the anxious waiting period, the ebullient spirits of Wilmington consoled themselves by refusing to sell supplies to the *Diligence* and the *Viper*. When a private bumboat attempted to do so, they seized it and threw its crew in jail.

Fort Johnston, that unredoubtable pile which had been built to protect Brunswick from the Spanish and had never fired a gun in anger, had the British ships in range. Colonel Hugh Waddell decided to capture it, but when he and his militia arrived at the fort they found its guns had been spiked by a *Diligence* landing party.

The bolt out of the gathering thunderclouds came on February

16 when the attorney general declared the seizure of the *Dobbs* and *Patience* in consonance with the King's law and ordered them to Nova Scotia for trial. Two days later the leaders of New Hanover, Brunswick, Bladen, and Duplin counties formed at Wilmington an Association Against the Stamp Act. Next day a crowd of 450 men chose Hugh Waddell to lead them to Brunswick. A letter to a friend in London gives Governor Tryon's version:

"The next intelligence I received was in the dark of the evening of the 19th, soon after 6 o'clock, by letter delivered to me by Mr. George Moore and Mr. Cornelius Harnett, bearing date the 19th and signed John Ashe, Thomas Lloyd, Alexander Lillington."

The letter informed Tryon that the people were marching "in hopes of obtaining a peaceful means of redress of their grievance from the commanding officers of His Majesty's ships."

After scanning this impossible request, Tryon declined the offer of a guard to assure his personal protection, and bowed Moore and Harnett out the door. That night 150 armed men surrounded Russellboro.

On the morning of the twentieth a delegation boarded the *Viper* and demanded the release of the *Patience.* Against Tryon's orders, Captain Lobb capitulated. Tryon was not quite left alone that night to face the rising tide of colonials. "Mr. Pennington, His Majesty's comptroller [he wrote] came to let me know there had been a search for him." The Governor took him in and supplied a bed for the night—*under* Tryon's, the scoffers had it.

The finale came next morning. At ten o'clock the citizens drew up within sight of Russellboro. A detachment of sixty, with Cornelius Harnett at their head, marched up to the doorway. Harnett requested that Pennington be turned over to the people.

"Mr. Pennington," the Governor replied, "came into my house for refuge. He is a Crown officer, and as such I will give him all the protection my roof, and the dignity of the character I hold in this Province, can afford him."

Harnett again hoped the Governor would let Pennington go, as the people were determined to take him out of the house if he should be longer detained, an insult they wished to avoid offering their governor.

"An insult that would not tend to any great consequence," Tryon replied, "after they have already offered every insult they could offer, by investing my house, and making me in effect a prisoner before any grievance or oppression had been first represented to me."

Pennington grew uneasy. He would, he said, go with the gentleman. Tryon, his last supporter gone, told Pennington to resign. When Harnett interposed that this would not be necessary, Tryon demanded his written resignation, and having obtained it, propelled Pennington outside with an angry: "Now, sir, you may go!"

The watchers raised a cheer at the appearance of Pennington. They marched him away to sign an oath that he would never issue any stamped paper in the Province of North Carolina. The *Diligence* sailed away with the stamps unpacked. People married and signed leases, made wills, and loaded lumber on board waiting ships, all without benefit of stamps.

Alfred Moore Waddell, historian and descendant of Colonel Hugh Waddell, may be excused some family pride when he wrote: "The only people in America who resisted with arms the landing of the Stamps on their soil, and the first who defied British power with guns in their hands more than 10 years before the Declaration of Independence, were the people of the Lower Cape Fear."

•

William Tryon's pride was hard hit. Letters back to England acknowledged the "most irredeemable failure" that he was ever called upon to pen. He had idle months now to gnaw on his hurt; yet out of it came an absorbing preoccupation. He would build a palace of dignity and grandeur, visible proof of the qualities of the mother country which the colonists had humbled.

The town of New Bern, on the broad triangle where the Neuse and Trent rivers meet, by happy chance lay eighty-seven miles south of Edenton and eighty-seven miles north of Wilmington. When it required two days in the saddle to reach New Bern from either Albemarle or Wilmington, this midway town was certain to be the choice as capital of the province. There Tryon would have a new start, away from the temptation to mix official duty with personal friendship. So he passed the late spring of 1776 sketching floor plans, including the master stroke of designing the palace as both the official place of assembly and the residence of the governor. The savings made by eliminating a separate building for the legislature would justify the cost of a ducal edifice, an elegance beyond the concept of untraveled colonials. Tryon wrote inquiries to London and discovered his perfect architect, John Hawkes.

On June 25 Parliament repealed the Stamp Act. Since its obvious failure as a revenue producer made this inevitable, the grand gesture of a major retraction was made in public, while in ministerial privacy the search went on to find a more soothing approach to the colonial milch cow. This eventually would be the Townshend Act taxes on tea, window glass, lead, and artists' colors; but of this the people of the Cape Fear were ignorant, and loud were the huzzahs for resurrected LIBERTY.

Governor Tryon made a felicitous speech to the Assembly gathered at Wilmington. The happy members of the Council and lower house chose a committee to prepare a response to the Governor's address. Of this committee, Maurice Moore would ultimately, as "Atticus," write withering criticism of Tryon; Cornelius Harnett and Robert Howe would be the only two North Carolinians exempted from a Cornwallis decree of general clemency; Edmund Fanning would become a British officer; and Joseph Hewes would sit in the Continental Congress. But at the moment they were of the King's own men.

A second committee of John Ashe, Fanning, and Howe was

told off to prepare thanks to George III "on the happy event of the repeal of the Stamp Act" and to forward their "love and duty to His Majesty's Royal person."

In this atmosphere Governor Tryon's request for £5,000 to construct a residence at New Bern passed by acclamation. Cape Fear neighbors were after all good fellows, with the makings of English gentlemen.

And so, perhaps, they were, except that their compliance in providing funds for Tryon's palace was based on the false assumption that London had capitulated on the Stamp Act. And Tryon, infatuated with his palace plans, had forgotten the back-country Regulators.

# 8 : The Regulators

In 1768 the old dragon of civil war did lift its evil head again and
try to swallow our country.

 ——Sister Anna Catharina

To John Lawson in 1708 the "pretty Risings and Levels between
the main Branches of the Cape Fair" offered land enough "to contain some Thousands of Families," and sixty years later they were
there from long journeys in time and distance originating in Saxony, London, and Ulster. The virgin soil gave them abundant
crops; their hogs fattened on the forest mast; rough cabins were
easily thrown up for shelter. The living was easy, although it was
a subsistence-and-barter living, with few puncheon floors and no
sidesaddles.

The first generation of pioneers in the piedmont found every
prospect pleasing and only the tax collector vile. There was not
enough hard money to go around. English, Spanish, and French
coins had drifted to London where the Board of Trade refused to
let the province replace them with printed money. A piedmont
farmer could get along by barter without having two shillings to
rub together, except when the sheriff from Hillsboro called on him
for tax payment. That meant borrowing from the local hoarder.
To this the sheriff was always agreeable, leaving instructions for
the debtor to follow him with the money and describing the route

by which he himself was returning to Hillsboro. With the borrowed money in hand, the farmer would set out to follow the sheriff, only to discover that the latter had taken a short cut and, arriving first at Hillsboro, had sold the farm in default of taxes. Twenty years of a couple's labor, the inheritance of their children, had gone into the official maw.

Suppose that the aggrieved farmer hired a lawyer . . . for entering suit on the docket 41s 5d to the clerk, who, in the absence of currency, took it out in work at 18d a day, or twenty-seven days of work for a few minutes of writing. An additional 30s to the lawyer, requiring nineteen more days of work, and "there goes your land to satisfy these cursed hungry caterpillars that will eat out the very bowels of our commonwealth if they are not pulled down from their nests in a very short time."

Any appeals against these injustices had to be addressed to the very people whose livings depended on taxes and fees instead of salaries. The sheriff lived well according to his initiative in distraining property for taxes. The county clerk had bought his office at auction and must top that in fees. The recorder could split one item into two and double his fee. None of this might have driven the victims to violence had the officials kept to known and legal fees. The one lawbook in the region which set the fees down in black and white was kept hidden from the farmers.

Under the weight of these evils, and with no answers to their pleas to the officials, restlessness brewed in farmer gatherings. It showed in the way that they received the news that the Stamp Act had been repealed. Orange County was of a mind to applaud the defeat of the will of Parliament. But their version of the triumph of the Americans came from Philadelphia rather than from up the Cape Fear. Hermon Husband, a Maryland-born Quaker in his late twenties, was in correspondence with Benjamin Franklin whose patriotic pamphlets he reprinted and circulated by saddlebag to the farthest farms of Orange County. It was natural to associate defiance of English taxes with Pennsylvania patriots rather than with tidewater planters who were part and parcel of the officialdom which was gouging illegal taxes from them. So when the farmers met at Sandy Creek to cheer the Stamp Act repeal, they contrived a mixture of praise for whatever the Assembly had done to stop British tyranny and a warning not to try the same thing upcountry:

> While the Sons of Liberty withstood the Lords In Parliament in behalf of true liberty, let not officers under them carry on unjust oppression in our own province . . . Take this as a maxim, that while men are men, though you should see all the Sons of Liberty set in office and vested with power, they would soon corrupt again and oppress, if they were not called upon to give an account of their stewardship. . . .

They sent this resolve to Colonel Edmund Fanning for transmission to Wilmington and called a second meeting at which ten county officials promised to be present. But the concept of officials being called upon to account to the people was distasteful to Colonel Fanning. He kept his people home and sent a messenger to Sandy Creek to tell the farmers that in his opinion their meeting was nothing less than insurrection. Sobered by this statement, the Sandy Creek men let their next meeting fall into the hands of a hotspur faction calling themselves Regulators. Under the leadership of Hermon Husband, William Butler, and Schoolmaster Rednap Howell, they sent this message to Fanning:

> We are determined to have officers of this county under a better and honester regulation . . . Think not to frighten us with rebellion . . . To be plain with you, it is our intent to have a full settlement of you in every particular point that is matter of doubt with this, so fail not to send an answer by the bearer.

Colonel Fanning changed his estimate of the movement from insurrection to treason. The moderate Sandy Creek men dropped back to an advisory role.

•

The year 1767 was the most free from care that Governor Tryon
was to enjoy in North Carolina. His political honeymoon held
with the Assembly. There was time for road building. The Regulator troubles seemed quiescent under the firm hand of Colonel
Fanning. Not that Tryon was indifferent to injustices to the back-
country men. During this year he wrote in their behalf to the Earl
of Hillsborough, Secretary of State for the Colonies and, most
helpfully, Lady Tryon's kinsman and his own patron. To Hillsborough Tryon pointed out the ills of a lack of provincial currency
and pleaded for permission to print money. This the Colonial Secretary refused. It was well enough to please his protégé but quite
another thing to interfere with Empire trade patterns.

Personal tragedy struck the Tryons early in 1767 with the death
in infancy of the only son they were to have. To divert Lady
Tryon, the Governor took her that spring on a journey to the foot-
hills of the Blue Ridge, where he met with the Cherokee to fix the
boundary beyond which white homesteaders would not be allowed to settle. The Indians accepted the first mountain range as
the treaty line. Several chiefs bore variations of the name "Wolf."
When they gave Tryon the title "The Great Wolf," it was a high
token of respect.

The favor of the savages and the cool air of their forest hunting
grounds were remote from tidewater bickerings. The Governor
and his Lady returned through a region to be entitled Tryon
County until later events were to scratch their name from the
maps. Yet a mountain and a pleasant mountain town are still
called Tryon in memory of this interlude.

On the return trip the Tryons visited the Moravians at Bethabara. The Governor was interested in their highly successful community projects. He was informed that whatever a Brother earned
was his own to keep, but that each contributed and shared in a
common pool of labor. Tools were handed to an apprentice on
credit, to be paid for in installments. Tryon entered orders for a

windmill, candles, butter, tallow, and flour, to be delivered by wagon to Brunswick.

Lady Tryon admired the children and their good behavior, and her husband diplomatically agreed with her. A musician herself, Lady Tryon sat at the pipe organ and Sister Krause joined her in singing a hymn while the Governor lent a humming accompaniment. That night the French horns played softly outside the Tryons' window.

That summer the Governor moved Lady Tryon and Margaret to Hillsboro, high in the piedmont hills. He himself had named the town in honor of his belted patron and kinsman by marriage, Lord Hillsborough. Tryon took one of the few frame houses in this log-cabin county seat. Here the pleasant interlude continued. The townspeople named Margaret Tryon Street after his small daughter. Hillsboro also afforded him the civilized conversation of Edmund Fanning.

There was a natural empathy between the well-educated Englishman and the brilliant Yale classics scholar. A common purpose to maintain law and order in the Carolina hinterland bound them together. Ten years younger than the Governor, Fanning had the vigor and will to prevent any such colonial impudence as Tryon himself had experienced at Brunswick. As a member of the Assembly, Fanning might help persuade that body to increase the £5,000 appropriated for the palace at New Bern.

Ground had been broken for the palace. Architect Hawkes's plans were in Tryon's hands. They showed that the £5,000 would cover no more than the land and the foundations. For this was to be the finest building in North America. The drawings showed a brick main edifice with stone trim. It was flanked on the left by a kitchen wing, on the right by a stable and carriage wing, both ample to support State affairs in grandeur. A paneled room was to house Tryon's library, and there would be a dining room where the entire Council could be seated, and a vast chamber in which the Assembly could convene. The Moores' Orton Plantation and Cornelius Harnett's Hilton could both be swallowed up by this structure. With its wrought-iron gateway and walled rear garden sloping to the Trent River, the palace would embody that Britannic puissance to which colonials also were heir, if they would but keep their interests in alignment with Mother England's.

It so happened that Fanning's enthusiasm for the larger palace appropriation would not be important when the Assembly met late in the fall of '67. Unanimously they voted the palace an additional £10,000. This would require a new poll tax of 2s 5d (several days of work by a piedmont farmer lacking specie) for three years. Governor Tryon palliated this by announcing that the poll tax for 1767 must be held to 7s, and by a strong speech that county sheriffs must not, upon penalty, extort more than the legal tax.

"The Sheriffs," Tryon told the Assembly, "have embezzled more than half of the public money ordered to be raised and collected by them."

•

By the spring of 1768 half of the Orange County men had joined the group who called themselves "Regulators" and the rest were sympathizers. They were first-generation pioneers with hands horny from ax haft and hoe handle, each owning a small farm and with no mind to lose it to royal officeholders. Their aim was to hold annual meetings with the officials to examine the county books and by "regulation" keep taxes and fees within legal limits. They were petitioners to, not rebels against, authority.

One April day in '68 the sheriff seized a Regulator's mare for taxes. A squad of mounted Regulators invaded Hillsboro and rode off with the recaptured mare at tether. In passing Fanning's house they fired rifleshots through the roof. Colonel Fanning called for a militia muster. When only a few responded, he led a foray to Sandy Creek where he arrested Husband and Butler and lodged them in the Hillsboro jail.

Negotiations began behind Fanning's back. The Reverend George Micklejohn, Hillsboro's Presbyterian minister, arranged

with the Regulators for a joint meeting on May 11. Before this
could take place, Fanning had informed Governor Tryon by
courier to Brunswick that the Regulators had sworn to pay no
more taxes, to kill all officers who tried to collect them, and to
arraign all officials "before the bar of their shallow understanding." He added that the Regulators were threatening to invest
Hillsboro for the rescue of Husband and Butler, and that he was
prepared to make a stand against them.

Fanning was right on only one point. A body of seven hundred
Regulators did appear at Hillsboro. Husband and Butler were
hastily released from jail, after promises that they would end
abusing the officers. The excited rescuers were further quieted by
the appearance of the Governor's secretary who in Tryon's name
told them that if they would petition the Governor and return to
their homes, he would see that entire justice was done them.

This was exactly what the Regulators had hoped would happen
at the May eleventh meeting. They at once wrote their petition.
But instead of sending it to Tryon, Fanning wrote his own version
of what the Regulators should say, letting them know that his
wording was the only one which would "go down with the Governor." In Fanning's draft the Regulators were to denounce their
past conduct as "illegal and unwarrantable," declare that they had
been mistaken in their charges against the officers, and promise to
throw themselves entirely on the mercy of Tryon.

The Regulators decided to bypass Fanning. They drew up doc-
umented charges against the sheriff, clerk, and register (being
Fanning himself) and sent them to Tryon, together with a request
for pardon for anything they had done contrary to the King's
peace and government.

Tryon's eyes were veiled by the misrepresentation and downright lies of Fanning, and perhaps by his feeling that so decent a
chap as Fanning should not be made the butt of country oafs who
shot through his roof, stole a mare belonging to the government,
and were evading taxes. His reply to the Regulators was chilly,
hinting at treason and its consequences, endorsing the vigorous

action of Colonel Fanning, and telling them to hold no further meetings.

Content that this show of royal authority would end the matter, he bundled Lady Tryon and Margaret into a chaise and set out to spend the summer at Hillsboro which, since it was Fanning's headquarters, was comparable to seeking the cool of a sylvan glade and sitting on a nest of yellow jackets.

Tryon sent word to an August first Regulator meeting that the attorney general would prosecute officials charged with extortion, and that the Regulators should pay their taxes to the sheriff. The Regulators replied that they themselves and the Governor were alike victims of these petty officials: "Seeing that these sons of Zeruiah are like to prove too hard for your Excellency, as well as for us . . ." So, in order to strengthen Tryon's hands, they would now submit their demands direct to the Assembly.

Before Tryon had time to recover from this impudence, a gathering of a thousand Regulators sent Tryon delegates to discover whether or not he was enlisting the Indians against them.

Somewhere along the way the Governor's patience cracked. Why couldn't they pay their taxes like proper British subjects? Who had started the ridiculous rumor that he would set his friends the Cherokee against them? If those thousand Regulator idlers had stayed home to work their farms they would have earned their tax money. They'd strengthen *his* hands, would they! And who the devil was Zeruiah?

Two days after the meeting of August 17, Tryon was in Salisbury recruiting the militia. The British military man had taken over. For the next month he held reviews and administered oaths of allegiance in Mecklenburg, Rowan, and Orange counties. It did not come easily. At rallies he read a letter in which four Presbyterian ministers pledged loyalty to government and heaped maledictions on the Regulators. The reading was followed by a liberal handing around of beer and toddy among the volunteers and thus reluctance to take the oath was overcome.

The Regulators were busy at their own musters. To the annoy-

ance of the Moravians (from whom Tryon had ordered two wagonloads of zwieback for his militia), Salem was chosen by the
Regulators as a drill ground. A herd of 150 hogs, accompanying
the Regulators as ambulatory bacon, broke into a Moravian field
of turnips and pumpkins, which escaped destruction only because
at the same moment bears attacked the hogs, killing some and
driving away the rest. The Moravian witness who reported this
dispensation of Providence—along with a Regulator threat to take
action on the loss of the hogs—wryly commented: "You can't
complain of bears at a Regulator meeting."

For his officers Tryon looked to the tidewater planters and his
official family. To a man they responded—James Moore and his
brother Maurice, the younger Alexander Lillington, John Ashe,
Cornelius Harnett—all the Sons of Liberty who two years before
had flouted Tryon on paying a Stamp Tax now joined him in
marching against the back-country tax delinquents.

No army north of the Mexican border ever boasted so high a
ratio of general officers to enlisted men. There were six lieutenant
generals, two major generals, three adjutant generals, two majors
of brigades, seven colonels, five lieutenant colonels, four majors
and thirty-one captains. Only 1,153 were privates. Politicians from
the banks of the Lower Cape Fear had something to save up for
their grandchildren, a military commission. Edmund Fanning,
John Frohock (he who had been beaten by angry farmers in the
Granville land dispute), Thomas Hart (the obnoxious former
sheriff of Orange County), eighteen Assemblymen, and six Councilmen marched with Tryon, who might well have addressed
them: "Gentlemen, today's meeting is not a council of war; instead you will convene in your capacity as members of the legislature." For these were the same men to whom the Regulators had
proposed to submit their cause in Assembly, the sons of Zeruiah
who were likely to prove too hard for the Governor to handle.

After all this, the impending battle dissolved into an exchange
of messages. The Regulators wanted to negotiate, not fight. Their
battleline of 3,700 farmers faced Tryon's force of half that num-

ber. Yet they sent across a meek request to know "the terms on which submission would be accepted." The council of war (Tryon was ill and absent) offered pardon upon a promise to pay taxes and not obstruct officers. There were dickerings about hostages, some arrests, then pardons, ending in a dejected trailing of squirrel rifles back to the farms. All the King's horses and all the King's men also marched right back again. The expedition cost the Province £4,844 and not a drop of blood.

The show of military might served its purpose of protecting the Hillsboro trials. Husband was acquitted. Butler and two other Regulators were fined and jailed. True bills against others were quashed. Tryon hoped leniency would dampen the last sparks of Regulation.

Next Fanning stood trial on indictments of having collected multiple fees when one only was legal. He was convicted on five counts and for each offense was fined one penny. His appeal eventually reached London where it disappeared in the fogs of the Inner Temple.

The Regulators, far from quieted, decided to try politics in lieu of armed rebellion. For a year they lay doggo, then in the summer of 1769 they ran members for the Assembly and captured a working majority of seats. Before this there had been no party lines in the Assembly. Charles Robinson, chosen by Anson County Regulators as their Assembly candidate, received the first political nomination ever made in America.

Husband was elected to replace Fanning in Orange County; Regulator Christopher Nation won over Frohock in Rowan. These victories brought about Henry Eustace McCulloch's comment in London: "The madness of the people must be great, indeed, to trust such wretches as Hermon Husband and Christopher Nation as their representatives."

A moment's pause in this farrago would have revealed the cause and obvious cure of the agitation. The Regulators had begun as mild protestants against thievery cloaked with official authority. Tryon admitted this—having once set the overcharges of the officials at £49,000—and his moves to stop it were many and sternly worded. But to scold county officials meant nothing to the principal beneficiaries of the system, the Assemblymen, Councilmen, registers, and judges. Moreover these officials regarded the attempt of the people to question official actions as treason and a direct threat to authority. The Crown officers and the tidewater planters could have benefited by heeding a forecast made by Brother Graff that Hermon Husband's pamphlets were "inflaming the minds of men and that the fire would spread beyond control." While it would not consume the planters themselves, Hermon Husband's bonfire would spread, along with others, up the Eastern seaboard into a general conflagration which would consume the notion that royal authority was exempt from responsibility to the people.

When the gavel opened the first Regulator-dominated Assembly in October 1769, Hermon Husband arose to read petitions from the piedmont counties; and Edmund Fanning was not there to edit them. The petitions pleaded for these reforms: elections by ballot, taxation on property instead of per capita, the issuance of paper money, small debts to be sued for without lawyers, a salary for the chief justice instead of fees, the restriction of clerks' fees, and an end to making land grants without regard to the legal limit of fifty acres. They requested, too, that the Established Church monopoly on performing marriage services be ended. Finally, they asked that Benjamin Franklin be appointed their agent in London.

The business of writing these proposals into bills was hardly under way when a messenger arrived from Virginia with word that its Assembly had been dissolved when it protested Townshend Act taxes. A meeting at the Raleigh Tavern in Williamsburg, George Washington in the chair, had broadcast appeals to all the colonies that each pass a nonimportation act against British goods.

Governor Tryon, disapproving of the Townshend Act as he had the Stamp Act, risked his own career by saying so, and was reprimanded in Parliament. His patron, Lord Hillsborough, saved Tryon's official head, but wrote him to dissolve his Assembly. The Regulators returned home empty-handed. Tryon in a letter to Lord Hillsborough decked his forebodings in the language of polite correspondence: "Confidence, my lord—that delicate polish in public transactions—has received an ugly scratch, and I fear we have no artists who can restore it to its original perfection."

•

Edmund Fanning, no artist in restoring polish to Regulator transactions, was sent to the 1770 Assembly from the new pocket borough of Hillsboro created by Tryon. No one step could better have guaranteed the reappearance of the rough and tough Regulator fringe. Perhaps Tryon no longer cared. He had been informed by Lord Hillsborough of his appointment as Governor of New York with orders to report there at once. This Tryon did not want to do, having only in June taken over the palace of his four years' dreaming; nor could he immediately leave the unfinished business with the Sons of Liberty and the Regulators.

A month after Lady Tryon, Margaret, and the Governor's beloved books had been installed in the palace, Cornelius Harnett called a six-county meeting at Wilmington to form one of those Committees of Safety (regarded by all loyalists as traitorous) which were spawning from Boston on down to the Carolinas. In comparison the Regulators were behaving decorously. This new petition to the Superior Court pled for a reopened door:

> Our only crime with which they can charge us is vertue in the very highest degree, namely, to risque our all to save our country from rapine and slavery in our detection of practices which the law itself allows to be worse than any robbery . . .

Tryon had agreed with this time and again. The Assembly foregathered in the great north room of the palace, facing Tryon on his raised dais in front of the high many-paned windows. Here was the setting for the relief of their acknowledged distress, within the framework of British law.

It might have progressed—was progressing in discussion of the reform measures interrupted a year ago by the message from Virginia—when tempers in the piedmont riotously exploded.

On Saturday September 22 James Hunter presented the Regulators' counciliatory petition to Judge Richard Henderson sitting alone on the bench for the Superior Court at Hillsboro. Far too many Regulators crowded the courtroom on the following Monday. Demands were made on Judge Henderson that he schedule pending Regulator trials at once and that he dismiss the jury and choose another. The Judge reasoned with them. They went outside to talk it over, gesturing with sticks in hand or tapping their thighs thoughtfully with switches. They intended trouble, and the appearance of a disliked lawyer, John Williams, touched them off. They fell upon Williams and beat him for a while, until it appeared that bigger game was inside the courthouse. Fanning had sought sanctuary on the bench beside Judge Henderson. They dragged him outside by the heels and drubbed him until, as Judge Henderson described it later, Fanning "by a manly exertion miraculously broke hold and fortunately jumped into a door that saved him from immediate dissolution." They badgered Fanning out again, but sent him to his home with orders to report in the morning.

Fanning duly reported. After huddling over their verdict the Regulators announced it to him: "Take the road and keep running until out of sight." Fanning ran. They next invaded Fanning's new dwelling, burned his papers, and exuberantly took the house apart until all that remained was studding and kindling.

Judge Henderson during that night had very sensibly ridden away. The crowd now swarmed into the courthouse where they brought out the docket to try their own cases, entering judgments and comment ad lib: "Damned rogue," "Judgment by default, the money must come from the officers," "Fanning pays but loses nothing." These learned commentaries, and the brutalities to lone men, were stupidities perpetrated at exactly the wrong moment.

When the Assembly reconvened in the palace to consider the Hillsboro riot, it expelled Hermon Husband but left Edmund Fanning to represent his invented borough of Hillsboro. Again the Regulators trudged down the piedmont streams to become a mob threatening New Bern. Tryon appropriated £500 to protect his capital. A bill against rioting was passed by the Assembly. Anyone indicted under it would have to appear within sixty days at New Bern or be declared outlaw. Then, being Regulators in sympathy, the legislators passed a bill embodying most of the reforms which, had they been in effect four years previously, would have quieted the piedmont countryside.

All this was keeping Tryon from sailing for New York, an assignment which glowed in rosier light as local politics grew foggier. He signed the riot act out of hand, too impatient to wait out the soothing application of the reform bills.

Schoolmaster Rednap Howell provided an excuse to move against the Regulators. He had written forty popular ballads, one of which ran:

> When Fanning first to Orange came
> He looked both pale and wan,
> An old patched coat upon his back,
> An old mare he rode on.
>
> Both the man and mare wan't worth five pounds,
> As I've been often told;
> But by his civil liberties
> He's laced his coat with gold.

Fanning, the Yale boy from New York, never did present such a sorry sartorial aspect. The Regulator satirist had let his wit run beyond facts, and now he had added further insult by writing a letter in which he threatened revenge for Husband's ill-treatment. The letter was intercepted and read to the Assembly. The fat was in the fire.

•

This time it would be no political lieutenant generals for Tryon. The British lieutenant colonel would himself lead the invading column from New Bern. The Cape Fear column he intrusted to Hugh Waddell, sound military man and hero of the fight with the Cherokee at Fort Dobbs during the French and Indian War. As with others of the Lower Cape Fear gentry, it was forgiven and forgotten that Waddell had led the expedition against Fort Johnston during the Stamp Act troubles.

It required a forty-shilling bonus to enlist each recruit, but early in May the two columns were marching inland with a rendezvous set at Hillsboro. Tryon reached his summer capital with a thousand men on May 9. General Waddell moved his Cape Fear column to Cross Creek and over the old buffalo trail to Salisbury where trouble awaited. A band of young Regulators, the "Black Boys of Cabarrus," charcoaled their faces and blew up a wagon train of ammunition. And across the Yadkin an unknown force of Regulators awaited Waddell's force. The general held his position and sent a courier to Tryon saying that the Regulator army was somewhere between the Deep and the Haw. Tryon set forth on May 12 to cross this territory in relief of Waddell. On the fourteenth he reached the banks of the Alamance where he rested over the fifteenth.

The Regulators spent that day milling around their encampment, with small stomach for a fight if they could find a peaceful solution. Dr. David Caldwell, a Presbyterian minister respected by both sides, went to Tryon in their behalf and was promised an answer the next morning. The temper of that reply was fixed when Tryon learned that the Regulators had caught and whipped Colonel John Ashe and Captain Walker. On the morning of the sixteenth, when Tryon's army was already moving forward in two lines spaced two hundred yards apart, the promised message reached the Regulators: Submit to Government and disperse within the hour.

What may be history's most noble yet least effective exhortation before joining battle was voiced by Captain James Hunter. The rank of captain was the highest in the Regulator army. Asked by fellow officers to take over-all command, Hunter declined, saying: "We are all freemen, and everyone must command himself."

In that same hour before the first shot, Hermon Husband consulted his Quaker conscience. Persuasion had failed; violence was at hand. He mounted his horse and rode off the field and out of North Carolina forever. Dr. Caldwell likewise sadly withdrew. Tired of waiting around for their show of strength to bring Tryon to his senses, the farmer-soldiers took to wrestling matches and horseplay. A veteran among them gave warning to be on the watch for a volley. In a few minutes Tryon's swivel guns lobbed the first shots.

The Governor's militia was almost as reluctant as the Regulators. It had required that Tryon stand in his stirrups and cry: "Fire! Fire on them or fire on me!" But once started there was two hours of fighting. Shots were fired from behind rocks and trees. One Regulator group captured Tryon's swivel guns, but they withdrew when they could not figure out how to work them. A general Regulator retreat through the wood left the field to Tryon, with nine killed and sixty-one wounded. Nine Regulators were dead; the wounded uncounted.

One of the captured Regulators was James Few, recognized as outlawed for his part in the Hillsboro riots in which Fanning's house had been destroyed. Fanning urged Tryon to hang Few on the spot, and this was done, as an act to strike terror into an already terrified and routed amateur army.

A compassionate account of the hanging of James Few turned up later in Moravian records at Salem. This would have it that Few, with the rope around his neck, was three times offered pardon by Governor Tryon, and each time refused to recant. The Governor turned aside weeping. "Crazy young rebel," said some. "Brave young enthusiast," said others. "Unnatural obstinacy to die rather than submit to lawful authority." The sum of the Moravian judgment was this: "If a man is so sure of the righteousness of his cause that he is willing to die for it, he deserves our respect if not our approval."

Tryon spent a week at Sandy Creek extending pardon to all who would take oath of allegiance to the King. Eventually there would be more than six thousand so swearing, and, when all this would be known in London, Tryon would be given the British Government's highest approval for his putting an end to Regulation.

On June 4 Tryon's and Waddell's forces were united at Bethabara. June 6 would be George III's thirty-fourth birthday. The happy occasion was set down in Anna Catharina's diary. Some prisoners were brought in, she writes, to take the oath of allegiance. Then the troops under arms went through the maneuvers that had taken place on the battlefield of Alamance.

To feed the Moravians' guests six oxen were slaughtered and the ovens set baking around the clock. Upon his departure the Governor smilingly noted that the bill for provisions was too small, no amount appearing for his personal entertainment. Tryon added "just another item to cover expenses."

All that remained was to try twelve of the Regulators as outlaws. A court martial at Hillsboro found all twelve guilty; six were hanged, with the army drawn up to witness.

•

Tryon left it to others to lead the columns back to the coast, and set off alone for New Bern and the preparations to take ship for New York.

After Alamance 1,500 Regulators climbed through the mountain passes to the Holston and the Nollichucky valleys on the other side of the Blue Ridge. There they would help Colonel Jack Sevier to create the State of Franklin, named for the Quaker who had been their teacher and their friend. Congress would eventually vote down the State of Franklin as the fourteenth State, and the Scotch-Irish Regulators would end their long journey as citizens of Tennessee.

Hermon Husband, with his keen nose for tax impositions whether at the hands of George III or George Washington, wound up as a member of the Pennsylvania revolt against Federal taxation of their stills, known as the Whisky Rebellion. Husband, condemned to death, escaped human bondage for the last time by dying of natural causes in a Philadelphia tavern.

Edmund Fanning, when the Revolution broke out, became an officer in the British Army. We hear of him for the last time as a beneficiary in the will of William Tryon, deceased at Norbury Park, Surrey, in 1788.

Tryon's palace outlasted its builder only ten years. Its last brilliant fête was a ball attended by President Washington. Too big to keep up, the palace made a good place to store hay. An old Negro woman also found it a convenient place to keep a few hens. Lighting her way downstairs with a pitch pine flare, and needing both hands to gather eggs, she set down her torch too near the hay. Flames gutted the main building and the kitchen wing of Tryon's pride. The bricks went into New Bern house construction.

The fact of Tryon's governorship of New York is the only memorabilia of public service carved on his Surrey gravestone. The Carolina years are omitted. Yet, was there perhaps nostalgia for that period in his naming of Edmund Fanning in his will? Or did the Cape Fear friendship last their lifetimes? At any rate it was a costly alliance for Tryon. At every instance where his integrity and humanism clashed with the upholding of traditional pride (his own and the Empire's), Fanning had persuaded him to make the poorer choice. Fanning deceived and cajoled him into some credence that his own hatred of the protesting colonials was justified. And after all, one did not condone it when an English gentleman is told to start running and keep on running until out of sight.

So the good things about Tryon were forgotten. Among his colonial contemporaries he was admired because they, too, held to his standards of gentlemanly conduct and fealty to the Ruling House. But the river-change working for a century on his fellow lovers of port and conversation at Brunswick was not permitted to a royal governor. So, out of the later bitterness of the Revolution, Tryon became both bloody and a tyrant, a reputation he deserved only a very little. As an unwitting influence in preparing North Carolinians to fight in the American Revolution, Tryon should be awarded honors. The events he had put in motion were to set the stage upon which his Stamp Act antagonist and Regulator ally, Cornelius Harnett, would now reorganize Patriot domestic and military forces through his office as chairman of Wilmington's Committee of Safety.

# 9 : *Winds of War Along the River*

We must exhaust our men, money, navies and trade. These are the four trifling articles we pay to the old scheme of arbitrary power. When will all the Kings of England learn how great they may be by the Constitution; how sure of ruin if they try to be despotic? Cannot the fate of the Stuarts teach even the House of Hanover to have common sense?

————Horace Walpole

Walpole had safely put his anger at Hanover arrogance into a private letter. In Parliament, Fox, Pitt, and Burke openly assailed the American policy of the Crown's Ministry. Yet in America the Crown remained untarnished, as being somehow removed from the policies which America so bitterly resented. English manorial life continued in mode along the Lower Cape Fear.

The fripperies of the drawing room were largely left to the females. In the taverns there were exclusively male matters to be discussed. During the relatively quiet first three years of the 1770s the trade of the Carolinas with England rose to its highest annual figure. The threepence a pound Townshend Act tax on tea was no burden, except as Parliament's opening wedge. That point needed settling.

The Wilmington talkers were of the same breed as the disputants in the Raleigh Tavern and Faneuil Hall. A Carolinian near to them in time describes Cornelius Harnett as one "who could boast a genius for music and taste for letters." William Hooper, Harvard graduate and law student with James Otis, brought his Boston intransigence to Wilmington. There was Colonel John Ashe "whose quickness of apprehension seemed intuition"; Samuel Ashe of stalwart frame and practical good sense; Dr. John Eustace "who united wit and genius and learning"; Colonel Thomas Lloyd, "adorned with classical literature"; Dr. John Fergus of stately presence, with velvet coat, cocked hat and gold-headed cane, a graduate of Edinburgh and an excellent Latin and Greek scholar; Judge Maurice Moore, "as a wit always prompt in reply"; Maclaine, "irascible but intellectual . . ."

Cornelius Harnett's country seat, Hilton, commanded wide acres above Wilmington. His gig brought him in minutes to this good company. He had as much to preserve through loyalty to the Crown as any man in the province. What made this forty-eight-year-old merchant turn revolutionist at the risk of his tall ships and his neck? What yeast was working in this region to make it withdraw from the eighteenth century sunshine of royal splendor into the Spartan shadows of a desperately chancy democracy?

With Harnett it was a thoughtful set of convictions. He had seemed a weathervane to every gusty dispute along the Cape Fear. In '65 he had faced down Tryon on the Stamp Act; in '68 he had joined Tryon against the Regulators; in '70 he was both in support of Tryon against the piedmont rebellion and Tryon's enemy on the new issue of the Townshend Act. In fact, Harnett had been veering where his convictions pointed. The Stamp Act he held in violation of the English Constitution. The Regulator's protests against tax frauds he felt were justified, but he could not approve armed revolt against a wholly domestic ill. When Parliament revived the external taxes levied by the Townshend Act, he again fought Tryon and would fight his successor, Governor Josiah Martin.

•

Martin, formerly a lieutenant colonel in the British Army, lacked Tryon's flair . . . "Insufferably tedious and turgid, his dispatches made the tired reader long for the well-constructed clear-cut impertinences of Tryon." Bore that he was to his contemporaries,

Martin was still honest and well-intentioned within an Empire framework. Along with Tryon's palace he inherited a mass of troubles.

One of his first acts was to make a tour of the Regulator country. His report to the British Government might have been written by Hermon Husband: "I now see most clearly that they [the Regulators] have been provoked by insolence, and cruel advantage taken of the people's ignorance by mercenary tricking attorneys, clerks and other little officers, who have practiced upon them every sort of rapine and extortion, and who have enlisted the aid of Government in order to cover their own transgressions."

This candor was not pure-grained. Martin was jealous of Tryon, and the truth about the Regulators was calculated to dim the victory of Alamance. Tryon had gone off to New York retaining the affection of the tidewater planters. The Assembly even affronted Martin by sending their state papers via New York for Tryon's transmittal to the King. The lot of the last royal governor of North Carolina was not a happy one.

Events played a tattoo up and down the Atlantic coast. In December 1773 the North Carolina Committee of Correspondence was formed at Wilmington, and in Boston Sam Adams' masquerading Indians tossed East India Company tea valued at £15,000 into the harbor. On June 1 an Act of Parliament closed the Port of Boston. Declaring the cause of Boston the cause of all, Wilmington sent the sloop *Penelope* to Massachusetts with the gift of 2,096 bushels of corn, twenty-seven barrels of flour and seventeen barrels of pork.

Josiah Quincy of Boston visited Cornelius Harnett at Hilton. There must have been sympathetic exchanges and plans for continued continental co-operation. Quincy left calling Harnett "the Sam Adams of the South." As such he found himself in another head-on collision with a royal governor.

The Battle of Alamance had wiped out all political strength of the Regulators in the Assembly at New Bern. Josiah Martin stayed on there in the palace. He felt that his report on the justice of the

Regulators' cause had won him solid upcountry friendships. He also held that the Highlander Scots were a potential Loyalist force. He confided in correspondence to Sir Henry Clinton in New York that North Carolina (excepting the impudent planters of the Lower Cape Fear) would rise in the King's name should the issue be drawn.

If it came to open fighting, these same planter-politicians were no novices. The Regulation campaign had given James Moore, Alexander Lillington, John Ashe, and Richard Caswell the feel of command. The Eastern county militia were used to musters and marches. And all this civil disobedience was woven of strands running through the hands of Cornelius Harnett who, through successive elevations to the offices of head of the Committee of Safety and the Provincial Council, was quartermaster general, chief of field operations, the hand of discipline against defectors, and the voice of the colony in bitter dialogues with Governor Martin.

The first Continental Congress meeting in Philalphia in September 1774 passed Resolves which called on the people to give up their sports—horse racing and cockfighting, plays and every species of extravagance and dissipation—in order that by this sacrifice the King and Parliament could be made to understand that loyal American subjects were serious in their pleas for redress of grievances.

Cornelius Harnett's Committee of Safety at once began to apply the Resolves to the people of the Lower Cape Fear. The gentlemen who intended to enter purses in the Wilmington horse races, "of whom we understand you are one," were notified that they would either withdraw or be under the disagreeable necessity of bearing public testimony: "Nothing will so effectively convince the British Parliament that we are in earnest in our opposition to their measures as a voluntary relinquishment of our favorite amusements."

It was not all that voluntary:

"Mrs. Austin, Madame: The ball intended to be given at your

house, this evening, is contrary to the Resolves of Congress. We warn you that your house cannot be at this service, consistent with the good of your country."

"Since merchants daily purchasing wines and other articles contrary to agreement . . . names will be published in the *Cape Fear Mercury.*"

"Resolved: that the permission of billiard tables in this town is repugnant to the Resolves of Congress. . . ."

The cockfight gentry and the frivolous fringe of the town at first defied these ukases. But the Committee members were the leading men of the community—Harnett, Moore, Hooper, Howe, Maclaine, Clayton, Quince—and the extralegal authority they assumed was made to stick. They printed the Continental Congress "Association" pledge of life and property to the cause of the colonists, and went in person to "wait on all housekeepers in the town, with request their signing it, or declare reasons for refusing, that such Enemies of their Country may be set forth to Public view and treated with the contempt they merit." The Madame Austins of Wilmington sent servants scurrying around the town to regret cancellation of evening diversions.

As the spring of 1775 brought its new crises, the Committee applied itself to matters hardly likely to retain the mother country's love. The ship *Diana* out of London was confiscated and her cargo sold at auction for £1,916. The proceeds were sent to relieve the sufferings of the closed Port of Boston.

The sloop *Mary* brought in five slaves from the West Indies. They were ordered reshipped and the bills of lading presented in proof of compliance.

Merchant William Hill received a shipment of tea on his brig *Sally.* Although the order had been placed before the ban on tea, Hill relinquished it on the ground that "The safety of the people is, or ought to be, the supreme law."

Governor Josiah Martin spent the first months of 1775 in his New Bern palace. In March he wrote General Gage in New York requesting that the royal standard and troops be sent to the Cape

Fear. Martin's messenger was captured and his move was made public with Harnett's comment: "Nothing shall be wanting on our part to discredit such diabolical schemes."

In April 1775 many moves were made on the transatlantic checkerboard. Parliament prohibited all colonial trade with Great Britain and with the West Indies, but—considering the need of the British fleet for Cape Fear naval stores—North Carolina was exempted from this ban. As soon as this news reached Wilmington the Committee of Safety rejected the exemption as "a base and mean artifice to reduce them into a deserter of the common cause of America."

In April the palace at New Bern became the scene of a humiliating farce. The elected Assembly met there at Governor Martin's summons. The rebellious and extralegal Provincial Council had named a "Provincial Congress" to meet in New Bern at the same time. Harnett was a member both of the Assembly and of the Congress as were most of the representatives. John Harvey was at once Speaker of the Assembly and Moderator of the rebel Congress. When Governor Martin sent his private secretary to call upon the Assembly to disperse the Congress, Mr. Moderator Harvey "in the twinkling of an eye would become Mr. Speaker Harvey and gravely receive his Excellency's message."

Martin issued a proclamation forbidding this unholy union. Not a man obeyed it. On the fourth day the Assembly adopted a resolution thanking the Continental Congress for their services. On April 8 Governor Martin dissolved the last Royal Assembly of North Carolina. British rule in the Province had come to an end forever.

In that same month of April '75 a dispatch rider left Boston with the news of Lexington and Concord. Fresh mounts galloped relay to New York, into the South and three days later to Wilmington. Cornelius Harnett read the dispatch and pressed into the hand of a new rider a scribbled note to planters along the route to Charleston: "For God's sake send the man on without the least delay, by night and by day."

Another rider was sent inland to Charlotte in Mecklenburg County. There on May 20 the citizens declared themselves "absolved from all allegiance to the British Crown." The document itself disappeared, but a second Mecklenburg meeting on May 31 spelled out the organization of an independent state in stronger terms than any other province had attempted. Provision for the purchase of gunpowder, lead, and flints underwrote the Mecklenburg intent.

•

Brunswick Town now became the seat of its fifth royal governor. Josiah Martin, escaping shameful treatment by a turncoat Assembly at New Bern, came there as a refugee. He planted himself and staff at Fort Johnston, uncomfortably close to his Brunswick enemies but within call of British men-of-war at offshore anchor.

Martin at once began work on a master plan. The first move was to sound out the loyalty to the Crown of the Regulators and the Scots Highlanders. The Regulators had no love for the tidewater politicians who had dressed up as lieutenant generals in Tryon's army. Martin now sent emissaries into Regulator country and was reassured by the reports they brought back.

Among the Scots were many gentlemen, some of them retired on half pay from the British Army, whose interests certainly lay on the side of the Crown. Being himself a Scot, he felt sure of his ground, and exploratory soundings confirmed him.

Martin wrote all this to Lord Dartmouth, Hillsborough's successor as Colonial Secretary. Whitehall saw the opportunity. North Carolina was the only one of the thirteen provinces where a hinterland might be expected to rise against the self-denominated Patriots of the tidewater. Geographically the Cape Fear was perfect for an invasion which would split the northern provinces from the South. There was a deepwater harbor for a British fleet to use as a base, and at the same time suppress the rebels along its shores. The arrival of a British force would clinch the loyalty of the upcountry. The traitorous colonials from Virginia would lose any hope of troops and supplies from the South and the fleet could starve out the separated segments of rebellion. It was an excellent plan, and might have worked had not the tidewater rebels been old hands at frustrating overseas authority. Lord Dartmouth let Martin know that Whitehall approved his plan and would implement it. Meanwhile, Dartmouth advised, it would be unbecoming for a royal governor to leave Fort Johnston for shelter on one of His Majesty's ships.

But there riding offshore was H.M.S. *Cruizer* and within Fort Johnston was its commander, Captain John Collett, as obnoxious a creature to Martin as he was to the colonials. To the Governor, Collett was a low fellow who, when notices were sent him to pay his just debts, "wiped his b—— s—— on the King's writs." To the colonials Collett was a rascal trying to entice Negro slaves to leave their masters and join his corporal's guard of Fort Johnston defenders.

Martin braved Lord Dartmouth's displeasure and moved headquarters aboard the *Cruizer*. Perhaps it was a bit infra dig to be skulking under protection of the *Cruizer's* guns, and so, as assertion of his authority, Martin issued a proclamation threatening death to anyone who should attack Fort Johnston. To make clear to whom he was talking he called Harnett and his Committee "false, seditious and abandoned men." The Committee answered him in kind:

"His Excellency Josiah Martin, Esq., hath by the said proclamation discovered himself to be an enemy to the happiness of this Colony in particular, and to the freedom, rights and privileges of America in general."

Yet, along with resounding gasconades, Martin's "wicked efforts of the tools of Government calculated to throw this Country into confusion," and Harnett's "resist force by force, unite ourselves, associate as a band in her defense against every foe," the door was still open a crack. Colonial resistance, Harnett said, would last only "until a reconciliation shall take place between Great Britain and America, upon constitutional principles, an event we most ardently desire."

The Committee of Safety had its internal foes—merchants pinched by the nonimportation act, many who were emotionally attached to the dignity of the British Crown, and those who scoffed at the notion that British power would suffer these amateur revolutionists to exist. One James Hepburn of Cumberland County spread the rumor that 50,000 Russians were in His Majesty's pay and already embarked to subdue the Americans. The Committee gave him thirty days in which to recant or be deported. It also ordered a tax to raise gunpowder funds, began hoarding saltpeter and lead. In July it called upon every Wilmington man capable of bearing arms, including apprentices, to enroll in one of the two militia companies being organized.

A few days later some "enterprising young fellows" decided to make an attack on Governor Martin's stronghold. The fort, shabbily built, had been repeatedly and unsuccessfully repaired to overcome its habit of shedding parts of its bastions every time a cannon detonated. Martin came ashore to order Collett to spike the guns, and was rowed back to the refuge of the *Cruizer*.

Two forces, under Colonels Robert Howe and John Ashe, sailed from Wilmington for a Brunswick rendezvous. On July 18 their combined militia happily destroyed the fort and burned Captain Collett's house. The prisoner on the *Cruizer* watched the flames of a royal installation reflect on the dark night surface of the Cape Fear, and began pacing an oaken deck for the duration.

A month later the Provincial Congress met at Hillsboro to establish a government duplicating in every respect that of the deposed royal governor and his Assembly. In October George III began recruiting Hessians for service in America. The Continental Congress had assigned a quota of 1,000 Tar Heels to be placed in the Continental Army under General Washington.

James Moore was chosen colonel of the first Continental regiment, winning by a single vote over John Ashe. In addition there were to be battalions of Minute Men. Wilmington's battalion was put in command of Alexander Lillington. A bounty of twenty-five shillings was given each Minute Man for his uniform: hunting shirt, spatterdashes (leggings) and black garters.

Governor Martin took comfort in the single vote which had won for Moore over Ashe, and reported to Lord Dartmouth that the resentment of John Ashe over losing the chief command "will cause some division here, for it seems he and his friends are raising men of their own authority, in opposition to Mr. James Moore, his brother-in-law." Josiah Martin had forgotten that the early Cape Fear grandfathers of Moore and Ashe had hunted together in the sport of badgering the proprietary and royal governors of North Carolina.

Ashe returned from losing the election (as reported by George Hooper) "in a state of prodigious excitement. His object was to raise a regiment and he accomplished it. You cannot imagine what a commotion he stirred up . . . He struck the chords of passion with a master hand. His words roused the soul like the roll of a drum or the roar of artillery . . . Every breast heaved, as if with the sentiment of the Athenian orator, 'Let us away! Let us arm! Let us march against Philip!' "

The recruiting fervor of Ashe, Moore, and Lillington warmed their friends into wearing legends on their hats: "Who will not follow where Ashe leads!"; "Who will not follow where Lillington leads!" The rolls filled for all three outfits. Martin's hope of an Ashe-Moore breach was disappointed; but the Governor's optimism had solid reasons for expecting recruits to the King's side among the Regulators and the Scots Highlanders.

# 10 : *Last Gathering of the Clans*

Speed bonnie boat like a bird on the wing,
"Onward" the sailors cry;
Bearing the lad who was born to be king
Ower th' sea tae Skye.

The thread of Flora MacDonald's life appears twice in the tapestry of history. As an unmarried Scotch lassie, diminutive of figure and beautiful of face, she saved Bonnie Prince Charlie from British capture at risk to herself and her people.

The other thread appears thirty years later, across the sea in the valley of the Cape Fear River. She was a matron now, fifty-four years old, the mother of seven children and wife to the Loyalist leader Allan MacDonald.

Posterity has chosen to remember the Grecian Urn image of Flora, she and her Prince remaining ever young and fair. That she lent her world renown to the British against the Americans is overshadowed by her earlier romantic adventure. Nonetheless, the tragic American episode far outweighs the glamorous girlhood exploit in its final effects. The defeat of Charles Edward Stuart at Culloden Moor in 1746 ended the Stuart dynasty and removed feudalism from its last stronghold in the Highlands of Scotland. But Flora's rescue of the Prince, gallant and charming in itself, merely assured that the last of the Stuarts would live out his brandy-fuddled years in Europe. Willy-nilly the Prince, the victorious Hanoverians would have stripped the Scotch lairds of the feudal power to summon their liegemen into battle. Blood fealty to a chief was on the way out; the drift was toward a limited monarchy and cabinet government. Flory's was a late flowering of chivalry, the purer for its doomed and bloody background.

In her second brush with history, in the Cape Fear valley of 1776, Flora MacDonald directly turned the course of the American Revolution during the critical early months when the colonists were wavering between patching up the quarrel with England or supporting an all-out and united rebellion. Flora and Allan (and, without her, Allan could not have done it) recruited a Loyalist Highlander Regiment to serve George III against the American rebels. The crushing defeat and capture of the regiment at Widow Moore's Creek proved that colonial militia could stand up to British forces in the field; and thereby not only North Carolina but the whole Atlantic coast was emotionally welded into one entity of defiance.

The Scots were double losers. Those who had been defeated and denied the old Highlander way of life after Culloden Moor now, in the span of the same generation, met defeat and exile at the hands of the American Patriots.

The motives behind the Highlander adherence to a hated House of Hanover are still hidden by the overlay of folklore and glamour created by the young Flora MacDonald on the misty Isle of Skye. In pondering the paradox of Scots willing to die for George III, I followed the trail from Culloden Moor to Widow Moore's Creek, with Flora and Allan MacDonald as guides and exemplars of the Highlander misfortunes.

•

In 1745 Charles Edward Stuart, twenty-four years old, tall, slender, redheaded and impetuous, landed in Scotland with a few followers. Many Presbyterian Scots resented Charles Edward, but the magic of the Stuart name and the daring of the handsome young lad raised Bonnie Prince Charlie an army for the invasion of England.

The Highland fighting man is at his invincible best in the fierce first charge, with claymore swinging and barbaric yells in duet with the pipes. The British retreated before them almost to London. But the Highlander dislike of massed maneuvers on the plains determined a countermarch back across the Border. At Culloden Moor, with rain and hail driving in their faces, the march-weary Highlanders were attacked and routed by the Duke of Cumberland's forces. For the last time a Scottish army had fought on its own soil.

The "Bloody Duke" of Cumberland let loose his troops in rapine and slaughter on the fleeing Scots and unarmed country people. In England a flower, Sweet William, was named after the Duke. In Scotland it was known as Stinking Billy.

For two months after the battle the Prince was a hedgerow fugitive. Friends secretly passed him on to the west coast of Scotland where he crossed the Minch to the Hebrides. The people of the Isles knew he was there. So did the British, whose ships patrolled the Minch while landing parties searched the fens and knocked on the doors of croft and castle. The fealty which had protected Charles on his flight from Culloden still held in the Hebrides despite a £30,000 reward on his head, enough to found a family dynasty. By mid-June the Prince was at Carradale, near the home of Flora and her brother Angus. With two companions, the Irish Captain Felix O'Neill and the schoolmaster Neil Mac-Eachainn, he led the redcoats a chase across moorland to an islet where it had been arranged Flora should meet them. In the long twilight of June 21 Flora walked to a summer shieling in pretense of looking after the cattle. The girl and the fugitives had their first talk by dim gleam of a shieling's peat fire. Flora was hesitant. The danger did not matter, but if an unmarried girl was to be found on the moor in the company of three men. . . . The hotspur O'Neill offered to marry her on the spot. An oath in the presence of witnesses would make it legal. Flora declined. The Prince appealed to her for help. The sensible MacEachainn talked tactics. The outcome was a merry-mad plan to dress the Prince as Betty Burke, Irish spinning lass, enter Skye on a pass signed by Flora's stepfather, Hugh MacDonald, and to take shelter at the house of another relative, Alexander MacDonald.

On Skye Flora fell into the hands of a British outpost where she was held until Hugh MacDonald—himself as a militia officer supposed to be in pursuit of the Prince—managed her release. Meanwhile the fugitives made an eighteen-hour march through bogs and icy rain. Charles's nerves were near the surface. His sleep in a bothy was broken by a boy's warning that the militia were due there to fetch milk, forcing the Prince to huddle under a rock ledge for three hours until the boy could signal him back. One cheerful meal in a shieling—a beef's kidney, heart, and liver roasted on a spit—was chaperoned by Lady Margaret MacDonald, with Flora and Anne McAlister as the Prince's guests.

There was laughter over the investiture of the Prince (over his trews and waistcoat) in the calico gown, quilted petticoat, mantle, and cap which transformed him into Betty Burke. What if he were halted and examined? That, the Prince replied, would soon disclose what he was! The over-tall gangling servant girl walked behind Flora's pony, hitching up his skirts to wade through the burns. They made it without challenge to Kingsborough, high on the cliffs of the Taternish peninsula. There for the first time since Culloden the Prince had friends at dinner, brandy with the men, adoration from the females, and, bathed and safe, slept between linen sheets.

There were more weeks of wandering before the Prince was picked up by a French ship and taken to Europe. Upon discovery of her part in it, Flora was taken to London and for a time confined in the Tower. Her connections were good, and on her release she was for a while the darling of hostesses and ballad makers. London could afford generosity toward a charming girl who had snatched the quarry out of the hands of the British man hunt, for Charles Edward was no longer a threat. The faint chance of a Stuart restoration let him live out his years at the bounty of France and the Papacy, but the young ardor drained away in disappointment, and the brandy which had warmed him on the Scottish moors reduced him to a concealed couch at the rear of his opera box where he could sleep off his vapors.

Despite the balladeers and later romanticists, there are no inklings that Flora's feeling toward the Prince were more than those of a spirited girl enlisted in helping a desperate man-on-the-run. She returned to Skye and married her distant cousin Allan, raised him a large brood, and worried with him over the sorry changes come over Scotland since Culloden.

Parliament had abolished the clans. The proud hunting tartan, the gay kilts for the nightly dance to the pipes were banned. The feudal power of the laird was gone and with it the laird's role to protect his clan and to allot the crofters workable farmland. Now the laird perforce became a landlord claiming rents. No longer were crofters oath-bound to give forty days' work a year and answer the summons of the fiery cross to rally armed for battle. Rents doubled. The small Highland cattle ran unfenced. Food for the bairns grew scarce. Grain for bread went into the distillery. Land was turned over to sheep for the profit to be taken when three pounds of mutton could be raised on the same land producing one pound of beef.

In 1750 Thomas Pennant reported that poverty had caused "such a depression of spirit on Skye that groups were emigrating to America." The *Edinburgh Advertiser* stated: "There are no beggars in America, the poor, if any, being completely provided for. Lastly, there are no titled, proud Lords to tryannize over the lower sort of people, men being there more upon a level, and more valued in proportion to their abilities than they are in Scotland."

In the Highlands the pipers were playing a new dance tune: *Going to Seek a Fortune in North Carolina.* Some immigrants brought in thousands of pounds sterling; mostly North Carolina gained printers, surgeons, bakers, clockmakers, silver casters, and husbandmen, many with all their possessions sold to pay passage. Given ten to twenty years of being their own masters, of spinning flax of their own growing, of walking their own deep furrows, these Highlanders became transmuted into Americans, rebellious when the long overseas arm tried to reach them.

It was different with most of the late-comers to the Cape Fear who were not given time to undergo a New World change. In the last stages of the Culloden Moor aftermath, the Highland land-owners and managers faced ruin from diminished rents and the departure of their crofters to America. Among these were Allan and Flora MacDonald of Kingsburgh. In 1773 a murrain killed three hundred of Allan's horses and cattle. Annabella, Flora's half sister, had already gone with her husband Alexander MacDonald to the Cape Fear. Flora's daughter Anne and her husband Alexander McLeod had sold their estate for £1,200 and were preparing to emigrate with their three children and eight indentured servants. Allan and Flora arranged to sail with them. Their two grown sons would make the voyage; Johnie, Flora's youngest, would remain in Scotland in care of a family friend. In a year Johnie would become a hostage whose safety against Hanover reprisal would influence Flora's decision in America to remain a Loyalist.

The McLeod and MacDonald families landed at Wilmington in the fall of 1774 with a retinue of fourteen indentured servants and baggage filled with silver plate, damasks, satin bedcovers wrought with needlework, wine services, drinking cups and calfbound books. Flora and Allan had come to recoup their fortunes. Nothing in their experience prepared them for the rejection of the arbitrary power of kings which had been leavening the colonial spirit for a century, and which had reached its crisis at the moment of their arrival on the Cape Fear.

Cornelius Harnett's Committee of Safety was at the time banning horse racing, cockfighting, and dancing, all this by way of showing King George that he could not tax their imports nor close a far distant port called Boston. The royal governor, Josiah Martin, had lost control over these mad colonials, and had fled his palace for refuge on H.M.S. *Cruizer* off Brunswick on the Lower Cape Fear. Within a few months after arrival, the MacDonalds would have to choose sides between the British Crown and the rebel Patriots.

The two families went upriver to Cross Creek, remaining there only long enough for the men to go farm hunting. Flora and Allan bided for a few months at Annabella's home on Cameron's Hill. On Sundays they took the ten-mile drive to Barbecue Church where the Reverend James Campbell made no secret of his leanings toward rebellion. The hatreds were already causing glares from pew to pew. The MacDonalds began search for a home away from these dissensions. They found it twenty-five miles west, a 475-acre farm which they named Killiegrey in nostalgic echo of the Atlantic surf pounding on the cliff below Kingsburgh.

Their new neighbors were of the same ilk, some of them like Allan on British Army half pay, exiles bent on reconstructing Highland life in the new land. Allan and Flora hardly had time to explore Killiegrey's orchards and farm buildings before Alexander McLeod came to inform them that Governor Martin had made him liaison officer between British headquarters on the *Cruizer* and the upcountry Highlanders. The Governor wished Allan to serve as his recruiting officer.

Where was the need for Allan and Flora to weigh choices? In their eyes an unruly buckskin rabble was attempting to overthrow constituted authority. One need not admire George III, but he could be tolerated if he represented the orderly British establishment of service and rewards. Allan's two sons were of age for that ancient prerogative, the military career. Could anyone doubt that the power which had crushed the Scots at Culloden Moor would make short shrift of the rebellious men of the Lower Cape Fear and their make-do militia? If the MacDonalds chose to join the rebellion, its certain defeat would bring reprisals against kinfolk still in the Highlands. Among them was Johnie, Flora's last-born.

•

On July 5, 1775, McLeod and Allan made an overland trip to Governor Martin at Brunswick. Cornelius Harnett got wind of it and dispatched patrols to capture the Scots. Failing in this, the Committee of Safety wrote a letter to Allan MacDonald demanding to know whether he had the intention "to raise troops to support the arbitrary measures of the Ministry against the Americans in this Colony." For reply Allan and McLeod accepted captaincies in the Royal Highland Emigrant Regiment.

Governor Martin, infatuated at having won over the Highlanders, would have done well to tune his ear to the sermon preached that summer at Guilford by the Reverend David Caldwell, the man who had sadly failed in mediation between Governor Tryon and the Regulators before the Battle of Alamance. The words of the Reverend Mr. Caldwell were a better windvane of up-country sentiment than the interested reports made to Governor Martin. Caldwell, their leading Presbyterian preacher, thundered his message to the Provincial Council then sitting at Guilford:

> We petitioned His Majesty in a most humble manner to intercede with the Parliament in our behalf. Our petitions were rejected . . . We have therefore come to that trying period in our history in which it is manifest that the Americans must either stoop under a load of the vilest slavery or resist their imperious and haughty oppressors . . . if I could describe the feelings which you will have of self-approbation, joy and thankfulness, or of self-reproach, shame and regret—I should have no difficulty in persuading you to shake off your sloth, and stand up manfully in a firm, united and persevering defense of your liberties . . .

The Council voted $125,000 in milled Spanish dollars for defense, departing for the first time from reckoning sums in British pounds.

Next month Governor Martin was writing Lord Dartmouth:

"The people are in general well affected and much attached to
me." He estimated that two thirds of the region's fighting men—to
exceed 30,000—would rally to the King's standard. Acting on
these estimates, General Sir William Howe sent a seasoned officer, Major Donald McDonald, into the Highlander country to
direct operations.

In October King George withdrew his fatherly protection from
all Americans. In his place the colonials substituted: In God We
Trust.

Governor Martin's reports impressed Whitehall. In no other
province was there such a potential Loyalist support. The King
himself decided to send seven regiments and two batteries under
Lord Cornwallis. Sir Henry Clinton would come down from New
York with 2,000 redcoats. A British fleet of fifty-three vessels
would converge on the Lower Cape Fear. This was no punitive
expedition. It was designed as a major campaign to make the
Cape Fear valley from the sea to the mountains a British enclave
and so separate northern from southern colonies. The plan contained one hedge: the use of the entire British force to subdue the
interior was contingent on a successful Highlander uprising by the
time of Cornwallis's arrival. If the Highlanders failed, the plan
would be abandoned.

Now Governor Martin must stop guessing about the degree of
upcountry loyalty and back up his optimism with facts. He sent a
Loyalist lawyer, Alexander McLean, into the interior to sound out
both Highlanders and Regulators. In December McLean returned
to report that 5,000 Regulators would answer the Governor's call
to arms. Christmas on the *Cruizer* was bright with assurance.
Lord Dartmouth's latest dispatch breathed confidence in "sub-
dueing, with the assistance of the Almighty, the said impious and
unnatural rebellion."

Now Martin bade McLean to return to Cross Creek with spe-
cific orders for all His Majesty's loyal subjects-in-arms to stand by
for assembly. Commissions were handed out. On February 5,
1776, a meeting was held to pick a date for the march to Bruns-

wick. The Highlanders wanted to wait until word should arrive that Cornwallis, Howe, and the British fleet had actually arrived in the Lower Cape Fear. But the four hotspur Regulators present insisted on an immediate muster.

Although this spirited motion was adopted, a skeptical Scot, Captain Donald McLeod, thought it prudent that he return with the Regulator delegates to see that their promised thousands of volunteers were not a mere paper muster. The next word to come back to Cross Creek from Captain McLeod was that the Regulators had scattered and were "skulking and hiding themselves through swamps and such concealed places." He could not even find a guide to conduct him out of their woods.

The King's cause was in fact not dear to the hearts of the former Regulators. They had rallied to defend their farms against royal taxgatherers, but after Alamance the same tax gouging had continued. Governor Martin had come among them and sympathized with their distress, yet they were weary of long marches in which they seemed never to have any attainable stake. They made promises and disappeared in to the swamps.

McLean turned westward into Highlander country. At Cross Hill (so called for the fiery cross summons of the Scotch glens), Martin found Allan MacDonald, Alexander McLeod, and Colonel Cotton camped with 500 Highlanders. Next day the pipes sounded the march to Cross Creek.

A reported 3,500 Scots and Regulators reported at the February fifteenth rendezvous at Cross Creek, but each morning of the next few days saw fewer in camp. It had been given out that Governor Martin and a thousand troops would arrive to escort the volunteers to the coast. Instead, they were now told that they were on their way to Nova Scotia to be enlisted in the British Army. That meant fighting their way through to Brunswick, possibly against neighbors and friends in the Provincial forces. As McLean told it later: "Suspecting that such a project was in view, one Captain Snead with two companies of Colonel Cotton's corps ran off with their arms that very night."

On the eighteenth of February 1,300 Highlanders and 300 Regulators marched from Cross Creek four miles downriver on the west bank. Next day "all the men with arms were ordered to parade, having in view to attack Moore's Provincial Army."

Colonel James Moore's First North Carolina Continentals had reached the southern bank of Rockfish Creek, near where it empties into the Upper Cape Fear. Moore was only three miles below the Highlanders' encampment. Major Donald McDonald, whom Lord Howe had made commander of the Loyalist volunteers, had 1,600 men of known fighting quality, yet they were merely assembled, not trained as a corps. How much had McDonald's intelligence informed him of the numbers and soldier skills of the Provincials?

Cornelius Harnett, now President of the Provincial Congress and commander of its military forces, had received word on February 9 that the clans were gathering. For the next three days at Wilmington there was an around-the-clock bustle of roll calls, commandeering of farm wagons, and sending them upriver with ammunition and commissary supplies. The year of preparation was paying off. Colonel Moore with his Continentals and Colonel Lillington with his Minute Men from Duplin and New Hanover counties began the march up the west bank to Cross Creek. Colonel Caswell with 800 militia had left New Bern to join the other columns. When the troops were en route, Harnett now had no other duty than exchanging acrimonious messages with Governor Martin.

London had accepted Martin's estimate of thousands of uplanders devoted to the person of their Governor and to the King, who would rise and hold in check the traitorous tidewater Patriots until Lord Cornwallis and Lord Howe's forces should arrive. The fleet indeed sailed from England, albeit tardily and then delayed by North Atlantic storms. Sir Henry Clinton's forces were held in New York awaiting word that the Highlanders had risen.

To while away the nervous days of waiting on both the British fleet and news of the armies on the Upper Cape Fear, Harnett and Martin sent daily couriers between Wilmington and the *Cruizer*, vying for the laurels in sarcastic invective. Harnett complained to Martin about British misuse of Fort Johnston: ". . . built by the People at a great expense for the Protection of their Trade and made use of for a purpose the very reverse . . . and to crown all, you Sir, have brought up the *Cruizer* to cover the landing of an army composed of highland banditti; none of whom you will ever see unless as fugitives imploring protection.

Sir, Your Obt. Serv't,

CORNELIUS HARNETT"

To this Martin replied expressing surprise at being addressed by "a little arbitrary Junto (stiling itself a Committee) under the Traitorous Guise of a combination unknown to the laws of this Country: the Revilings of Rebellion, and the gasconadings of Rebels are below the contempt of the Loyal and faithful People [the Scots] whom I have justly stiled Friends of Government."

For all this bluster, the *Cruizer* had been receiving Wilmington supplies by bumboats without interference. Now Martin chose to make a demand beyond reason:

It is expected & hereby required that the Inhabitants of the Town of Wilmington do furnish for His Majesty's service one thousand barrels of good flour on or before Saturday next.

Jo. MARTIN

Cruizer Sloop of War
Off Wilmington

Captain Francis Parry had indeed moved the *Cruizer* to a position off the town, whose inhabitants began throwing up breastworks and moving their families into the woods. A note was rowed ashore by Captain Parry's gig: "I expect to be supplied by six this evening. If His Majesty's ships are in the least annoyed it will be my duty to oppose it."

This was on February 27 when, unknown to either of the pen-

and-ink antagonists, the Highlander and Patriot armies were drawn up within a few miles of each other on either side of Widow Moore's Creek.

In answer to Parry's threat to come fetch the thousand barrels of flour by force, Harnett sent a dispatch in which he found it difficult to conceive what need His Majesty had in this part of the world for so much flour. If Parry should destroy Wilmington, Harnett said, its people would "have one consolation left, that their friends will in a few days make ample retaliation upon those whom your Excellency thinks to dignify with the epithet of friends of government."

Shortly after this was delivered late on February 28, both Harnett and Martin received the news that the armies had met at dawn at Widow Moore's Creek, and that in a few minutes of fighting the ambushed Highlanders had been defeated and captured.

Captain Parry next day, on behalf of his hungry crew, tactfully forgot the thousand barrels of flour, and sent to the Committee of Safety a note begging for a few sides of beef.

# 11 : The Bridge at
# Widow Moore's Creek

Through one of the early Moore plantations on the coastal plain a creek meandered at a sluggish two miles an hour. On the marshy verges of its upper reaches the Venus's-flytrap caught and digested insects exploring the flower's inner sweetness. North of Wilmington the creek cut through the forest in black water thirty feet wide and almost as deep where the current cut around the curves.

In eighteenth century fighting, this negligible stream counted as an obstacle, the last one on the road to Wilmington eighteen miles away. Toward its one bridge the Loyalist Highlanders would march as unwitting of strong jaws as the victims of the Venus's flytrap.

•

Brigadier General Donald McDonald, in command of the Highlander Emigrant Regiment, had started from Cross Creek down the west bank of the Cape Fear, bound for Brunswick one hundred miles south. On the night of his first encampment he learned that Colonel James Moore's First North Carolina Continentals were only four miles ahead. A Cape Fear tributary, Rockfish Creek, lay between the two armies. McDonald held a council of war.

His duty was to avoid conflict and reach the coast with his troops intact and ready to be transported to Nova Scotia. Express riders had informed McDonald that the expected British armada had not yet arrived on the Lower Cape Fear. The only evidence of British aid sure to be at Brunswick would be Governor Josiah Martin stamping the deck of the *Cruizer* in rage at the nonappearance of the forces which Lord Dartmouth had promised him. McDonald knew that his 1,600 troops outnumbered any single rebel column, but he must maneuver so that no two of them might join against him.

Terrain was all important in what was now developing into the first campaign of movement in the Revolution. McDonald had fought under Gage at Boston, but that was a battle of investiture. Now he must somehow counter the advantage Moore had in a native's knowledge of the country between Cross Creek and Brunswick.

The best route was the one he was on, but Moore and Rockfish Creek barred the way. McDonald decided on a gesture to test the caliber of the rebels' resolve in the face of British authority. He gave orders that a parade and rally to the standard be held next morning.

It came off splendidly, with a quick step to the pipes and a halt to raise bonnets in a huzzah for the King. The only sour note was discovery that during the night one of the Regulator companies had gone over the hill and left word that "their courage was not warproof."

Let them go. Like Gideon's band, the Scots and remaining Regulators were now fined down to the real fighters. McDonald sent a stiff note to Moore ordering him to lay down his arms or "suffer the fate of an enemy of the Crown."

This was not all bravado. Both sides were subjects of the Crown. General Washington's chaplains were still putting the

King's name into their prayers at roll call. Sam Adams and the New England Patriots were declaring themselves merely against "the tools of the Ministry" and ready at a word from the King to restore their allegiance. Might not these North Carolina rebels think twice on the penalty for treason?

The answer came quickly back from Moore: "Take oath to support the Continental Congress or be treated as enemies of the constitutional liberties of America."

So be it. McDonald studied his maps. While the west bank road was by far the better, Moore's position behind Rockfish was too strong for assault. The alternate choice was to return to Cross Creek where boats were available to cross the Cape Fear. The lower ground on the east side was herringboned with marshes and rivers running obliquely into the Cape Fear, but there was one well-used road to Wilmington which crossed the South River by bridge and the Black by ferry. The last barrier, Widow Moore's Creek, was also bridged, and from there it was only eighteen miles to Wilmington and a juncture with Governor Martin's warships.

On February 20 McDonald marched back to Cross Creek, ferried to the east bank and sank his boats.

Colonel Moore let him go. Caswell was on his way across Duplin County with 800 militia and Minute Men. Ashe's independent rangers and Lillington's Minute Men were approaching from Wilmington. Since the Scots would be covering a probable ten miles a day, Moore could direct his converging columns to meet at a point east of the Cape Fear where McDonald could be intercepted. The Orange and Guilford County militia, coming to his aid from the west under command of Colonels Thackston and Martin, were ordered to occupy Cross Creek.

Moore chose Corbett's Ferry on the Black River as the place where the three tidewater columns should meet to oppose McDonald's crossing. He himself and his Continentals dropped thirty-five miles downriver to Elizabethtown where he proposed to cross the Cape Fear and attack McDonald from the rear. A day's wait for supplies kept Moore at Elizabethtown until February 25, but couriers kept him informed of McDonald's progress southward and the converging movements of his own forces. Plans were proceeding to his satisfaction.

•

James Moore, the third of his name in America, had his share of family contentiousness and daring. He had in his command English, Scotch-Irish, Germans, French, and Patriot Scots. They were not summer soldiers. Many had gone through the Regulation campaign. For the past year they had trained under the fiery Ashe, the sagacious Caswell, and the gallant Lillington, and had been supplied with uniforms and arms through the Spartan severities of Cornelius Harnett. The Highlander Emigrant Regiment was in for a fight.

On February 23, 1776, McDonald marched down the east bank road where it followed high ground between the South and Black Rivers. On the twenty-fourth his Light Horse scouts reported that Caswell was four miles in front. Acting on this dubious intelligence, he turned north to cross the Black River five miles above Corbett's Ferry. There a Negro pointed out a sunken flatboat which was used next morning as a bridge over which the Scots crossed to pick up the road to the bridge over Widow Moore's Creek. Now Brigadier McDonald himself, leading a mounted detail, came across sounder evidence of Caswell's near presence. He captured a train of twenty-one bullocks and two wagonloads of meal bound for Caswell's camp. From the drivers he learned that Caswell had entrenched below on their side of the Black. Two Scots officers, McLean and Frazier, were sent with a few men to take a position on the west side of the Black, near Caswell's supposed camp, and there, with drum, pipes, and rifleshots, to "amuse" Caswell into thinking that the main Scots force was still on the other side ready to make a crossing.

Caswell had indeed been surprised by McDonald's upper crossing of the Black, but he had a few wiles of his own with which to amuse McDonald. From the Black River to Widow Moore's Creek there is only one high ground route, running down a narrowing tongue to the Widow Moore's Creek bridge. McDonald was now in a slot with impassable marshes on either side. Caswell had fixed the place of battle by luring McDonald into precipitant pursuit of his own far smaller force.

On Sunday the twenty-fifth McDonald sent one Hepburn to Caswell under a flag of truce, with the usual offer of reconciliation if the Provincials would return to their duty and lay down their arms. Hepburn received the usual scornful reply, but his mission was successful in picking up the location of Caswell's camp. At this point Brigadier McDonald was stricken ill and left in a farmer's house. The command went to Colonel Alexander McLeod, who had arrived with McDonald to recruit the Highlanders for the King.

A Highlander council of war, acting on Hepburn's information, decided on an immediate attack while Caswell was still on their side of Widow Moore's Creek. They would follow the Old Country ways of clan fighting. Broadswords were put into the hands of eighty picked Scots who would form the attack thrust. The rallying cry was "King George and Broadswords." The signals for the attack were "Three cheers, the Drums to beat, the Pipes to play."

The Highlanders marched in three columns, ready to form line of battle before Caswell's army. But the advance discovered a camp so recently abandoned that the fires were warm and several tethered horses indicated a panic flight.

Caswell had sacrificed a few horses to create that very impression. In the dark he had crossed the bridge at Widow Moore's Creek with his main force, then detailed a squad to rip off the boards and grease the sleepers with soft soap and tallow. Colonel Lillington's Minute Men had arrived and were ordered to dig trenches a few hundred feet back from the creek and out of sight of the bridge. Lillington's boys in spatterdashes and black garters manned the forward position, with Caswell to one side in reserve. They doused all fires and awaited dawn.

•

The best laid schemes of mice and men gang aft a-gley. The High-landers broke camp at one o'clock on Tuesday morning the twenty-seventh and in darkness plodded through swamps and thickets for two weary hours. Within an hour of daylight they reached their objective, a woods facing an open space through which the road passed to the bridge. Line of battle was formed on the verge of the woods, although this formed the rim of a funnel through which they would have to pour into the narrow outlet over the bridge, and that with its sleepers greased to the slickness of poles at a country fair.

General McDonald was gone. The Highlanders shivered in the February predawn, seeing no room for broadsword play, no en-emy to afright with clan war cries. Yet the three cheers, the drum and the pipes were signaled for the attack. McLean and forty men advanced to the bridgehead. In the faint dawn, too dark to iden-tify friend from foe, a Provincial sentinel heard McLean and chal-lenged. The Scot answered in Gaelic, thinking that some of his own people might have crossed the bridge. There was no an-swer. McLean fired his own piece and ordered his men to fire. Colonel McLeod and the eighty broadswordsmen reached the bridgehead and began to cross. Some fell off the greased stringers into the water, but McLeod and most of his party crossed and advanced on the double to within thirty paces of Lillington's con-cealed breastworks. There they crumpled under a blast of swan shot and musket fire. McLeod fell with twenty bullets in him. Forty-nine other Scots were killed. One Provincial militiaman, John Grady of Duplin, was killed, the first North Carolinian to fall in the Revolution.

The Highlanders had made their thrust, and in the glens back home they would have rallied to fight another day. As it was, their remaining officers called them back from the bridge and marched them by first daylight to the camp they had just left. McLean, firer of the first shot, later described this dispirited rendezvous:

We found we had but two barrels of flour to serve the whole army, that the men were not to be kept together and that the officers had no Authority over the men. A Council of War being instantly called it was proposed that the Army should retire to Cross Creek and there fortify themselves until Governor Martin's pleasure should be known, to whom an express was sent the day before but that we understood he was taken by the Enemy, still another would be sent to him, which remonstrance had no weight. In short we found it needless to persist any longer in endeavoring to keep the Army together, therefore thought it most advisable to destroy the Ammunition to prevent its falling to the Enemy's hands.

After the council, the Loyalist McLean and three other Scot officers took horse for Cross Creek, thinking themselves a small cadre to hold onto and fortify that place. But Cross Creek was in the hands of Thackston's and Martin's Patriots, and the Highlanders' feckless ride served only to prevent their own capture.

Within a few hours after the battle, Caswell's victorious men were joined by Moore's Continentals. The Highlander camp was taken without resistance. There was considerable booty: 350 guns and shotbags, 1,500 muskets, 150 swords and dirks, 13 wagons, £15,000 in gold, an altogether useful store for what lay ahead.

It required two weeks to round up those of the Highlander-Regulator army who had not waited with their officers to surrender. Some eight hundred privates and subalterns were gathered at the juncture of Little River and the Cape Fear and there released on parole. The Gaelic newcomers had lost stomach for royal adventure. Many of them had taken the King's oath upon Governor Martin's promise that each would receive two hundred acres. Now they would have to work for their land, and perhaps the more value it.

•

Among the captives were Captain James Hunter, the Regulator military man who at the moment of joining battle with Tryon at Alamance had advised each freeman to be his own commander. Prisoner also was the Reverend George Micklejohn, a species of

clerical weathervane. Micklejohn in preaching to Tryon's troops
at Hillsboro had advised that twenty Regulators be forthwith
hanged. Next he appears offering prayers at the Provincial Congress which substituted a Patriot Government for Josiah Martin's
abandoned Assembly. Now the Reverend Mr. Micklejohn, like the
Vicar of Bray, Sir, had veered again to the side of the putative
winner, and found himself in the unfriendly hands of James
Moore.

The Highland crofters (three were Allan MacDonald's indentured servants) could be safely allowed to return home. The Scottish clans would never again send out the battle call in North
Carolina. Their officers were of a different breed, still on half pay
from the British Army, imbued with caste loyalty to the Crown if
not to its current wearer. Some of their friends and relatives were
in George III's Scots Guards. Their kinfolk in Scotland were vulnerable to Hanoverian reprisals. They could not now be converts
to that new enthusiasm—part self-assertion, part bred in a new
land's spacious generosity—called Americanism.

Allan MacDonald and the two sons with him in the Highlander
army were put in jail at Halifax, first stopping point on their prisoners' journey to Philadelphia. Flora was left to mourn at the Killiegrey plantation. But her son-in-law, Alexander McLeod (not to
be confused, as some historians have been by the identical names,
with the McLeod who fell before Lillington's breastworks), had
escaped after the battle and would eventually reach New York
and arrange safe conduct for Flora, his wife Anne, and their children.

News of the Highlander defeat reached the Lower Cape Fear
on the afternoon of the same day. Confident Josiah Martin had
been training the *Cruizer's* guns on frightened Wilmington and
demanding a thousand barrels of good flour. Now he delegated all
negotiations with the Committee of Safety to Captain Parry, who
sent Cornelius Harnett the significantly reduced request "must
beg you send a few quarters of good beef."

Governor Martin himself was not quite that discouraged. His

fellow optimist, Alexander McLean, whose original report had inspired Martin to assure Lord Dartmouth that 30,000 back-country people would rally to the King's standard, had escaped capture by Caswell and by night travel had made his way overland to the *Cruizer.* His report was exactly what Martin wanted to hear. The people "such as we durst discover ourselves to" were loyal and "would assemble upon seeing a proper military force." Martin now had confirmation of his fixed idea, that somehow, sometime a British army would enter North Carolina and be the rallying point of Loyalist opposition to the rebels. To keep his standing as an analyst of the situation he had to belittle the defeat at the Widow Moore's Creek. To the Ministry at London he wrote that "the little check the Loyalists have received will not have any extensive consequences. All is reversible by a body of troops penetrating into the country."

London accepted this glossing over of a smashing defeat. The armada of Sir Peter Parker's fleet and the troops of Sir Henry Clinton and Cornwallis, although delayed by Atlantic spring storms, were on their way to the Cape Fear. Tories in their London clubs were reassured by *The Gentleman's Magazine* that the affray at this ridiculously named stream was of little consequence as "they only reduced a body of their own, supported by no one body of regular troops."

Realistic intelligence agents would have told London that the three-minute ambush at Widow Moore's Creek had raised a whoop of sheer joy and confidence in North Carolina, and that its reverberations had boomed along the Atlantic coast to Boston. Wrote one North Carolinian to a Northern friend: "You never knew the like in your life for pure patriotism." Another was reported in the *Remembrancer:* "Since I was born I never heard so universal an ardor for fighting prevailing, and so perfect a union among all degrees of men."

Samuel A'Court Ashe, descendant of the firebrand Colonel Ashe of the Independent Rangers, summed it up in his *History of North Carolina:*

The ease with which a well-devised and widely extended insurrection had been quelled excited an ardor that stirred the Revolutionists from the seaboard to the mountains. The iron had entered into their souls in the time of peril, and now in the exultation and rejoicing there was mingled a higher resolve, and suddenly the nature of the contest changed. Theretofore reconciliation had been desired; now, as if by magic, the watchword became independence.

President Harnett summoned the Provincial Congress to meet at Halifax. With New Bern and Wilmington both vulnerable to the approaching British fleet, the village of Halifax on the Virginia border was safe and equidistant from coastal and inland counties. Allan MacDonald and other captured Scot officers were lodged in the Halifax jail, uncomfortable reminders that defeat does not carry with it the goodwill of the defeated and that in the province many hopes were alive that the British would invade and restore royal authority. All delegates to the Provincial Congress had arrived by April 4, greatly relieved at the choice of inland Halifax, for forty British warships under command of Sir Henry Clinton had arrived the week before and were riding at anchor in the Lower Cape Fear.

Was the heady victory over the Highlanders working up to too dangerous a sentiment for independence? A letter to the Congress from John Penn, North Carolina delegate to the Continental Congress at Philadelphia, was circulated at Halifax:

> Our dispute with Great Britain grows serious indeed. Matters are drawing to a crisis. They seem determined to persevere and are forming alliances against us. . . . Can we hope to carry on a war without having trade or commerce somewhere? The consequence of making alliances is perhaps a total separation with Britain. . . . My first wish is that America be free; the second, that we may be restored to peace and harmony with Britain upon just and proper terms.

In other provinces the leaders were still reversing the order of Penn's wishes: restoration of peace with Great Britain first, independence only if that failed. The general theory was to preserve the rights of Englishmen within the Empire. There was a reciprocal contract; the colonies owed obedience to the King; the King owed his colonial subjects the rights enjoyed by Englishmen at home. Almost a year after the shedding of blood at Lexington, this theory still held in Boston and in Williamsburg. But not in Halifax. There the delegates for the first time abandoned the fiction that the Ministry and Parliament were the responsible villains and put the onus also on the sacred person of George III.

On April 8 Cornelius Harnett was named head of a committee "to take into consideration the usurpations and violences committed by the King and Parliament of Great Britain against America, and the further measures to be taken for frustrating the same, and for the better defense of this Province."

Harnett and his six committeemen holed up for three days drafting this resolution, then on April 12 submitted a report which the eighty-three delegates unanimously adopted. It was the first official declaration of independence by an American Colony and the first recommendation to the Continental Congress that independence should be declared by all the colonies. The last paragraph read:

Resolved: That the delegates for this Colony in the Continental Congress be empowered to concur with the delegates of the other Colonies in declaring Independency, and forming foreign alliances, reserving to this Colony the sole and exclusive right of forming a Constitution and laws for this Colony, and of appointing delegates from time to time . . . to meet the delegates of the other Colonies for such purposes as shall hereafter be pointed out.

This cutting of the Gordian knot at Halifax severed the remaining thin line to loyalty. Sam Adams wrote in Philadelphia: "The convention of North Carolina has revoked certain instructions which tied the hands of their delegates here. Virginia will follow the lead . . . the hostilities committed in North Carolina have kindled the resentment of our Southern brethren, who once thought their Eastern friends hot-headed and rash."

On May 15 Virginia passed similar resolves. Richard Henry Lee instructed Virginia's representatives to "propose that these United Colonies are and of right ought to be free and independent States."

Within three months of the action at the bridge over Widow Moore's Creek—an insignificant discomfiture in London but a spiritual spark to a colonial powder train—the concept of United Colonies had been spoken aloud. In another two months the Declaration of Independence would be signed at Philadelphia, and, the news having reached North Carolina, Cornelius Harnett would be carried on shoulders through a hilariously happy crowd.

•

The Halifax Resolves were not without effect on the British invaders of the Lower Cape Fear. Governor Martin left the *Cruizer* for Sir Henry Clinton's flagship. On May 3 Lord Cornwallis arrived with his seven regiments. One regiment was put in camp on Baldhead, five were bivouacked at the burnt-out ruins of Fort Johnston. Now was the time for Martin's push inland to rally the thousands of Loyalists he was still certain awaited only the arrival of the British task force. But when the newly arrived British commanders had observed the situation close at hand—a royal governor cooped on one of His Majesty's ships, helpless against an aroused countryside—they were not impressed by Martin's pleadings.

Cornwallis issued a proclamation of amnesty to all North Carolinians, excepting Cornelius Harnett and Robert Howe. Harnett was the chief local rebel and Howe the General of North Carolina troops who had helped defeat the British at Norfolk's Battle of the Great Bridge. Harnett's residence, Hilton, was out of reach. Howe's Kendall plantation was visible to the British fleet. On May 12 Cornwallis landed 900 men at Orton. They pillaged and burned General Howe's house and outbuildings, and returned with twenty cattle as spoils of war. Later Russellboro and Bellfont were also burned.

These diversions filled the time of awaiting orders for disposition of the British forces. The London decision was for Cornwallis to make an attack on Charleston. The Cape Fear valley as a conquered British salient between northern and southern colonies, had been abandoned by Whitehall.

A final landing party set fire to Brunswick Town and St. Philips Church. With a pillar of smoke from burning Brunswick on the starboard shore, the British armada sailed down the Lower Cape Fear, with sixty-three captured cows and the last royal governor of North Carolina.

# 12 : *Cornwallis Wins a Battle and Loses an Army*

For four years after the Battle of Widow Moore's Creek the Cape Fear valley was free of the major armies of the Revolution. Whig-Loyalist hostilities occasionally boiled over into the seizure of Loyalist farms and exile of their owners to Nova Scotia. But the act to confiscate Loyalist properties was unevenly applied. One canny Loyalist, Alexander McKay, put his land in the name of his Patriot son John, who dutifully returned it when the war was over.

The acquisitive Jennie Bahn McNeill never lost to Whig or Tory. When a British squad seized her mare, a slipped bridle and a whack on the rump from Jennie sent her property galloping out of British reach.

Jennie Bahn was born in 1720 as Janet Smith. When she was nineteen she sailed from Scotland with her parents and brother Malcolm. Her mother died on the voyage and Jennie became the woman of the family. In 1739 the Smiths homesteaded along Trantham's Creek. The giant sailor-woodsman Red Neill McNeill had still a dozen years of trailmaking when Jennie first lighted his longleaf pine cathedral with the candle of her red hair. When more Scots began to change the forest to tillable land and grazing meadows, they gave her the rare name of Jennie Bahn, meaning the Fair One. Jennie Bahn's descendants still keep being born in the valley, some with the brown-gold hair and blue eyes suggesting imprimatur by Jennie. For she was both fair and vigorous. Land was her love. She chose as her husband one Archie McNeill (no kin to the Big One) whose contemporaries gave him the title of Archie Scrubblin', meaning No Account. While Archie gave his attention to the cider barrel (decently aged), Jennie Bahn surveyed newly bought lands by sending a slave at a brisk walk until she rang a bell, whereupon he planted a stake, changed course and turned full rectangle to enclose a nice tract which years later would be subject to "cowbell litigation." Jennie acquired many thousands of hillside acres to graze five hundred cattle. Each autumn she set out as her own drover. Virginia was one of her markets, Philadelphia another. The tale appears that Jennie Bahn McNeill and Benjamin Franklin somehow contrived dissimilarity into friendship.

•

From 1776 to 1780 the valley was a market garden and cattle range for Washington's army. Flax ripened and went through its tortuous course to the spinning wheel. Great droves of hogs trotted to Virginia.

Cornelius Harnett as President of the Provincial Council chartered fast sailing boats which slipped through the inlets to the West Indies for small arms, gunpowder, salt, clothes, and shoes. Letters of marque were issued to privateers which brought back British booty to make up for British trade.

During its four years of freedom from invasion, North Carolina sent its soldiers south to the defense of Charleston, west to fight the Cherokee, north to endure Valley Forge. Of them Charles

Pinckney of Charleston said: "They have been so willing and ready on all occasions to afford us all the assistance in their power, that I shall ever love a North Carolinian."

Cornelius Harnett spent three years as a member of the Continental Congress. The initial Patriot fervor had tapered off into grudging support of the common cause and mass desertions from Washington's army. Harnett wrote back to Wilmington: "For God's sake fill up your battalions, lay stores, put a stop to the sordid and avaricious spirit which has affected all ranks and conditions of men." He longed to be at home where he had been useful: "If I once more return to my family, all the devils in hell shall not separate us." He began to suffer greatly from "my old companion, the gout." In 1780 he did return, in time for the second invasion of North Carolina by Lord Cornwallis.

Josiah Martin is perhaps unique in that a great nation accepted from him the same bad advice on two separate occasions, each with disastrous consequences. His foolish optimism in 1776, which caused Great Britain to mount a major offensive on the false intelligence that thirty thousand Tar Heels would spring to the Crown's cause, was repeated five years later, this time at the expense of Lord Cornwallis.

The strategy to divide the colonies by investing a vital river had not been abandoned by Whitehall. After failure on the Cape Fear, plans were put into operation to capture the Hudson-Lake Champlain-St. Lawrence waterway by having General Burgoyne come down from Canada and Lord Howe ascend from New York. Burgoyne's defeat at Saratoga by Horatio Gates ended the project. The British, in stalemate with General Washington, in 1780 turned again to the South as the place to employ their strongest land and sea arms.

It began well with the capture by Sir Henry Clinton's fleet of Savannah. A naval and land attack and siege put Charleston into British hands in May 1780. On June 5 Cornwallis was put into command of a British army comprising crack units, and assigned to roll up resistance through Georgia, South Carolina, and North

Carolina. In Virginia he would find reinforcements for the final reduction of the rebellion.

A large bland man of forty-two, Cornwallis had been educated at Eton and Cambridge. In this march through rebel country he held both military command and responsibility for re-establishing British civil control in conquered provinces. Josiah Martin rode north from Charleston with Cornwallis, in furtherance of the project to reseat him as royal governor of North Carolina . . . among those many thousand citizens whom Martin imagined were so attached to his person. This was the crux of the plan, for the three thousand troops in the Cornwallis command were too few to guarantee success; North Carolina was counted on to supply the needed strength, and thereafter to become an unobstructed highway for the march into Virginia.

The nature of the fighting on the way through South Carolina was not the sort to inspire devotion in Tar Heel breasts. Major Banastre Tarleton, chief of cavalry for Cornwallis, combined genius with sadism. He left the field strewn with dead and wounded enemies multiple-hacked by the swords of his dragoons. In an engagement at Waxhaws south of Charlotte, Tarleton's victory over a Virginia force led by Colonel Buford tallied 100 dead, 150 so fiercely hacked that they had to be paroled where they lay, and 53 allowed to surrender.

The hatred between Carolina Tories and Whigs had been smoldering during the four years when the major fighting was taking place in the North. Now Tarleton's blood bath at Waxhaws inspired 1,300 citizen-Tories to march on Whigs camped at Ramseur's Mill on the Catawba. In this "Battle of Neighbors" the pick-up uniforms were so alike that enemies mingled. The Whigs won. Those who came to claim the fifty dead bodies of friends and relatives on both sides never again rose against each other in that neighborhood. But as the scent of the beast trailed deeper into North Carolina the lesson was forgotten.

Cornwallis spent the summer of 1781 in the northern tier of South Carolina counties, much annoyed by the hit and run forays of Marion the Swamp Fox. Relieved of serious British pressure in the North, the Continental Congress determined to send its best fighting force south to meet Cornwallis. The command was given to Horatio Gates, hero of Saratoga. With him was Baron de Kalb and the cavalry leader Dan Morgan. They assembled at Coxe's Mill on the Deep River and confidently set out southward.

Insofar as the confidence was based on their commander, it was misplaced. General Gates took no more precautions than if it were a route march in friendly country. The encounter came at the South Carolina town of Camden. Cornwallis, marching at night to avoid the daytime August heat, was aggressively on the move; Gates in camp. The British discovered Gates at 2:30 A.M. of August sixteenth and attacked at first dawn. Cornwallis had his greatest victory. A third of the Continental soldiers were killed on Camden field. Baron de Kalb died there of eleven wounds, athwart him the bayonet-stabbed body of an aide who had thrown himself down to protect his general.

Save for one frightened horseman, Horatio Gates was the first to speed free of the dangerous battle area. He made what must be a record for generals retreating on horseback—the 230 miles to Hillsboro in seventy-five hours. The pothouse verdict held that his "Northern laurels had turned to Southern willows." Congress retired Gates and gave his command to Nathanael Greene.

Josiah Martin, savoring in advance his return as North Carolina's governor, declared that that province was "rescued, saved, redeemed and restored." Cornwallis, too, after Camden, was looking ahead to Loyalist recruits flocking to his banner, once South Carolina was left behind. In September he crossed the border into Mecklenburg County where his foraging squads and cavalry were given a shockingly dis-Loyal reception. Tarleton described Charlotte as "a veritable hornet's nest." Cornwallis consoled himself by characterizing Mecklenburg as the most rebellious section in America. He had had the "strongest professions of Friendship" from other Tar Heels and anticipated no further trouble from them. To reap the first fruits of this friendship he sent Major Patrick Ferguson on the march toward the hill country north of Charlotte, in full force to meet any known Rebel bands in the region. It was a recruiting mission. In Ferguson's baggage train were a thousand extra rifles to be handed out to Loyalist volunteers along the way.

Expecting Ferguson to return with redoubled strength, Josiah Martin issued a proclamation calling on the faithful subjects of His Majesty with heart and hand to join the British Army. All younger men might enlist in a corps under Martin's own command. Bounty: three guineas in hand and a section of land when the rebellion should be quelled.

Major Ferguson received intelligence that large bands of irregulars—mountain men from Virginia and over the Blue Ridge—had been on the march for weeks and were now joined in a force larger than his own. Ferguson planted his army on the flat top of King's Mountain, confident that its steep wooded slopes could not be stormed by an untrained buckskin rabble.

From the mountaineers' encampment 900 picked horsemen rode to attack Ferguson, whose view of the impregnability of his stronghold embraced no knowledge of the western Indian fighters, unhorsed now and slipping through the rainy day's dripping undergrowth at the foot of King's Mountain. Campbell of Virginia, Shelby and Nollichucky Jack Sevier of the transmountain contingent led columns up three separate sides to divert and divide Ferguson's defenders. With handholds on small trees and rifles at the slant, they fought their way up singly and reformed on top in mass bayonet charges. Ferguson died there. An hour brought unconditional surrender, with 242 killed or wounded and the capture of 664 redcoats and Loyalists. Fifteen hundred stand of arms were taken by the mountain men, along with the mythical Loyalist recruits who were to have borne them.

The news of King's Mountain raised cheers from the Patriots and for a while quieted the Loyalists. The saddest among the

King's subjects was Josiah Martin, whose enlistment proclamation announcing the "restoration of royal rule" was being simultaneously circulated with the word that taking the King's three guineas had been no bargain for Ferguson's Loyalist band.

It was a bitter taste of Martin's promised Tar Heel loyalty. Cornwallis withdrew into South Carolina to ponder strategy. But the encouraged Continentals were on the aggressive. Dan Morgan's mixed cavalry and infantry crossed into South Carolina to a place named Cowpens from its annual roundup and branding of cattle headed on the drive to Charleston. Here Morgan chose to fight it out with Tarleton. The Americans took station in three lines, the front one with orders to fire and retreat to the second position, fire again and join the third. To Tarleton it seemed a frightened flight. But at each stage he met new volleys and at the last one an American bayonet charge. In a cavalry duel going on at the same time, Tarleton fared no better. The defeat set the alarmed Cornwallis on the northward march with his full command. He crossed into North Carolina above Charlotte on February 1, 1781, with the pick of the British Army, among them the Black Watch, Welsh Fusiliers and Queen's Guard.

Cornwallis must now continue his efforts to build up his strength with North Carolina recruits. Nathanael Greene was in the field against him with a numerically inferior army, yet Greene himself was acknowledged to be one of Washington's ablest generals. No Horatio Gates he.

Cornwallis issued his own proclamation to North Carolinians. It forbade his own people from arming Negroes. It banned outrages against civilians. His presence on their soil, he said in a shrewd appeal to wavering Tar Heels, was solely to maintain their rights as English subjects.

Instead of the easy journey to Virginia, Cornwallis spent three months in pursuit of the wily General Greene, compelled to forage for 2,500 hungry men during the cold winter months in a countryside which concealed its cattle head-to-rump in the swamps and denied him both supplies and recruits. He might have gained some Loyalist adherence were it not for two serio-comic episodes of mistaken identity.

Near present Burlington 200 Loyalist recruits on their way to join Tarleton heard what they supposed to be the approaching hoofbeats of Tarleton's cavalry. They stood respectfully by tho side of the road to let the column pass. Tarleton was in fact still a mile away. The troopers were those of Light Horse Harry Lee who, taking a second look at the watching recruits, knew them for Loyalists and fell upon them hip and thigh.

A second body of Loyalists from Deep River, marching in the half-light of dawn, were mistaken for Patriots by Tarleton's dragoons, who hacked them savagely before the error was detected.

If Cornwallis was unhappy with his Tar Heel reception, so were the invaded Patriots. Word had reached Wilmington that General Greene was in retreat toward the Virginia border. The Provincial Council, aiming to support their armies with a million pound loan, found they had merely sparked inflation. A day's work was reckoned at $250. The Council paid $12,000 for a horse. At Charleston and Camden there had been great losses of North Carolina militia and Continentals. It was a dismal winter.

But Nathanael Greene had not let them down. His retreat to the Dan River, made without loss of men or baggage, drew Cornwallis 250 miles from his supply base. Greene had increased his force from 1,400 to 4,000 men, sufficient in strength to engage Cornwallis. The latter pursued him to the now flooded Dan, and retired south again to Hillsboro. Here the drums rolled, the King's standard was raised, and Josiah Martin was again invested as royal governor of North Carolina. Martin at least had his political ambition fulfilled, but of Loyalists attached to his person there were none.

Once more the rolling creek-crossed countryside between the Deep and the Haw, to which the first Quakers had come to escape the brawls and battles of the unregenerate, beheld armies maneuvering on the land. Greene was now between Troublesome Creek and Reedy Fork, shifting camp each night to confuse Cornwallis.

The British were west of Alamance Creek, near the battlefield where ten years before Governor Tryon had defeated the Regulators. The decade had brought the Upper and Lower Cape Fear peoples into a common American alliance, excepting those who had lost at Widow Moore's Creek or had listened to Martin's blandishments.

At Guilford Courthouse on March 15, 1781, Cornwallis "won a battle and lost an army." Greene had some 4,000 men, Cornwallis 2,253, but the British were elite and battle-seasoned troops. Greene's tactics were those Morgan had successfully used at Cowpens. In the first two lines Greene placed militia with orders to fire three shots and retreat. His reliance was on the hard core of 1,725 Continentals in the third line. When the hard-bitten British veterans came in sight, the first two militia lines obeyed only the retreat part of their orders. The redcoats bulled their way through and had at the Continentals bayonet to bayonet. "I never saw such fighting since God made me," Cornwallis said later. "The Americans fought like demons."

Greene, seeing his units too scattered for rallying, skillfully withdrew them, in defeat yet with such enemy losses that Cornwallis was scotched as a threat, and the grand design of conquering the South went with him. In London, Horace Walpole turned one of his phrases: "Lord Cornwallis has conquered his troops out of shoes, and himself out of troops."

Cornwallis left seventy of his wounded "to the humanity of General Greene." He bridged the Deep at its eastward bend along the piedmont escarpment, and began the 150-mile march down the Cape Fear to Wilmington. That town had been for two months in the hands of Major James H. Craig, sent there by Cornwallis to hold the coast while he was traversing the back country. The obsession that North Carolina would rise for the King was in Craig's mind too. Unlike his general, Craig used murder and arson.

When Craig first landed at Wilmington, Cornelius Harnett had taken the town's funds to a place of safety and himself continued down country as fast as his "old companion, the gout" permitted. The disease had taken over his whole body. He became bedridden in the house of a friend. There Craig's dragoons found him. They made him walk until his legs could no longer uphold him. They flung him over a horse's back like a sack of meal, and in this way Harnett made his last entrance into Wilmington.

Cornwallis was there at the time, perhaps unaware that the leading rebel citizen was dying in Craig's bull pen. A decision engrossed Cornwallis. He had left Lord Rawdon in command of the conquered coast from Savannah to Charleston. Should he now return there, or march to Virginia where 3,700 promised troops were already awaiting him? Cornwallis worked off his discontent by writing letters to Sir Henry Clinton, complaining that General Greene had inconsiderately declined a second battle and, instead, had gone south with probable intent to fight Rawdon. Irreplaceable officers had been killed at Guilford Courthouse. Not a single Loyalist had taken the King's three guineas. To turn south against Greene would be foolhardy. The only fair prospect lay in reaching Virginia and the reinforcements. To that course he now made up his mind.

Five years before this, Cornwallis had rescued Josiah Martin from H.M.S. *Cruizer* and carried him away from the Cape Fear. Now on the last of April 1781 he again had Martin in his keeping, on a dreary last journey to official oblivion.

During the three months of the British Army's marches across and up and down the Cape Fear valley, the discipline enforced by Cornwallis had held his civilian Tory camp followers under some control. But in the Tidewater the brutal example of Major Craig had encouraged assaults on anyone who had not taken Craig's loyalty oath. The Tories now flanked Cornwallis' northward march. Whigs went into the woods; their women watched their possessions stolen and their houses burned. Their best fineries now adorned the camp-follower women. Except for some harassment by Alexander Lillington's militia, the great beast wound its way unopposed toward Yorktown.

•

Townspeople persuaded Major Craig to parole Cornelius Harnett. The damage had been done. On April twenty-eighth Harnett died. He was buried in the St. James churchyard with the "utmost frugality," having expressed in his will the opinion that expensive funerals were ostentatious folly. A vestryman of St. James, he, like Jefferson, remained reticent regarding his relations to a personal God. His tombstone bears Pope's couplet:

> Slave to no sect, he took no private road,
> But looked through Nature up to Nature's God.

With him died the last of The Family, that group bound by blood, marriage, and sympathies who had settled and ruled the Lower Cape Fear since 1725. The first generation had seized the river lands to establish their slave-labor plantations. They had been alternate allies and foes of proprietary and royal governors. Cornelius Harnett was the final product in the transformation of the first adventurers into statesmen of a new nation. The last of the second generation Moores, Judge Maurice Moore and General James Moore, had died in 1777 in the same house on the same day. Cornelius Harnett, second generation European man and first generation American, drew down the curtain on the Cape Fear's changeling period.

# 13 : *Violence in the Valley*

When in April 1781 Cornwallis marched north to Virginia, there was left a vacuum in which guerrilla surprise attack and personal revenge replaced the rules of war.

There were only two allegiances, British or American, but these were fragmented. The Loyalist Scots, landed and educated, set themselves apart from the Tory partisans, who were attached to the Crown by the same motives that pilot fish attach themselves to the lordly and all-conquering shark. The Highlanders thought Tories very low fellows and winced when necessity made them hunt with them as one pack. Never would a Scot acknowledge himself under Tory command.

The Patriot enemies of this Loyalist-Tory mesalliance were in the majority yet held small practical authority. Their young men were south with Greene or north with Washington. The Provincial Congress had no troops able to stop guerrilla fighting. It met at Hillsboro or what town it could, passed measures and hoped for the best.

Into this already crowded field of antagonists rode a twenty-five-year-old partisan leader mounted on a draft horse, Scaldhead

Dave Fanning. He was no kin of the Yale scholar and sustainer of
royal authority, Edmund Fanning. It was simply North Carolina's
misfortune to have two Fannings.

Scaldhead Dave was born in Wake County in 1756. He ran
away from his job as apprentice loom maker. Half naked, his head
afflicted with the "tetter worm," he found shelter with the John
O'Daniell family at Hawfield in Orange County. Here he was
cured of his ailment, although made bald and self-conscious about
it for life. At Hawfield he added reading and writing to a dare-
devil courage and a sense of timing which made him a superb
horse tamer.

His career in North Carolina began as an "outlier" and bush-
whacker for Cornwallis. When the British departed and left Major Craig to harry the North Carolina Patriots, Fanning and Craig
discovered a mutual liking for surprise raids and house burnings.
Craig gave him ammunition and sent him back to Coxe's Mill on
the Deep River where Fanning spent the early spring of '81 recruiting his troopers. It was not Fanning, however, who was the
first to show how merciless to each other civilian partisans could
be.

•

Colonel Thomas Wade and other Patriot families of Anson
County had fled northward ahead of Cornwallis's advance and
now, in May 1781, thought it safe to return home. They ferried
the Cape Fear above Cross Creek and camped for the night at
Piney Bottom, a small stream now within the boundaries of Fort
Bragg. One of Wade's men during a farmhouse stop had stolen a
piece of cloth which a servant girl, Marian McDaniel, was saving
to make into a dress for Sunday display at Barbecue Church. It
was a foolish thing to do in hostile Highlander country. The news
of Marian's stolen cloth went by horseback to Loyalist houses.

John McNeill, one of Jennie Bahn's sons, prepared for himself
an elaborate alibi. He spent the afternoon at the house of a Patriot
leader, Colonel Folsome, at sundown saying good-by and jogging

casually around the bend of the road. He was a good horseman and knew at what points along the road to Piney Bottom he could trot or push to the gallop. There were forty miles to go in the dark, yet he was certainly at Piney Bottom in time to participate in the massacre of Wade's party, for the next morning McNeill returned her cloth to Marian. By that time it had cost fifteen lives.

The surprise 3 A.M. attack had begun with a sword hack which cleft the head of a twelve-year-old boy of Wade's party. The Loyalists killed whoever could not make it into the woods on time. They set fire to the baggage and were back in their homes by dawn. After the war, John McNeill stood trial for the Piney Bottom murders, but the jury, incredulous that the ride could have been made from sundown to the time of the attack, acquitted him. His neighbors gave him the name of "Cunning John."

Colonel Wade recruited a hundred men to take the field in revenge. Now it became open warfare, the angry Colonel Wade against both the Highlanders and the partisan Tories. Fanning on June 8 was formally chosen leader of his troop. With these credentials and a batch of captured Whigs as gift to Craig, he rode to Wilmington. There on July 5 he was presented with a rich suit of regimentals, epaulettes, sword and pistol, and a commission as colonel of the Loyal Militia. Craig had secured an astute back-country commander with mobile cavalry bands in four counties. Fanning now issued official field orders, all very British regulation, but his weapons were cruelty and terror, as indeed were those of his Whig enemies.

•

On July 17 a court-martial of Tory prisoners was to be held at Pittsboro. At dawn Fanning's riders surprised and captured the officers of the court, three delegates to the General Assembly, a colonel and subalterns, fifty-three in all now bound for the humiliation of swearing on the Holy Evangelists of Almighty God their true allegiance to George the Third, or, alternately, a spell in Craig's prison ship. Those who refused to take the oath were marched toward Wilmington. At McPhaul's Mill, a Highlander rendezvous, Fanning halted to bait the Governor of North Carolina, Thomas Burke, a doctor and an able man bearing up stoutly in an impossible situation. Fanning's prisoners wrote Governor Burke a joint letter pleading that he end his mistreatment of Tories in consideration that they themselves were being accorded "the utmost respect and kindness by our commanding officer, Colonel Fanning . . ." That this was written at gun point appeared later when one of the prisoners, James Williams wrote Governor Burke: "I am told your Excellency understood our letter from McPhaul's Mill. We were very unhappy there."

•

A Whig colonel, Philip Alston, a violent man eventually killed by a slave whom he had mistreated, headed a party which came upon Kenneth Black, the Loyalist who had given shelter to Flora MacDonald after her eviction from Killiegrey. Black, attempting to escape, was shot. He fell on his face and was beaten to death with his own musket. Alston duly informed the new widow, killed two of her beeves for the evening's entertainment, and set off for his home, the "House in the Horseshoe," standing on the west bank of the Deep below Coxe's Mill. There Fanning next day besieged him.

Alston stationed snipers inside the house. Mrs. Alston lay prone on a bed to offer the least target. Her two children stood on a table inside the fireplace, their bodies safe in the sooty brick enclosure. A British officer, attached to Fanning as an observer, called for a charge and upon exposing himself was shot dead. A farm wagon loaded with hay was backed up to the house with a view to setting it on fire. Alston's snipers accounted for that detail.

When eight men had been killed and the siege went fecklessly on, Mrs. Alston, perhaps moved by small smothered cries up the chimney, appeared on the veranda with a white flag and a plea for honorable surrender. This Fanning granted. The dead were buried. Philip Alston took the King's oath. In exchange for his surrendering peacefully, the House in the Horseshoe became one of the few along the Deep River to survive the summer of 1781.

Fanning in early August captured Cross Creek and added some highly surprised Patriot leaders to his string of prisoners for Wilmington delivery. It was probably on this trip that Craig and Fanning laid a plan for the capture of Governor Thomas Burke.

On the return upriver Fanning made camp at Elizabethtown, the Bladen County seat on the west bank of the Cape Fear. Here the Loyalist Colonels Slingsby and Gadden had four hundred troops, some of them Craig's redcoats, taking a respite after a series of raids. Fanning warned Slingsby that he was holding a dangerously large number of Whig prisoners. Next morning he set off for the Deep and missed the Battle of Elizabethtown.

Slingsby had taken the precaution to beach all small boats on his side of the river against any notion the Whigs might have of surprising his camp. There were one hundred Whigs still at large, all of them refugees from burned homes. Among them were the heads of Bladen's first families, Robeson, Brown, Owen and Morehead, Scots whose people had been there long enough to break British leading strings. They had a spy in the person of a young girl who sold eggs in the Tory camp. She reported roystering going on in Elizabethtown and a letdown in vigilance. That night the Whigs undressed on the east bank, bundled their arms and clothes atop their heads and forded the river. Since no dams then existed to raise the stream's level, the ford permitted the smallest Whig to cross with his chin raised above water. They shook themselves, dressed and moved on Elizabethtown just before dawn.

It was as the girl had said. From a sodden sleep the Tories awoke to bullet and bayonet. Slingsby and Gadden were killed. Their Whig prisoners were set free to join in the slaughter. The worst of it happened in a deep V-wedge gorge which began at the town's main street and dropped sharply to the river. Fright poured the Tories into this seeming shelter where they were easy targets for muskets on the ravine's edges.

•

Colonel Wade had recruited 450 Patriot militia to attack the Scots Highlanders under Colonel Hector McNeill, "Old Hector" to distinguish him from the younger Hector who was Jennie Bahn's son. The rivals met at Betti's Bridge on Drowning Creek. Reluctantly Old Hector had allowed the distasteful Fanning and forty of his partisans to join in the engagement. This was a fortunate decision for the Highlanders. Fanning's swift strike at Wade's flank turned the battle into a rout. Wade was denied his revenge for Piney Bottom, and lost 250 mounts to the Tory-Loyalist coalition.

•

Craig and Fanning had put their heads together on the coup of capturing the Governor of North Carolina and bringing him hostage to Wilmington. That, they thought, would break the back of the Rebel government. Now Fanning began to weigh his chances. Governor Burke was at Hillsboro. The notion of surprising a civilian in his night clothes was agreeable to a man who brooded strategy in the saddle while softer men were sleeping. But his rangers were too small a force to bring it off alone.

There was the larger Highlander corps whom he had aided in defeating Wade at Betti's Bridge. If they would play his game the taking of Hillsboro would be possible.

The most formidable Patriot army now in the field was that of General John Butler, at the moment busy recruiting between the Haw and the Deep. Fanning and the Highlanders agreed on a plan, first to make an open start in Butler's direction, secretly to separate into three columns and converge on Hillsboro at dawn. This satisfied the Highlanders as retaining their identity. Fanning had his needed reinforcements.

At seven o'clock on the foggy morning of September 13 two Loyalist columns and Fanning's entered Hillsboro, not yet quite awakened to the day's serious business of planning riddance from the state of their Tory enemies. Governor Burke, his Council, a

Continental colonel and seventy-one soldiers were captured with the expenditure of a handful of powder. The jail guard, learning the Governor was taken, ripped the Whig deertails from their hats and substituted Tory oat straws. In the mist and confusion they might have escaped had not Fanning recognized them. Raising a cry, "The Rebels! The Rebels!", Fanning brought his sword down on a guard's head. An iron plate under the guard's cap saved his pate and broke the sword.

The rest of the morning was spent in looting stores and broaching rum kegs. A few Tories were too drunk to move out at noon, and were later captured by rallying Whigs. The Governor and other prisoners were marched away under the charge of Captain John McLean, a teetotaler.

•

The sloping banks of Cane Creek, a day's march southwest of Hillsboro, first saw white men's cabins when the Quakers settled there to be away from the company of those who thought fighting was the only way to settle disputes. But violence chose Cane Creek for its own. The armies of Cornwallis and Gates passed that way. Now Fanning and Old Hector McNeill camped there with their valuable captives, and there General Butler caught up with them.

There were six hundred in the Loyalist camp and only four hundred Patriots, but prisoners were a hindrance to the larger force and Patriot tempers at the capture of their governor were at hornet heat. The engagement lasted for hours. Patriot Colonel Robert Mebane in full enemy view passed a hatful of powder along his line and, wiping his hand over his sweaty forehead, wound up his heroics as a blackamoor. Colonel Hector McNeill was killed. His command passed to young Hector McNeill, Jennie Bahn's son, who had not yet lost an eye to his father-in-law's thumb. It was Fanning who saved the Loyalist day by crossing the stream and attacking the Patriot rear. A musket ball broke Fanning's left arm. His men spirited him off to Brush Creek.

The Patriots, undefeated yet fearful that the Governor and his party might be killed, broke off the battle. Butler followed down the Cape Fear until the Loyalists reached Bladen County and Craig reinforcements. Craig received his distinguished hostage, but had barely a month to enjoy custody of the Governor before word came that Lord Cornwallis had surrendered his army to General Washington at Yorktown. Craig sailed down the Lower Cape Fear. North Carolina, given over to "frolicking" over the victory, was free of British occupancy but not of its own hatreds, nor of Fanning.

•

Scaldhead Dave astride a draft horse had become Colonel Fanning mounted on his mare Bay Doe. He held that title and his partisan command for eight months after Yorktown. Craig was no longer there to send him medicines and ammunition, so Fanning took to looting and burnings. With no one to whom he might send prisoners, his killings increased.

In April Fanning married a sixteen-year-old Deep River girl. What was to have been a triple wedding—reduced by sudden death to a double wedding—is described by Fanning in his *Narrative:*

> Captain William Hooker and Captain William Carr agreed to be married with me. They both left me to make themselves and their intended wives ready, and the day before we were to be coupled, the rebels before mentioned, with those good horses, came upon them. Captain Hooker's horse being tied so fast he could not get him loose, they caught him and murdered him on the spot. Myself and Capt. Carr were married and kept two days merriment.

During the first months of 1782 Nathanael Greene defeated Lord Rawdon at Eutaw Springs and still further hedged in the hungry British from foraging beyond Charleston. The end was in sight there. In North Carolina Governor Burke returned to Hillsboro to hold treason trials. Colonel David Fanning, holding himself local British authority, threatened tenfold reprisal if any of his men were hanged at Hillsboro. Scaldhead Dave had come far in war and diplomacy. But his last adventure in North Carolina concerned only a horseman's dismay at loss of his mount Bay Doe.

The mare was stolen from him by a whisky runner. From then on the matchless speed of Bay Doe kept her beyond reach of her lesser-mounted master. In a week of pursuit Fanning wounded one man and killed another, without recovering his mare. Lord Rawdon was about to embark from Charleston. To be left behind meant death for Fanning at the hands of the Patriots. He sailed on the *New Blessing* for Saint Augustine. His wife went with him, suffered with him months of misfortune in Florida, and eventually sailed with him to Nova Scotia, where she bore him a son and lived to see grandchildren.

Nova Scotia was also the last home of a son of Jennie Bahn McNeill and Archie Scrubblin'. He was Daniel, appointed by Cornwallis as captain in a Loyalist regiment. Daniel named his place on the Avon River "Loyal Hill." He was grandfather of a distinguished physician and legislator, Daniel McNeill Parker.

Jennie Bahn died in full possession of her resolute mind and her real estate. This was in 1791, one year before Cross Creek changed its name to Fayetteville, becoming the first of many American towns to commemorate the Marquis de Lafayette.

The admirers of Jennie Bahn raised a fund to have a shaft hewn from the granite ribs of Scotland and shipped to her Upper Little River grave. Unhappily it slipped from a barge into the waters of the Cape Fear, and there, buried in silt, it rested but was not forgotten.

In the new nineteenth century Jennie's monument was raised and its pointed tip was reared properly over her remains. But the mass of the shaft found its way to a stonecutter's. Its suborned blocks were laid as foundations stones in the growing city of Fayetteville, the Cross Creek of the pioneer days, now the hub of the wheel of post-Revolutionary Tar Heel life.

# II : The Nineteenth Century
## *Revolutionists into Rebels*

# 1 : *What Price* Liberty?

When the war ended, the people were in poverty, society in disorder, morals and manners almost prostrate.

————Archibald Debow Murphey


Independence came at a price to the first generations of American
citizens along the Cape Fear. During the Stamp Act troubles at
Wilmington, a hand on the sawdust pulse of LIBERTY had detected
a faint beat of life in the effigy. Huzzahs and the clinking of mugs
of rum celebrated the breaking of the first leading string from
Mother England. When all the strings were broken and English
law and order sailed away with Lord Cornwallis and Governor
Martin, there was no Provincial authority strong enough to sort
out the disorder and calm partisan hatreds.

The leaders of the Revolution had met the crisis with courage
and verve. But it was well for Moore, Harnett, and Ashe that they
had died face to the foe, before the bright armor of war should
tarnish in the foggy aftermath. Their sons would find small glory
in taxing people who had no money, or in trying to persuade the
kin of exiled Loyalists into working on roads side by side with the
sons of Patriots murdered by David Fanning.

There was desperate need of the former foes' getting together
on common projects, road and bridgebuilding most especially.
Plantations back from the river must have roads on which to move

their tobacco. Without a way to market, the small farmer lived on his own corn and fat back, clothed himself in homespun, and had no silver for taxes or tools. And whereas in the pioneer years the mere fact of ownership of land had made isolation tolerable, the pioneer's children wanted to market their surplus; they craved a town to visit, and the jingle of spendable cash.

The valley was crowded with them now, it being the heartland of what the first United States census in 1790 discovered to be the fourth most populous state in the new Union. It also had the worst transportation system and *ipso facto* was the poorest state in the Union.

From Burrington to Tryon, the royal governors had urged the building of roads as a first necessity. The highway along the Atlantic coast, "the road used by gentlemen who make the tour of the continent," touched Brunswick and Wilmington. The road up the west bank of the Upper Cape Fear had been pounded hard by the marching feet of the British and Continental armies. Across the Deep and the Haw rivers went the Great Trading Path, an immemorial Indian trail following high ground from Virginia to South Carolina.

Cross Creek was the hub of five roads. They served the farmers living along them, but by the end of the Revolution there were tens of thousands of back-country men with no outlet to road or river.

The Legislature passed an act to build feeder roads. Having no funds for the purpose, it invented the stratagem of having county courts appoint road overseers and bestowed on them the authority to compel local labor to build and maintain local roads. On call were to be all white males from the age of sixteen, all Negro males twelve years and up. The results were mere widened trails pocked with mudholes and stumps. When the route passed through a longleaf pine forest, there was the hazard of dead trees, boxed for turpentine and illegally left standing. Summer storms sent them crashing across the road, sometimes across a passing coach. Travelers from the outside, among them President Washington, searched for invectives to describe the dreariness of these highways.

A Northern visitor complained that he was "forced to crawl along a slippery log whilst a Negro swam over the horses." One Hussey, lost on horseback in the pine wilderness near Lockwood's Folly, struck flint to steel for a comforting pitch-pine fire and "spent the night in fighting wolves attracted to the light from the wilds." At daylight he "ascended a tall sapling to look out for land and saw Wilmington and the ferry house not far off."

Elkanah Watson of Massachusetts observed that "travelers with any pretensions to respectability seldom stop at the wretched taverns, but custom freely sanctions their calling at any planter's residence, who seeks to consider himself the party obliged by this freedom."

The lack of taxes to build roads stemmed from sectionalism which in turn traced back to lack of communication between sections. An Assemblyman elected by a Gaelic-speaking constituency was not likely to vote for a road needed by people across the river whose accent still bore a trace of Erse. This dreary cycle had begun when royalist governors had used the fee system to bilk country people and so had created lasting piedmont distrust of the coastal planter hierarchy. To this antagonism the Revolution had added the hatred shared among Loyalists, Tories, and Patriots. Why build a road headed into enemy country?

While this failure of land transportation in North Carolina helped strangle recovery from the Revolution, the real villain in the tragedy was the Cape Fear River. Roads in time can be widened, smoothed, made adequate for growing trade and travel. A river remains just as geologic ages shaped it and handed it over for the use of a people. The Cape Fear, which had lured the pioneers into its basin, now proved too small and cranky to serve as the Atlantic outlet of a matured commonwealth.

•

The bowsprits of tall ships projected over Boston's cobbled water-front. Ocean tides swept through the Narrows to the doorsteps of Manhattan's countinghouses. Rows of tall Georgian houses surveyed the Delaware. The James River planter loaded tobacco at his own wharf. Charleston's proud Battery rose on the profits of sea and river trade. The Cape of Fear, battleground of Atlantic rollers and river currents, stood inhospitable guard over the shipping lanes to Wilmington.

The hurricane-carved New Inlet and the Frying Pan Shoals were not difficult runs for schooners and brigs in the coastal trade. But the skippers of transatlantic ships of more than two hundred tons registry preferred not to thread the Shoals while peering over the side at sandy bottoms roiled by the passage of their keels.

Once inside, the sand of the channel changed to the mud of the Flats, a silt bank reaching from Brunswick to Wilmington and making the channel shallower each year as the river unburdened its eroded upcountry earth.

Trade recovers quickly from wars. Wilmington had products which the outside world wanted. Lumber, barrel staves and shingles, naval stores, deerskins, tobacco and rice kept Wilmington alive as a trading port and the social center of plantation life. A good growing season could rebuild a house burned by the Tories, with something left over to bet on the horse races and cockfights.

The estuary was still the planters' main highway, the periauger their favorite craft. The great shaft of cypress, hundreds of years old, was adzed and burned to make a hull. This oversize canoe was then sawed down the middle, one or two planks inserted, and ends fashioned for prow and stern. The periauger could sail a dozen tierces of rice to Wilmington. If the wind failed during an outing, the family could shelter under an awning while six Negro oarsmen propelled the periauger to town or a neighbor's wharf.

The plantation had survived the war. Four families in New Hanover County owned more than ten thousand acres each, the majority more than four hundred acres each. Slaves were the farm hands. Every pleasure vehicle was taxed five shillings the wheel. A

town which had been ravaged during the British occupation by
Major Craig could not forget the terror and the dead. People and
politics had moved upriver. Wilmington would remain a pleasant
river town, its gentility preserving itself against wharf manners
and morals. The sand of the Shoals and the mud of the Flats
would prevent its growth from promising colonial town to great
American port.

•

The Upper Cape Fear, even to its first travelers appearing the
"color of malt beer," meanders through marshes for the first few
miles above Wilmington. Willow roots cling to the first flood-
gouged banks. The cypress begin to form thickets along the shore
line. Hardwoods and pine take over the high ground. The west
bank becomes a small vertical cliff of shale, limestone, and sea
detritus carved into a layer cake by the compounded power of the
river and that of the rotating earth.

Ten miles above the estuary the solid forest walls both banks.
Excepting for wharves and steps cut in the bank, it must have
appeared this way to Indian and white canoe paddlers. The cypress canoe had become the farmer's carryall. It could float two
horses or the entire family. Once a hundred canoes carried the
countryside to a funeral.

The canoe's great cousin, the periauger, did the heavy lifting. It
could be loaded with a hundred barrels of pitch. On it a score of
immigrants could make the inland journey. A Negro crew manned
the oars. Poles pushed the boat over the shallows. When the river
was in spate, ropes were wrapped around trees and the craft
hauled past the worst water. In flood, periaugers had to be
beached. Yet there were those moments when a properly quarter-
ing wind and a straight stretch of river allowed the sail to relieve
the strain on taut shoulders. The thirty-mile journey around the
horseshoe bends from Wilmington to Elizabethtown required
more time than a man would take on horseback.

From both banks of the river marched the majestic longleaf

pines. The adopted Indian method of girdling thinned the forest slowly. A century more of felling would still leave virgin timber. In the far forest reaches the kiln tenders lived as lonely as charcoal burners ever were in the Black Forest. Some of them had indentured themselves to escape the London slums. Some had huddled in Dublin or Edinburgh when the tenantry of their farms had been bestowed on the reigning favorite, the wool-bearing mutton. If they were now distilling turpentine a day's journey from other people, it was that they had listened to the siren call of free land in the New World and from lack of luck or ability had failed to become freeholders. The penalty was severe. Some of the kiln tenders became "clay eaters." As children they had popped bits of cabin chinking into their hungry mouths. Pellagra and hookworm plagued their listless lives. They would remain the valley's poor whites, until the longleaf pines were all gone, and twentieth century medicine would learn to treat their ills.

•

Elizabethtown on the high west bank throve from river traffic and as seat of Bladen County. The "Tory Hole," that gulley whose wedge cut into the town's main street, was daily reminder of the dawn surprise attack in 1781 when Patriot invaders trapped the Tories in the ravine and slaughtered them to the last man. Their sons and brothers could live as neighbors now on the high farmlands west of Elizabethtown, but in the Legislature they would not agree on common action for the common good. Road bills regularly failed of passage.

Some of the Lower Cape Fear families established plantations on the Upper River. The first John Baptista Ashe, who died at Grovely Plantation in 1734, sired soldiers, judges, statesmen, and historians. The mile-square land on the Upper Cape Fear, which he patented in 1730, later in the century was held successively by William Bartram, brother of the botanist John Bartram, and by General Thomas Brown, one of the Patriot leaders who had stormed Elizabethtown. There were marriages among Bartrams,

Browns, and Robesons, producing numerous progeny which for a century and a half looked to the great house, Oakland, as their home place.

Oakland was built by General Brown in 1781. It escaped the house burnings of the last violent years of the Revolution. Its floors are of six-inch heart pine, its hearth wide for hospitality. The General's study windows command the river on one side and the landscaped approach on the other. The General earned his repose. As a prisoner on one of Major Craig's ships at Wilmington he had contrived a rum-drinking bout with his two British guards, keeping his own head clear and befuddling the others to the point where it seemed hilarious to swap his uniform for one of theirs. He walked through the town in his British togs, commandeered a rowboat and maneuvered through the anchorage to safety up-river. There he had the triumph of being arrested by a Continental sentry and revealing himself to a brother American officer. Oakland's brick walls were his reward for days of hiding out in a hollow tree, its kitchen a climax to jerked beef and spring water taken on the run in Tory territory.

•

William Bartram the younger, nephew of the Cape Fear planter and son of the botanist, in his own right was author of *Travels through North & South Carolina*. His two visits to Cross Creek spanned the settlement's first growing years. Going up river in 1757 from his Uncle William's plantation—where in his *Travels* he noted "a great variety of very curious and beautiful flowering and sweet scented shrubs"—he came upon the sister settlements of Campbellton on the river and Cross Creek a mile inland. Between the two of them there were only twenty inhabitants. There was a mill on one of the "cross creeks." Indians traded at Campbellton.

Twenty years later Bartram returned to find "a fine inland trading town, on some swelling hills." Here the periaugers ended their eighty-mile haul from Wilmington. Voyage by voyage over the years they had moved the center of valley life from the estuary to

Cross Creek. Here the Moravians fortnightly sent their wagon trains; rafts were assembled and loaded; country people came to grind their corn and to have fun at military musters and on court days. Bartram's second visit in 1777 records a city of more than a thousand houses, "a vast resort of inhabitants and travellers and continual brisk commerce by wagons from the back settlements."

•

Above Cross Creek a succession of rapids and falls barred further navigation to periaugers. The raft still made its serpentine way from the fall-line to the sea, for the raft was built in units which singly slid down white water and were assembled below. The detachable vertebrae of the completed snake was the "clamp," so named from the crosswise clamps at each end which held together a dozen squared longleaf logs. A settlement was bound to appear at the place where the rafts were put together and manned for the long lazy float to market. Below Smilie's Falls that settlement became the town of Averasboro.

The site had everything to recommend it. Nearby an old Indian trail had become a north and south trading path. The King's Highway running north from Cross Creek passed through it. A gristmill and a ferry across the Cape Fear had been there since 1740. Here the low east bank offered the advantage of a landing for pole boats whose upriver advance was stopped by Smilie's Falls.

In 1766 Alexander Avera bought 350 river-front acres. In ten years the place had a tavern, a cooperage to turn out tar and turpentine barrels, a tannery, and that back-country phenomenon, competing stores. After the Revolution the crossways became a rough and tough river town, with ambitions and the energy to undertake an obvious major enterprise—the extension of river navigation past white water into the rich farm market beyond the fall-line. Canals would do it.

The establishment of the Cape Fear Navigation Company in 1796 started a land boom on the Upper River. The first project was to bypass Buckhorn Falls with canals and flumes over the feeder creeks. Surveyors with line and level, slaves with pick and shovel, ran the red earth into a ditch around Buckhorn Falls and southward toward Smilie's. Engineers blasted the soft rock with gunpowder. Mile by mile the canal reached downriver until it encountered the granite ridge above Averasboro. There the gunpowder merely blackened the rock, and the completed section above would remain as a jumping place for small boys and a hazard for cattle. The Upper Cape Fear had delivered its first defeat to would-be conquerors.

Averasboro was in the same geographic location as Georgetown on the Potomac and Richmond on the James. A hard-to-wear-down rocky ledge ran from Virginia southward at an ever-widening angle from the Atlantic. This created the fall-line over which all piedmont streams flowed. The first smooth water below these cascades was the head of navigation to the coast. But below Georgetown and Richmond their rivers flowed unobstructed to the sea, and deep enough for the biggest ships of their times. Georgetown and Richmond could ship goods directly to Boston or London. Averasboro could not entertain the crew of a 200-ton ship. There were the falls above Cross Creek between it and London. In the vital half century after the Revolution, when great trading ports were being created elsewhere along the Atlantic coast, the Cape Fear throttled its trade.

•

Another geological quirk diverted piedmont beef and bacon, cotton, tobacco, cereals, and black walnut logs from the Upper Cape Fear valley to the competing states of Virginia and South Carolina. The rocky underpinnings of the upper piedmont slanted the mountain-born rivers southeasterly into South Carolina or northeasterly into Virginia. It was easier for the North Carolina piedmont cotton planter to reach the Yadkin and Catawba routes into South Carolina, and for the grower of black tobacco to send his products down the Tar and the Roanoke to Virginia. The Cape

Fear's tributaries, the Haw and the Deep, although in a more direct line to the sea, were blocked to navigation by the fall-line.

This ancient earthly accident had great effects on the three contiguous states. Piedmont Tar Heels bought supplies from Virginia, read Virginia newspapers, married Virginia girls. Or, if they utilized the Catawba, they formed bonds with Columbia and Charleston. When two thirds of their trade could not reach the Cape Fear, the old sectionalism between the piedmont farmer and the planter coast found new reasons for political disunity in North Carolina.

Still, the lines to Virginia and South Carolina were none too strong. Most Tar Heels settled down to live as frontiersmen on their isolated farms, handicrafts their source of household goods, the church the hub of their devotion and schooling, the tavern an outlet for their bonny brawls.

•

Despite all these hardships it was a growing time. When Bladen was created as the first county back from the Lower Cape Fear, it was still considered that Carolina extended to the "South Seas." That conceit of the Lords Proprietors was decade by decade whittled down at the opening of the piedmont and the discovery of the Blue Ridge bastion to the unknown West. While Indiana lawyers would some day have to wrestle with deeds based on Bladen County claims, Bladen itself early faced the fact that people needed to live within a day's horseback ride of the county seat; and so it subdivided into Cumberland, Harnett, and Orange counties and these into newer ones.

In the post-Revolutionary period many tracts were set aside for new county seats. Dwellings and stores appeared on the surveyor's grid. The new courthouse had a stairway to its first floor, leaving space beneath for folk to squat on the cool hard-beaten earth, to lie about the sagacity of their coon dogs or make matches for cockfights. On a court day the proceedings going on above their heads, plus pulls on the rum jug, could end in a ring of spectators around an all-out fight. The grim frontiersman tactic of knotting a man's hair in one fist and using the other hand to gouge out an eye could still stop short of mayhem if the worsted man could in time bawl out: "King's Curse!"

Such cloddish barbarities were not in the true mode of county life. Respectable God-fearing folk drank raspberry shrub on shady verandas and saw to it that their children learned their letters. In the river towns—some now due the title of cities—the tread of buckled shoe and satin slipper seemed to the awed eyes of country cousins not unsuspect of alliances with sin.

•

The miasma of guerrilla warfare still hung in the post-Revolutionary air. There was no social, economic, or racial group that could speak for all of North Carolina on the most important decision it had ever had to make, whether to join the new Union or try to make it alone as a sovereign and independent political unity.

Eleven of the states had ratified the United States Constitution by the time the Assembly met at Hillsboro in July 1787 to consider its position. Internal tensions go far toward explaining why North Carolina, which had done its full share in opposing King George, now erupted in accusations that George Washington was a "damned rascal" for having signed the Constitution, and blistering counterattacks from the Federalists that the opposition to signing consisted of fools and knaves.

There was a certain sectional consistency in all this. The planters of the Lower Cape Fear never had disliked the power over money and affairs which Parliament had wielded, and the lawyers, merchants, and officeholders went along with this concept of a ruling elite, providing that they themselves composed it. What they had disliked was Parliament's attempt to cut them down from wielding comparable power in their own bailiwick. Perhaps it was not quite that crude, since the planter rebellion against England had a strong New World leaven of shared authority with all American citizens. Yet there was a carry-over of the passion for

power-plus-democracy of the planter Patriots of 1776 into the enthusiasm of the same men for the proposed Constitution of the
United States in 1787. They wanted a strong central government
which could provide a stable currency and present a common
front to European friends and foes. So the planter rebels against
Parliament became the defenders of a strong federal government.

By their own lights the piedmont farmers were also consistent,
Parliament, both in its proper person and as reflected by Royal
governors and their coastal allies, had taxed, cheated, and fought
them. They had fought back, against Tryon in the Regulation and
against England in the Revolution, yet now in their own new independent nation a power was rising in Philadelphia which
smacked suspiciously of the old arbitrary British power.

At Hillsboro the farmer antifederalists were on their home
grounds, a day's canter from where they had stood up, if unsuc-
cessfully, against Tryon at Alamance and Cornwallis at Guilford
Courthouse. Now they were ready to listen to the predictions of a
Baptist preacher, Lemuel Burkitt, that the Federalists planned to
raise a standing army of 50,000 to crush the liberties of the people.
Willie Jones, a talented aristocrat schooled at Eton, jumped class
lines to become the antifederalist leader. A man of the people, the
Wilmington blacksmith Timothy Bloodworth, told them that the
Constitution would set up a "monarchial monarchy." Well, hadn't
a crown been suggested for George Washington?

After eleven days of debate at Hillsboro the antifederalists
blocked ratification of the Constitution by a vote of 184 to 84. It
was not a complete rejection. The Patriot preacher David Caldwell, along with Willie Jones and others, approved signing the
Constitution providing that there were amendments protecting
the civil liberties of the people. This stand was not without influence at Philadelphia. Congress was impatient to bring North Carolina and Rhode Island into the fold. In some degree the adoption
of the Bill of Rights came about because of the recalcitrant position of the Hillsboro Assembly. That body disbanded after agree-

ing to meet on November 16 at Cross Creek for another vote on ratification of the Constitution.

•

Over the summer opinion veered half circle. Respected Federalists—James Iredell and the war hero William R. Davie—campaigned for ratification. Iredell epitomized it by presenting a choice whether "we shall be truly a union, happy in ourselves and respected by the rest of the world . . . or an irreconcilable scattered people."

The taverns of Cross Creek were loud with argument that fall. Could the interests of the farmer and the merchant be separated? No, not when North Carolina as a separate nation would face the tariffs of the rest of the American states and suffer foreclosures by foreign creditors. A Sovereign Republic of North Carolina would be at the expense of raising its own armed forces and paying the salaries of its Ambassadors to the Court of St. James, Paris. . . . On the fifth day of the Cross Creek convention the resolution for ratification passed 195 to 77.

•

Two years later, in December 1789, the Assembly again met at Cross Creek and distinguished itself by voting to establish a State University "to consult the Happiness of a rising Generation and endeavor to fit them for an honorable Discharge of the Social Duties of life." Having made this magnificent gesture, the state which "tugged and fumbled at its purse strings a long time before she could get them open," thought to save itself cash by a vague arrangement for selling public lands for a university building fund, and graciously permitting private donations of money and lands. A grudging loan of $10,000 was eventually changed to an outright gift through the urgings of General Davie. It was the only public money in support of the university for nearly a century.

Cross Creek in its growing pride became weary of being named for an oddity of nature, especially since the efforts of the two creeks to push each other off course had been negated by a man who built a milldam on the site. The combined towns of Campbellton and Cross Creek voted to honor the Marquis de Lafayette, and Fayetteville it became and is.

One insult to Fayetteville was the rejection of its logical claim, as head of Cape Fear deepwater navigation and seat of the Assembly, to be the permanent capital of the state. That same Hillsboro convention which had refused to ratify the Constitution had voted to locate the capital "within ten miles of Isaac Hunter's plantation in Wake County." No sober choice could prefer a "broom-sedge patch" in Wake County to the urbane facilities of Fayetteville. But it was difficult to explain that the Wake County advocates had plied convention delegates with ample beakers of cherry bounce just prior to the vote. It was now too late for Fayetteville's outrage to be effective. The appointed committee bought Joel Lane's plantation in Wake County for £1,378 and laid out a town to be called Raleigh.

Later a foray of Fayetteville gallants, fortified by cherry bounce or its belligerent equivalent, set out upon the King's Highway and en route met a Raleigh delegation as primed for mayhem. The effective use of wagon spokes, rocks, and bare knuckles invalided a respectable number of both parties, without unseating Raleigh.

•

Another committee appointed by the Legislature surveyed the geographical center of the state to decide on a location for the new university. They settled on the site of New Hope Chapel, thirty miles northwest of Raleigh. A high ridge gave a prospect over the green carpet of farm and forest to the horizon. On January 15, 1795, Chapel Hill opened its doors, the first state university in the United States to do so. Hinton James, who had traveled 150 miles to become Chapel Hill's first student, won a second citation for immortality by being for two weeks the entire student body.

The University of North Carolina was a seed dropped into

otherwise sterile scholastic soil. There were a few academies for those who could afford ten dollars a term, but no public schools. Newspapers were weeklies which relied on casual private correspondence to report events months old. The Assembly voted road and river improvements without providing the money. When children grew up to discover that there were too many of them to share the family farm, they crossed the Blue Ridge to the virgin soil and forests of the West, or ventured south into the opening cotton country. North Carolina slumbered its way into the nineteenth century. It became known as "the second Nazareth," or "the Ireland of America," and, when Washington Irving's story would have its great vogue, it would be called "the Rip Van Winkle State," "Old Rip" for short.

# 2 : Sinners, Sails, and Paddle Wheels

The call on the sinner to seek salvation rang in the Cape Fear backwoods country long before the Revolution. A missionary from New England's Great Awakening, Shubal Stearns, brought the shouting revivalism of the Separate Baptists to Sandy Creek in 1755. Stearns had the modulated voice of entreaty, the thunderous tones of denunciation. His hands could soothe or flail. The pioneer farmers, oppressed by their taxgatherers, were moved to tears and cries of joy at this proof that a man of God cared for their souls and would fight the Devil himself to save them. Many fell to the floor in convulsions of ecstasy.

A Presbyterian preacher, the Reverend David Caldwell, came from Pennsylvania to Alamance in 1765. In the Northern split between the conservative Old Side and the revivalist New Side he had chosen the latter. He opened a log college near Guilford Courthouse and there, among many others, trained James McGready in Gospel militancy. McGready experienced a personal crisis. Convinced of his own sanctity, one day he overheard it being challenged. If such doubts could assail him, how greatly the palpable sinners needed to be alarmed to their peril of damnation. He found words to appall the most callous, in his sermon on "The End of the Fool" whose "soul was separated from his body and the black flaming vultures of hell began to encircle him on every side . . . sinking into the liquid, boiling waves of hell . . . among all the rubbish and off-scouring, the filth and refuse of the moral world, which a holy God deems unfit for any other place."

Members of the Old Side persuasion burned McGready's pulpit and wrote a warning in blood for him to depart, which he did.

After the hiatus of the Revolution, other circuit-riding preachers from the North made their harvests of salvation among the lonely, isolated people of the Cape Fear, among them two great preachers, George Whitefield and Francis Asbury. Yet conversions were not always lasting, and lapses from the dreariness of keeping farm were frequent and unrestrained.

The veterans of the Revolution were coming on to middle age. To drink heavily when given the chance, to bet, fight, and swear had been outlets from the boredom of camp life and the hellish months on British prison ships. Bad habits persisted. No farm was long walking distance from a crossroads tavern where a jug hanging by its handle to a pole promised a keg and tumblers inside.

Independence Day was a general invitation to get drunk. Muster days, after a token drill, were given over to matching the fighter champion of one neighborhood against another's. The muscled competed at throwing sledges, the nimble in jumping ditches. Gander pulling was a favorite. An elderly gander with a well-greased neck was hung by his feet to a limb. The merriment came in watching the galloping horsemen miss the swinging bird or being yanked out of the saddle by the force of his grasp and the resistance of the tough bird. Before the day's rout was completed, these organized sports gave way to impromptu fist fights and eye gouging.

Family recreation was more refined, if alcoholic in mild or wild degree. When persimmon beer and sweet potatoes regaled a corn shucking or fence building, frolicking and flirting kept mete bounds. If the whisky jug was passed, the host collected inert bodies and aligned them neatly on his puncheon floor.

To the farmwives these masculine releases from drudgery were denied. The quilting bee abetted neighborliness. The church was their weekly solace, the dance frolic a gaiety permitted by their preachers. But a combination of faraway influences and near-at-hand family troubles was preparing an outbreak of religious emotionalism in which the church banned the fiddle as the Devil's instrument and condemned the hard drinker to hell.

The fever ran down the coast from New England to Georgia. Among rural people it had appeared in Europe over the centuries, usually after such calamities as the Black Death. Perhaps the French Revolution, with its godlessness and blood bath worked an influence on the American Great Revival. The Cape Fear valley, as rural as any, was susceptible.

Mrs. David Caldwell in the summer of 1801 led others in praying for a revival. It came with the suddenness of revelation. The pastor, raising his hands in benediction after a communion service, found no words to dismiss them. The awkward silence was broken by a voice crying: "Stand still and see the salvation of God!" Cries as of the day of Pentecost shook the rafters. Restraints broke into a babel of exultation and pleas against damnation. Entranced bodies lay for a time on the floor and arose in a state of joy and praise. No one left until after midnight.

The fever spread through the valley. No church could hold a tithe of the sinners who came by the hundreds to the open fields where board pulpits were erected and a team of preachers prepared for days and nights of singing, exhortation and the triumph of confession. They came by families, as calm and expectant as though it were an outing to a county fair. They pitched cloth tents or knocked together bark shelters. The children chased each other and the dogs barked. The first hours of the meeting went by in friendly handshaking and singing. The preachers were no more exhortative than in their accustomed church services. Then, as the burden of collective sin grew unbearable, a stricken cry touched off pent emotion into the inexhaustible energy of speaking in tongues and contortions of whirling, jerking bodies. In the calms between mass spasms the preachers flayed the unrepentant and pleaded with the souls teetering on the anxious bench between heaven and hell.

For the women the camp meetings were a glorious release from chores begun before dawn, from nursing bruised menfolk who had spent the family pennies on liquor and gaming. The revivalist preachers told them no more of sin and salvation than they heard weekly at their own churches. And it was more comforting to see their men stricken to the floor by the voice of God than by the lip of a whisky jug. Then, there was food to be prepared for days of meeting, a ride through the countryside, and new friends. For single women there was an added excitement. In the high pitch of self-revelation it could appear that the Lord wished her to marry a certain person. The Reverend Joseph Moore reported: "It was said some old maids who had nearly gotten antiquated, managed in this way to get husbands."

Toward the end of the Great Revival the "exercises" deteriorated into excessive bodily jerks, into going about on all fours barking or mewing. God-defying wretches who had come to meeting for no good purpose, applied hot coals to the feet of those stretched on the floor.

When the Great Revival was spent, camp meetings periodically were held until the Civil War—into our times in rural backwaters. They had put the people of the valley into circulation, and had greatly increased Methodist, Baptist, and Presbyterian membership.

The gentry avoided revivals except for occasional curiosity seeking. Their wives were fully occupied with their households and servants. Their daughters were taught a delicacy of thought and manners alien to the rude antics of camp meetings. Curiously, a reflection of camp meeting unworldliness appeared in genteel dress. Necklines and padded silhouettes of Paris fashion in 1800 were replaced by loose gowns which prevented even a glimpse at a girl's throat.

The planters of the Lower Cape Fear, from Wilmington to Fayetteville, had their own period of excitement ahead of them. The War of 1812 brought privateers back to Wilmington with captured English merchandise. The first river steamboat was only around the bend of time.

•

England's highhanded impressment of American seamen in 1812 drove the United States into a brash declaration of war. There was no land army fit to face British invasion. New England, helpless against British attack by sea, moved to secede from the Union. Led by Henry Clay and John C. Calhoun, the young War Hawks in Washington held the shaky structure together and hurled defiance at the vastly stronger foe. Again, England's involvement in a European war left her only one hand free to deal with America. The War Hawks adopted the sound plan of issuing letters of marque to unleash American privateers on British shipping.

Cape Fear shipwrights, used to the building of small vessels, now launched ocean-going ships with live-oak hulls and cedar planking. The guardian Frying Pan Shoals and the Outer Banks gave coastal North Carolina the time for shipbuilding and safe retreats from enemy pursuers. Admiral Cockburn threaded his British fleet through Okracoke Inlet, made unkind observations on the adequacy of the harbor, and carried his small triumph back to sea.

Tar Heel naval heroes emerged. Captain Johnston Blakely of Wilmington commanded the first of the gallant line of American ships named *Enterprise*. Later, in the twenty-two-gun *Wasp* he roved the English Channel destroying merchantmen and two enemy warships. Undefeated, the *Wasp* sailed southwest into the oblivion of unreported ships. North Carolina adopted Blakely's daughter and paid for her education.

Otway Burns was born on Queens Creek, in seafaring Onslow County. In 1812 he was a skipper operating out of Beaufort. There he armed the *Snap Dragon*, a smart Baltimore clipper, with twelve-pounders on each side and a pivot gun, his crew of seventy-five being provided with fifty muskets and four blunderbusses. From Beaufort the *Snap Dragon* set out as a member of that "volunteer navy empowered under Congressional letters of Marque and Reprisal" to lay hands upon the floating wealth of Great Britain. This Otway Burns did, from Newfoundland to Ecuador. The log of the *Snap Dragon* during the spring of 1814 records two barks, five brigantines, and three schooners taken at a valuation of $1,250,000. The promised British reward of $50,000 on Commodore Burns's head went unpaid.

The *Snap Dragon* was named for a game in which raisins were snatched from burning brandy. Her skipper had the physique and heart to snatch safety from danger. Once a shore party found rum and the company of Caribbean charmers preferable to life aboard the *Snap Dragon*. Burns, facing them alone, was told as much. It was not in good Regular Navy tradition, but their captain drew his cutlass and flayed the rebellion out of them.

He did not win all his engagements. One well-armed British merchantman fought off his boarding party and maneuvered so as to ram the *Snap Dragon*. With four men killed and two disabled, Burns let the prize sail away while he limped back to port under jury rigging.

The last cruise of the *Snap Dragon* left Otway Burns on shore suffering an attack of rheumatism. The British ship *Leopard* opened concealed guns on his vessel. Acting skipper Lieutenant De Cokely was killed. The *Snap Dragon* was taken to England where Dartmoor prison held the crew until the Treaty of Ghent.

At Beaufort, Otway Burns built the steamboat *Prometheus* and navigated her south through the Frying Pan to become the first paddle-wheeler to churn the waters of the Cape Fear. All Wilmington crowded the waterfront on the gala day of her trial run. When *Prometheus* turned the Dram Tree, the bells sounded and cannons boomed. On the bridge Commodore Burns in cocked hat, blue coat, and epaulets, raised his speaking trumpet and called to his engineer in seaman's volume enough to reach Market Dock: "Give it to her, Snyder!" The paddle wheels warped her alongside. In the celebration that night the taverns resounded with happy bellowings of "Give it to her, Snyder!" For years along the river it remained a rallying cry, as "Geronimo!" rouses the Marines and "Kilroy was here" touches nostalgic G.I.s.

Good times appeared to have returned to the river. America had won respect abroad. Commerce throve. The Cape Fear built other paddle-wheelers for the run to Fayetteville. Bills of lading on Liverpool were issued by merchants of the town known to their fathers as Cross Creek, now a city of three thousand people, outranking Wilmington. Ladies and gentlemen found courage to be passengers on the white-coated monster, a hundred feet long and fifteen-foot beam. At the wail of the steamboat's whistle, plantation wharves built for periaugers became dense with cheering whites and blacks. At intervals the boat would ease her prow onto a sandy shore. From the high bank the crew toted down armsful of resinous lightwood from great piles accumulated there by plantation slaves. The refueled boat backed off the beach; paddle wheels splashed; black smoke plumed overhead. A new vista of trees, always the same, opened ahead at each tortuous bend of the river until the tidal calm of the last reaches brought arrival at Wilmington in the incredible time of twelve hours from Fayetteville.

The gentry of the Lower and Upper Cape Fear profited in morale and purse by this new outlet to market. But the back-country roads remained mere paths across fields and through forests; the small farmer was as isolated as before. It cost half the value of a crop to get it to market. Money was short for taxes and purchases. Excepting the river towns and the piedmont villages, the valley was as homespun and illiterate as ever.

# 3 : *Tar Heel Dreamer*

I love North Carolina, and love her the more because so much injustice has been done her.

——Archibald Debow Murphey

The move to shake the Rip Van Winkle State out of its long sleep began in the General Assembly in 1815 when Archibald Debow Murphey offered his Report on Transportation—by river, by canal, by turnpike. He spoke as Senator from Orange County where foodstuff rotted in the farmers' barns and the granite ridge of Smilie's Falls still blocked traffic going down the Deep and Haw, and made Averasboro the last upriver stop.

Murphey knew both town and crossroads from his years as a circuit-riding lawyer. He had spent miserable nights in flea-ridden one-room taverns. Since court days were local holidays, the legal cavalcades invariably left the saddle to encounter "noisy, drunken company, troublesome and indigent clients." The countryside was blasted by idleness and poverty. Murphey, who could speak for both the rude poor and the genteel rich, fretted against the isolation which was throttling the back country. To his friend Thomas Ruffin he wrote from Fayetteville: "In the Towns one found decent and well informed Men . . . who look well and live well. But the Mass of the Common People in the Country are lazy, sickly, poor, dirty and ignorant."

This low estimate of rural Tar Heels was not Murphey's last word on the subject, for he saw them stricken into slatterns and tobacco-chewing scarecrows for lack of any touch of trade or schooling. Their children were beautiful, until the young girls aged under devotion to the hoe and the cooking pot; and the boys matured (in Murphey's words) in the school of poverty which, "if left to itself, runs wild—vice in all its forms grows up in it."

But in these wild untended children—even in their poverty— Murphey found a pool of talents: "Providence in the impartial distribution of its favors, whilst it has denied to the poor many of the comforts of life, has generally bestowed on them the blessing of intelligent children. Poverty is the school of genius; it is a school in which the active powers of man are developed and disciplined . . . from this school generally come forth those men who act the principal parts upon the theatre of life; men who impress a character upon the age in which they live."

Upon these two concepts—that the opening of trade routes by river, canal and turnpike would bring prosperity, and that wealth would support schools to educate the poor—Murphey built his hopes for bringing North Carolina out of the doldrums. His forum was the General Assembly, and there his voice was powerful. His eloquence would win their votes for both of his great projects. But the massive conservatism of the planters and politicians of the East would deny the appropriation to bring his planning alive. Not until both he and his opponents were dead would his concepts change the face of the state.

•

Archibald Debow Murphey owed English descent to his Debow mother. His father, a colonel with Nathanael Greene in the Cornwallis campaign, had Irish and Dutch ancestry. The bloodlines of the Cape Fear pioneer groups had had time to intermingle when Archibald Debow was born. The boy attended one of the three classical academies in the state, that of the Reverend David Caldwell at Guilford. Books were scarce. His love of reading was based on chance access to three unrelated volumes, an abridged *Don Quixote,* Voltaire's *Life of Charles the Twelfth of Sweden,* and an odd volume of *Roderick Random.* He entered the second class to matriculate at Chapel Hill and graduated in 1799, with a record so brilliant that he was at once appointed professor of ancient languages. In 1801 he was admitted to the bar and well on his way to becoming the most admired Tar Heel lawyer of his times.

His passion not to be shut out from nature and books was one foible which would have a bearing on his career. At the age of twenty-four, while still teaching at Chapel Hill, he wrote a friend how irksome it was to be "shut up within the Walls of Colledge . . . in vain does nature spread her Green Carpet for those who are destined to one perpetual round of Business . . ." Well, it was spring and the undergraduates were neglecting Business that day in preparation for a ball that evening, and Murphey the professor was not out of earshot of the music. Seven years later, as a young lawyer, he was complaining that: "the Prime of Life is to be spent in Vulgar Pursuits, in getting a Competency to support a family, and providing a Pittance for Old Age." A Micawber streak in his nature would forestall his enjoying even that Pittance; would lead him into bad investments and signing friends' notes—would even clap him in debtors' jail. But while his Prime of Life lasted he cut a wide swath in the affairs of his times.

The Senator from Orange County who arose to present his Transportation Report in the General Assembly was a spare man of "fair complexion, eyes bluish grey, face soft and delicate as that of a lady." Those of the Assembly who had opposed him in court knew that the musical voice and persuasive manner could evoke any emotion Murphey wished from a jury, and had heard that affront to the court's dignity, a Murphey-cozened jury breaking into applause. "If," it was said, "he did not talk the jury out of their wits, he talked his own wits into the jury."

His December 1815 speech won him the chairmanship of a joint committee on Inland Navigation, with authority to make surveys of canal and sluice sites. The political philosophy of the conservative eastern counties was this: Taxation for any other purpose than preservation of life, liberty and property is contrary to the principles of republican government. The tidal basin and Upper Cape Fear planters were doing well enough. They had the river to transport their cotton, tobacco, and naval stores. Why should they pay taxes to dig ditches for piedmont farmers?

Murphey countered their politics by claiming it the duty of the government to aid the enterprise of its citizens, to offer them facilities for marketing their products. He linked the prosperity of the East and the West as one unity. He promised that the joining of all areas by river, canal, and turnpike would double land values and triple production in five years. He reminded them that in the past twenty-five years, for lack of roads and waterways, two hundred thousand North Carolinians had emigrated to the waters of the Ohio, Tennessee, and Mississippi "in quest of that wealth which a rich soil and a commodious navigation never fail to create in a free state."

A fillip to the gentry was Murphey's suggestion that the provincial towns of Fayetteville and Wilmington, under his plan, would become centers of trade and culture, the nuclei of civilized society. The Legislature listened, and for one sectional reason or another (Murphey had lures for both the planter and the small farmer) it passed his bill and for the first time committed state taxes and private money to a joint enterprise. In the world calm which followed the defeat of Napoleon, a fever for public works developed. John C. Calhoun, one of the War Hawks owning glory from uniting the nation in the War of 1812, now threw his influence toward internal improvements.

The fight for inland improvements was being won in other Atlantic coast states. New York's five million dollars to dig the Erie Canal finally staged that frenzied day when Governor De Witt Clinton arrived at New York by canalboat from Buffalo; emptied a vial of Lake Erie water into the salt Atlantic harbor. In Virginia $500,000 had been voted for inland improvements, in South Carolina $1,000,000. A year after his first speech, Murphey faced the Legislature with detailed plans based on intervening surveys.

Four rivers beginning in North Carolina flowed in parallel courses toward the sea. Only one of them, the Cape Fear, reached the Atlantic in Tar Heel territory. The other three not only turned into South Carolina but changed their names upon crossing the border. From rhododendron glens in the Blue Ridge the Catawba flowed through the fertile piedmont plain, turned due south across the state line and became the Wateree, eventually floating Tar Heel hams and wheat into Charleston under its third name of the Cooper River. The Yadkin also rose in the Blue Ridge, passed through eight million North Carolina acres and, when approaching South Carolina, showed its intentions by becoming the Pee Dee. Once safely into Gamecock territory it assumed the name of Great Pee Dee and moved Tar Heel cotton into Georgetown. The fickle Lumber River, a smaller Tar Heel stream paralleling the Cape Fear, veared south to become South Carolina's Little Pee Dee in honor of its juncture with the Great Pee Dee, itself born the Yadkin.

Murphey proposed to amend nature by digging canals from the Catawba to the Yadkin and—low down but still safely within North Carolina—from the Yadkin across the Lumber to the Cape Fear. That river would then be the central artery of navigation in the state.

The Legislature and the people for the first time saw the odd physical features of their state and what might be done to end the situation in which South Carolina on one side and Virginia on the other were marketing four million dollars' worth of North Carolina exports to the three million dollars' worth which made its way to foreign ports through Fayetteville and Wilmington.

The Legislature approved Murphey's bill. It granted modest sums for state participation in canal building, and encouraged private subscription. Below the fall-line the town of Haywood sprang full-blown from the wilderness. Land values along the Upper Cape Fear went to speculative prices on faith that the Buckhorn and Smilie's Falls would be bypassed by Deep and Haw flatboats. There was a new confidence that the trade and political bondage to Virginia and South Carolina would be broken. At Murphey's suggestion, a Scotch civil engineer, Hamilton Fulton, was hired to survey the waterways, at a salary of $6,000 sterling, twice that paid the governor. It was all brightly promising, until the cantankerous habits of man and nature threw Old Rip back into disastrous sectionalism.

•

As the tide of pioneer European peoples had swept up the Cape Fear, each generation had defied the power of Eastern authority. The early planters defied the proprietary governors. Their children rebelled against Parliament. The Regulators challenged the Lower Cape Fear hegemony of royal governor and planters. Archibald Debow Murphey was the first man to placate the rivalries between piedmont and coast by showing both parties the profit to be gained by combining forces. Clear the rivers of snags, mud, and sand. Bypass the waterfalls. Push turnpikes across the piney barrens. Make cities as civilized and wealthy as the deep-sea ports of Boston, New York, and Charleston: "Upon this subject let party spirit be hushed into silence; and uniting together in one feeling for North Carolina, let us all aspire to the honor of laying the foundation of her glory and her prosperity."

Yellow fever decimated Wilmington. A national depression slowed Cape Fear commerce. The canal digging went forward, but in separate stretches along the route according to whether or not local pride set the dirt a-flying. No connected ditch ever carried Yadkin water to the Cape Fear. The Legislature grew niggardly. When they cut his salary, Hamilton Fulton returned to Scotland.

But the people came to know their state better. Elisha Mitchell, a scientist acquired by Chapel Hill from Yale, published a geological survey of North Carolina. A map of sectional sentiments, however, would have shown the old rivalries still there. The

planter and merchant east kept control of the Legislature, by refusing to admit new western counties, by keeping the requirement
that to vote for a senator a man must own fifty acres. As the appropriations for inland improvements grew smaller, Murphey's
pleas took on a tone of anger. He turned his hopes for funds toward Congress in Washington.

Since the formation of the Union, North Carolina had paid
twenty million dollars in revenue to the Central Government. And
what had North Carolina received in exchange? ". . . two miserable Light Houses, one at Cape Hatteras, the other at Bald Head:
and two wretched Forts . . . What is the cause of this neglect? It
is to be found in the supineness and apathy of the State. We are
never thought of until the election of a President of the United
States is coming on; and then we are complimented for our *good
sense,* our *stern Republicanism,* and devotion to the *good cause;*
we are tacked to the Virginia ticket, and we vote accordingly.
When this Farce is over, we are laughed at for a few weeks, and
no more remembered . . ."

Murphey's voice did not reach Washington. There Nathaniel
Macon had been Representative since 1791, Senator since 1815.
He was guardian of the planter interests of North Carolina and
the entire South. A conviction against frittering away national
money—he had voted against a mausoleum for President Washington and against furniture for the White House—was not likely
to bend on behalf of canals for upstate farmers.

The silt grew deeper on the Flats, so that ships must anchor and
lighten their cargoes to Wilmington. The granite ridge of Smilie's
Falls held back traffic both ways. Speculators in river-front land
went bankrupt, Murphey among them. In 1821 he sold his estate,
The Hermitage, to his friend Thomas Ruffin, and acquired a small
Hillsboro house where during winter months rheumatism confined him indoors. The fight for his canals and river navigation
was over. He gave himself to his other dream, public schools for
Tar Heel children.

His hope had been that river outlets for its products would

make the state rich enough to build schools, hire teachers, and end the state's monumental illiteracy. Again, he was talking to the future.

"The State," he told deaf ears, "must take into her bosom the poor children, and feed, and clothe, and educate them, at the public expense."

Even he did not propose this for every child; but at least those with some proof of genius and future usefulness should be put through primary school, the promising ones winnowed out for free secondary education, and the surviving brilliant ones sent on to the University.

Murphey at the 1827 Chapel Hill Commencement gave the Dialectic Society address to the graduating class, using the occasion to advance his hopes for North Carolina. Education must kindle the light of learning, otherwise "in the wilderness civilization declines and manners and language degenerate, as witness the snuff-sniffing, indolent turpentine distillers."

•

Eighteen months after his honors at Chapel Hill, Murphey was put in the Guilford jail for the required twenty-day period before the "swearing out" that he was not worth forty shillings in any earthly substance. Sheriff Jimmy Doak agreed with his prisoner that the cell was not sufficiently lighted or ventilated, and observed Murphey's request that the door be left open. Judge Cameron, after visiting Murphey in jail, advised the sheriff of a risk to himself in leaving the door open since in law "it might be considered an escape: but let us go back and consult your prisoner; he knows the law."

"Mr. Sheriff, my friend," said Murphey with a sad smile, "it will be safest for you to lock the door on me."

After his term in jail, his private letters alternately wished that death might relieve his sufferings and glowed with the prospect of a financial windfall. Acquaintance with a French chemist, who had a new method of extracting gold from low-grade ore, persuaded Murphey to buy his own mine. In July 1829 he wrote Thomas Ruffin that he was "erecting 4 small Furnaces for the Purpose of fluxing the Ores . . . if as rich as they appear to be, I ought to make $600 per week . . ." The next January he wrote to his son Sam: "I cannot commence Life again without some Money." For years he had collected materials for a proposed history of North Carolina. The state had approved such a project, the author to be supported by a lottery. One of Murphey's last letters was to his protégé Bartlett Yancey. The lottery, he wrote, was certain to raise $12,000 to support him during his congenial labor. But he died February 1, 1832, and was buried at Hillsboro under a headstone as simple as that of his predecessor "representative man of the Cape Fear," Cornelius Harnett.

# 4 : *Fight Against the River*

Ships under sail still dominated the Lower Cape Fear estuary. The privateers of the late war with England had borne such names as *Snap Dragon* and the *Lovely Lass of Wilmington*, affectionate christenings to go with clean slim hulls and the pull on halyards of fist and forearm. Now came the steamboat *Prometheus*, aptly named for the mortal who had snatched from the gods the fire of heaven. On family pleasure trips from Wilmington downriver to Smithville, the steam boiler would soon replace the six swinging oars of a periauger's crew.

But it was the Upper Cape Fear which hailed the steamboat with the greater joy. On the estuary, tides could be awaited to go your way. The relentless flow of the fresh water of the Upper Cape Fear fought poles and oars every foot of the way from Wilmington to Fayetteville. The new flaming monster needed only to be fed lightwood and long draughts of water.

Soon after the first voyage of *Prometheus*, James Seawell at Fayetteville built the steamboat *Henrietta*, a side-wheeler with the speed to make Wilmington in less than twelve hours. Captain Benjamin Rush ran her for forty years. Before half that time there were seventeen steamers on the Upper Cape Fear, and many long warning pulls on the whistle cord before rounding the bends.

The steamboat created a river trade and social life. Produce was ready at the wharf for a quick run up the plank and stowage on the first deck. Children waited for the whistle of the *Cotton Plant, Magnolia, North State, Scottish Chief* and *Flora MacDonald.* Sometimes the family went on board in best bib and tucker, bound for the excitement of Wilmington, and on the way leaned enraptured on the rail to watch brown water churned white against a wall of solid green. At dinner the captain made one big family of them all.

In the early years, the steamboat was the only transport to take the burden off men and their beasts. Wagon trains still made the slow haul from Fayetteville to Philadelphia. On the hill above Fayetteville, the drivers from upcountry made their camp, sometimes two hundred at once. Townspeople came to watch them over their cooking fires. Some were mountain men who had driven their great covered wagons over the stony trails of the Blue Ridge.

Through river and turnpike trade, Fayetteville became the largest Tar Heel city, with 3,532 people counted in the 1820 census. At the intersection of its two main streets stood Town House where the General Assembly in 1789 had ratified the United States Constitution and chartered the University of North Carolina. Upstart Raleigh claimed the Assembly now. Town House was used as a market place where citizens could buy river shad in season, country produce, venison, beef, and fresh pork. Some difficulty had arisen over the naming of the square surrounding Town House. The land had been donated in 1790 by James Hogg. A delicacy about naming the market place Hogg Square had brought a first compromise to honor the donor with James Square, and a subsequent exaltation to St. James Square.

Here on March 4, 1825, Fayetteville had its high moment. The Marquis de Lafayette arrived to visit the first American community to adopt his name. "Guest of the Nation," the hero of two transcendent Revolutions had entered North Carolina under an escort of Mecklenburg Cavalry, in token of that county's valiant stand for independence. At the Clarendon Bridge over the Cape Fear the General was met by local artillery and the Fayetteville Light Infantry, all ranks marching in formation through six inches of Person Street mud to Town House and the platform erected for the ceremonies. A military band ended its flourishes, and in the following quiet Judge Toomer found apt words to wed the life purpose of Lafayette to the American democracy his sword and his diplomacy had sustained:

"We are plain republicans . . . Instead of pageantry we offer you cordiality and the grateful homage of devoted hearts . . . You, Sir, have been the steadfast friend of liberty, in every period of your life. In youth you fought the battles of freedom; in age, you advocated the rights of man . . ."

The General made a brief reply in kind. He was enjoying himself. His guard of honor was composed of three Fayetteville citizens who had served in his command fifty years before. At a ball that evening in the new Lafayette Hotel he spent two hours chatting with enamored ladies and their escorts. Next day, in male company at the Masonic Lodge, a toast was raised to "The Memory of Washington—He was a friend of Lafayette." The General raised his glass: "To Fayetteville—May it receive all the encouragements, and obtain all the prosperity which are anticipated by the fond and grateful wishes of its affectionate and respectful namesake."

•

Judge Toomer was one of those who heeded Archibald Debow Murphey's jeremiads on the state's poor transportation and schools. The Judge used the Town House platform that day to invoke the "spirit of Internal Improvement," telling his captive audience:

We place our confidence in the liberality and exertions of succeeding Legislatures. Colleges will be endowed; roads will be made; rivers will be opened; our resources will be annually developed, and Fayetteville, at some future day may be worthy of the distinguished name it bears.

The Legislature's first chance to redeem these pledges came three years later when citizens of four Deep-Haw counties—entranced with what railroads could do for piedmont prosperity—petitioned for the building of an experimental railway uphill from the Cape Fear at Campbellton to St. James Square, a distance of a mile. The money was voted. This was to be an improvement on the Northern practice of casting iron wheels with inner flanges to grip the rails. Down Person Street were laid convex wooden rails upon which were placed concave iron wheels. The tight embrace of this joining of wooden rail to iron wheel produced a marriage of much friction and no forward progress. Railroads, the prediction went, aren't practical.

•

Fayetteville was both the head of river navigation and the hub from which five roads spoked out into the valley's farms and forests where porkers fattened and the chevrons cut in the bark of longleaf pines dripped their valuable juices. Fayetteville dreamed of turning these dreary rutted turnpikes into plank roads, with tolls to pay for their cost and return a profit. They would be "Farmers Railroads," all converging on the warehouses and wharves of Fayetteville.

There was precedent for the plank road. More than a hundred were in use in the North, mostly short ones for crossing bogs and sand, yet demonstrations in a small way of what North Carolina could do on the grand scale. Tar Heel roads would thread longleaf pine country where the coppery trunks made endless vista above the sienna-needle floor. There were waterfalls to power sawmills. An era of national prosperity had put capital into Tar Heel banks.

So Fayetteville launched itself on a plank road venture during the 1840s and 1850s, when other places were bidding for railroads. Forty miles north, the Cape Fear and Yadkin Railroad began to lay the future of the piedmont. At Wilmington a railroad was projected to Raleigh and on to Weldon where Virginia rivers and railroads would be tapped. But Fayetteville had twice been bitten by the Iron Horse. No more convex wooden rails nor Legislative disappointments for Fayetteville.

•

The longest plank road ever built was the Fayetteville and Western, beginning at the Market House in St. James Square and reaching to the Moravian town of Bethania in Forsyth County, 129 miles of adzed heart of pine logs, the "Appian Way of North Carolina." The squared stone of the Italian Via Appia still forms the roadbed for Ferraris and Fords. Today in Harnett County a tobacco farmer sometimes plows up a length of ancient wood over which a Moravian driver once urged his six-horse team. There will never be another highway like the plank road to Bethania. The longleaf pines are gone, and the seeds of the scrub pine which slept under the sienna-needle forest floor have usurped their place in the sun. In the plank roads themselves the longleaf logs had only a span of eight years before they wore out and had to be replaced.

•

They laid the first section headed west from the Market House to the top of Haymount. On the base of two-inch-thick stringers were placed three-inch planks running crosswise, with a two-inch layer of dirt on top. A prophetic voice in the *North Carolinian* made the point that "The rumbling of carriages on that part of it in town, and the solid tramp of horses' feet, will give us new noise to get used to."

From Haymount the road had been surveyed centuries before by buffalo herds bound for pasturage along the river. Avoiding water crossings where they could, the buffalo had found the high ridge which slants northwest and dips only once to let the Lower Little River pass. The planks were laid and placed under toll as far as Lower Little River by April 1850. In its heyday the Fayetteville and Western gladdened the hearts of stockholders. The year of 1854 saw twenty thousand produce-laden wagons rumble over its planks. The *Fayetteville Observer* chanted happily: "Our plank roads have been worth hundreds of thousands to the country they have penetrated."

Land values rose along the plank routes. In 1853 a 5,000-acre tract, valued at fourteen cents an acre a few years before, sold for two dollars an acre. But a more permanent gain was the coming of the travelers to know each other. On this social and cultural hope springing from plank roads the *Tarboro Southerner* for December 18, 1852, commented:

> They will encourage the cultivation of the ornamental and beautiful . . . They will set the most steady agog now and then, and by awakening their curiosity lead them to see a little of the world . . . They will bring the powers of science into action at the very door-sill of our stand-still friends, and teach them the advantage of intellectual advancements.

An example of cultural advance in the use of language appears from the experience of some farmfolk who used the Fayetteville and Western to visit a sophisticated household. In this home the visitors found a new word, "gravy," which to their astonishment was "a high falutin' name for sop."

At the height of the movement there were five hundred miles of plank road under toll in North Carolina, built at an average cost of $1,500 per mile. Tolls ran one-half cent per mile for a man on horseback, two cents for a two-horse wagon. Canny citizens cut through the woods to bypass the tollhouses and continued blithely on their way as though they owned the planks. Some of those planks were from trees drained for turpentine and so subject to quick rot. Repairs were costly. Company charters were amended to permit "stone, gravel or other materials than planks." Dividends fell off. The railroads began to cut heavily into plank road traffic. The speculative fever abated. When the final tally was made it was found that the total of all dividends paid by plank roads did not equal the original cost of their construction. By 1860 the Legislature was ordering companies to remove the worn-out and rotted planks as hazardous to travel. The towns which had chosen railroads grew apace.

•

The immutable Upper Cape Fear could not keep pace with its new transportation rivals. Yet there were stubborn men who would not accept as final past failures to get boats up the rifts to the piedmont. The rumble of wagon wheels over plank roads was not music to the rivermen. They wanted the long wail of a steam whistle announcing a paddle-wheeler's arrival at Haymount.

The Frying Pan Shoals and the Flats of the estuary were acts of nature with which no digging equipment of the period was able to cope. The real fight began upriver from Fayetteville. There was no single high waterfall such as the Potomac's. In invading North Carolina the fall-line ridge had fanned out into half a dozen small barriers. Buckhorn Falls was the highest. The others on the stretch to Fayetteville would hurl a raft downstream at full spate, but were impassable at all times to periaugers or paddle-wheelers. Each decade as the Promised Land of piedmont filled up with farmers, as the Blue Ridge valley bottoms came into crops spoiling for a way to Eastern markets, the succeding Cape Fear generations swore to dig or blast a way through to the waters of the Deep and the Haw.

Those two rivers had an all but common origin. At a point a few miles east of Salem, their sources were so close that a cow could drink of the Deep and within ten minutes browse her way over to sample Haw waters. That stream and its tributaries took a south-easterly bend through Quaker country; the Deep veered in a wider curve westerly past David Fanning's headquarters and Alston's House in the Horseshoe, and united with the Haw above Buckhorn Falls. Their juncture came to be known as Mermaids' Point, in honor of the mermaids whom authority cited as beaching there to wash the Atlantic Ocean salt out of their hair. Other advantages obtained at this place of meeting rivers.

Seven miles up the Deep was the Egypt coal mine with a six-foot vein at the 423-foot level, and nearer the surface were black oxide deposits, very promising for high-grade iron mining. Add smelting to farm products as riches to tap, and the incentive for a waterway was compelling.

The inadequate means to do it meant heartbreak. They built fires on projecting river rocks and, when these were hot enough, poured on vinegar to split them. Before dynamite, there was only black powder for blasting; it could not budge the granite of Smilie's Falls. Then in the 1850s they came around to the lock and dam weapon against their enemy the river.

By late 1855 the job was done, a lock and dam around every point of swift water from Fayetteville up to the town above Mermaid's Point, now known as Haywood. As a putative metropolis Haywood was almost as old as the Cape Fear Navigation Company. In 1799 surveyor Jonathan Lindley had drawn a plat for it, with streets a hundred feet wide and two acres allotted to "orphans."

Haywood had been no more than Ambrose Ramsay's Mill and Tavern when Lord Cornwallis and Nathanael Greene had stayed there, separately, in 1781. By the 1850s it had pretentious summer residences and the hope that rested on river travel. Bob Brown ran a fifty-room hotel. Miles Stephens' bar was well patronized, until on March 11, 1856, it was precipitously emptied at the shriek of a steam whistle announcing that the *John H. Haughton,* Captain Matt Brady in command, was arriving from Fayetteville.

Captain Brady tied up below the ferry landing, the first paddle-wheeler to trail pitch-pine smoke across the Chatham County hills. Miles Stephens' bar did well that night, too well for the next day's peace of mind of Captain Matt.

While cutting lock and dam trees in the Beaver Dam Swamp the previous summer, the Haywood timbermen had been visited by a party from Averasboro across the Cape Fear. Some talk emerged on the comparative stinging powers of Beaver Dam and Chatham County mosquitoes. Red Saunders of Chatham took off his shirt, lay face down on it and asserted he could lie without flinching for an hour of Harnett County mosquito attack. He had sweated it out almost to the end when Billie Avera—distracting attention from the sufferer by pointing overhead and yelling: "What the hell's that?"—tossed a live coal on Red's back and produced the effect which no local mosquito had achieved. The Chatham contingent had bet their timbering wages on Red's mosquito tolerance. Now, in Miles Stephens' bar, they innocently offered Captain Matt to pay their way to Averasboro on his return trip, and, not innocently, arrived at sailing time with concealed coshes, brass knuckles, and ample drinking liquor.

Captain Brady had a mashed nose from an encounter with a paddle wheel, and was as tough as he looked. When on the trip down the Haywood passengers began tilting bottles and trying out brass knuckles on the railing, Captain Matt and his mate put their heads together and decided not to stop at Averasboro where, from remarks overheard, they could only conclude that they were ferrying a revenge expedition against those who had won their money on the toss of a live coal. The *John H. Haughton* had passed Averasboro before the avengers caught on and demanded a return to Averasboro. Captain Matt's forbidding nose, temper, and a horse pistol kept course toward Fayetteville. On the last leg the frustrated avengers tossed everything loose overboard, including some of their own members, and spent a reflective night in the Fayetteville lockup.

Aside from what of the Haywood crowd remained on board, Captain Brady landed 135 bales of cotton. The Deep-Haw country had a water route to Wilmington, to Europe. There was rejoicing. It lasted to the satisfaction of Haywood and Fayetteville for a few months longer than three years.

Freshets sweep down the Cape Fear every spring, invading Fayetteville and spreading more widely over the low-lying east bank country. A devastating freshet in the fall suggests that a Caribbean hurricane had veered inland and dumped its water cargo on the Upper River basin. On September 11, 1859, a walloping freshet swept away all locks and dams from Haywood to Fayetteville.

•

The 1850s had seen a three-way push for facilities to open the way to markets of other states and transatlantic countries for Tar Heel products. The plank roads had returned to the forest as humus, yet had opened highway routes for the future. The river had broken the fortunes of her opponents, yet had stirred in their hearts much gallant opposition. In the Tirza churchyard, in the ghost town of Summerville, is the grave of Colonel Archie S. McNeill, grandson of Jennie Bahn McNeill. He had lost in the long fight against the river. A bridge he built was swept away by a freshet. In the period before Smilie's Falls was circumvented by a lock and dam, Colonel McNeill had wrestled with its rocks, gunpowder against granite. When he was dying, many years after this bout, he called upon his friend Zachary Taylor Kivette to perform a last rite. A piece of the granite which defeated him must be his headstone. It was not simple to haul a piece of blasted river rock sufficiently towering to honor a spirit as indomitable as granite, but Kivette managed, and the Colonel's gravestone has five powder drill marks to prove it.

•

The Iron Horse was the final winner. Its principal backer was John M. Morehead. As Governor of North Carolina in the 1840s he had picked up the Murphey plan to salvage the state, and with vigor and intelligence had used the better conditions of his own times to put transportation and schooling into efficient running order. He became, after his term as governor, the founder and president of the North Carolina Railroad. An echo of Archibald Debow Murphey sounds in the report of ground breaking for Morehead's railroad on July 11, 1851:

> . . . the whole State, her entire people, have come forth in their might and majesty battling in the cause of internal improvements . . .

Morehead discarded *laissez faire*. He linked railroads, rivers and harbors, and turnpikes into one system. His rails, at one moment in the international race to build railroads, were the longest in the world, 223 miles from Raleigh through Hillsboro and on to Charlotte. The crescent of cities strung along the route which William Lawson pioneered in 1708 became the forerunner of the prosperous Tar Heel piedmont.

One of the railroads in the late 1830s, the Western, was being laid toward the Egypt coal mine on the Deep. In 1860 it was ten miles short of Egypt. In 1861 it closed down. The Confederate States of America took it over and pushed it to within reaching distance of the coal it would need for Navy bunkers and the manufacture at the Fayetteville Arsenal of guns for the Army of Virginia.

# 5 : *Five Steps to Rebellion*

A period of 135 years intervened between the first permanent settlement on the Cape Fear and the outbreak of the Civil War. In seven short generations the ten-million-acre basin of the river and its tributaries had filled with separately arriving European peoples, the English and Irish first on the estuary, the Scots Highlanders on the Upper River, the Moravians, Scotch-Irish, Huguenots, Germans and Swiss coming in on the wilderness trails from the North. The American Revolution had bound them into an unstable amalgam which had disintegrated in the aftermath of the Tory-Patriot hatreds.

The lack of education and ways to trade and visit each other kept the post-Revolutionary generation of Upper Cape Fear people in rural self-reliance—and left political controls in the hands of the landed gentry of East North Carolina. They seemed on the whole an unlikely assemblage to offer their lives in the common cause of the Civil War. The catalyst which combined them into one people was the emotional crisis over slavery. North Carolinians themselves were divided, only a slim majority voting secession. Once committed, every tenth Confederate soldier was a Tar

Heel. The descendants of English, Irish, Scots, German, and French settlers became Southerners.

There were tariff and power-politics issues between South and North, but the heat of anger which exploded the shells over Sumter was long smoldering in the relations between the Negro and his master, between the planter and the nonslaveholder, and in their combined front against criticism from the crusading free-soil states of the North.

The overlapping careers of five men along the Cape Fear may be taken to trace the emotional and economic transition from the arrival of the first Africans to the catastrophe of Americans divided in war.

"King" Roger Moore may stand for the generation which established their plantations by slave labor.

The Reverend David Caldwell, born in the year of Moore's arrival on the river, 1725, influenced the military, religious, and schooling phases of an emerging people until his death in 1824 at the age of ninety-nine years.

Levi Coffin, the Reverend Mr. Caldwell's young Quaker neighbor at Guilford, argued slavery with the aged Presbyterian divine, and went on his Quaker way to become president of the Underground Railroad.

Frederick Law Olmsted, Yankee intellectual, traveled the South in the 1850s, to make up his own mind on the wildly conflicting positions of Abolitionists and Southerners.

Hinton Rowan Helper, a native of what had been Regulator country, affronted the South, and tortured emotion on both sides of the Mason-Dixon line, with an inflammatory book against slaveholders. As he was a Southerner, this was a New Abolition voice.

The Negro for most of these 135 years on the Cape Fear had a leading role in the drama, but no lines to speak. Negroes were as voiceless as the children of Israel were in the land of Pharaoh— before Aaron and Moses spoke for them. Until the Civil War, the life of the slave is shown us only through white eyes, but the minds of those whites who left records of what they observed were obsessed by conflicts in their law, their religion, and their domestic life. The British African Company and the New England slave importers had opened the world's greatest Pandora's Box.

•

King Roger Moore and his brothers James and Nathaniel brought their slaves to the Lower Cape Fear from their Goose Creek plantations in South Carolina. Their Africans were domesticated and trained, among them brickmasons to build Roger's Orton Plantation and carpenters to erect Nathaniel's two-story frame house on the waterfront of his new town of Brunswick. When the cooking fires of the Indians raised a column of smoke across the river from Orton, King Roger led a black battalion to rout the red men out of the region.

Slaves cleared the land and built plantation houses for twenty miles up the high west bank of the estuary. They tended the garden crops, slaughtered the hogs and cured the meat, manned the oars of the periaugers, drove the coaches, and carried out the work of the household.

The field hands were already skilled from Goose Creek days in cutting "boxes" in the longleaf pine trunks to catch the sap for distillation. Turpentine was the planter's money crop; he organized his slave work crew for maximum production; he provided enough food to keep muscles supple and eyes accurate with ax and ladle and cooper's rive.

No other American immigrants had greater adjustments to make than did the African captives. One recently landed group, held near the sea, nightly worked themselves up in the singing of chants of their homeland, until some ran into the water separating them from Africa, and were drowned.

The soldier-planters of the Lower Cape Fear held the power in the Assembly at Wilmington. After the first fifteen years of dealing with some unruly slaves they passed, in 1741, a code for punishing slave infractions, basing it on the eighteenth century common law of England which listed two hundred offenses subject to the death penalty. Multilation, branding, and whipping were inflicted for misdemeanors. When these were the only means the eighteenth century could devise to curb the crimes of white people, it was inevitable that the code should carry over to the regulation of slaves holding over their masters the menace of conspiracy and violence. The 1741 law carried the death penalty for conspiring to rebel. The penalty for lying was to have an ear nailed to the pillory, cut off at the end of an hour and the other ear similarly treated. A runaway slave might be killed "by such ways as he or she shall think fit," without accusation of the killer.

This code, passed by tidewater planters—first generation Americans used to Old World justice—eventually covered the entire province. As the back country and the piedmont filled up with Moravians, Quakers, Highlanders, and Scotch-Irish, it became their law even though few at first owned slaves, even though the back-country farmers who acquired slaves usually worked side by side with them in the fields or forests. Actually the code was too rigorous for common use, and in time it softened and lapsed. But its spirit was always there to be invoked, in times of panic fear of slave conspiracies, and at all times by the minority of masters with cruelty or fear in their own natures. A scholar on the subject, John Spencer Bassett, professor at Trinity College (now Duke University), scanned the entire course of slavery in North Carolina and summed it up: "A master's treatment of his slaves corresponded relatively to his treatment of his children; good father, good master; careless or cruel father, careless or cruel master."

King Roger Moore, Eleazar Allen, and Cornelius Harnett, Sr., all died at mid-eighteenth century, ripe in years and rich in property, the last of the first-generation planters on the estuary. Their nephews and sons distinguished themselves in the Revolution. They gave black slaves guns and uniforms, and granted freedom for their willingness to fight under their command. The concept of the rights of man for which they were fighting caused a second look at the institution of slavery.

In 1774 the Freeholders in Rowan County resolved that "the African trade is injurious to this Colony." In the same year the First Provincial Congress at New Bern went further in resolving "that we will not import any slave or slaves, nor purchase any slaves imported into this Province by others from any part of the world after the first day of November next."

Many Novembers would pass with that pledge forgotten. There was a stalemate between those who favored keeping the Negro in ignorance and those who wished him able to read the Bible. The nineteenth century opened with two disparate but equally emotional impacts—the Great Revival and slave uprisings.

•

The Reverend David Caldwell's ninety-nine years spanned the period from the pioneering to the maturity of the piedmont settlements above the Upper Cape Fear fall-line. He was born in Lancaster County, Pennsylvania, in 1725, the year the Moores led their slaves north from Goose Creek. He graduated from Princeton in the class of 1761. In 1765 he was sent to labor as a missionary in the Buffalo and Alamance settlements, just in time to become sympathetically involved in the struggle of his Regulator neighbors against thieving tax collectors. It was Caldwell who tried unsuccessfully to mediate between Governor Tryon and the Regulators before the Battle of Alamance. When in the next few years the larger storm began brewing between England and the colonies, Caldwell became a highly vocal Patriot. By 1775 the British were organizing the Scots Loyalists, and in August of that year Patriot delegates met in Hillsboro to form a Provincial Government to replace the dispersed Royal Assembly. The Reverend David Caldwell preached to them, on the text that: "The slothfull shall be under tribute."

The sluggards he had in mind were those who would not volunteer to fight against Great Britain. After a first half hour of homilies on "many a fine estate has been wasted by sloth and inattention," the Reverend Mr. Caldwell finally got around to twisting the Lion's tail: the King's failure to promote the public good, the Boston Tea Party, civil liberty, the arbitrary British Parliament, and a final clarion call on Americans to "stand up manfully in a firm, united, and persevering defense of your liberties."

In passing his farm, seven years later after the Battle of Guilford Courthouse, British soldiers stopped long enough to burn Caldwell's library and all of his sermons they could find. Cornwallis had learned that the thousands of Regulators, whom he had expected to join his army out of revenge for their defeat by tidewater planters at Alamance, had fallen under the influence of their Patriot pastor.

In the year of his arrival in the piedmont, Caldwell had started a classical school. In the post-Revolutionary doldrums it became a shining light. Fifty boys each year sat under his instruction in Greek, Latin, philosophy, and mathematics. Five of them would become governors of states, three members of Congress, preachers, lawyers. At first he prepared boys for Princeton; when the University of North Carolina opened he sent them to Chapel Hill, Archibald Debow Murphey among these latter.

This valuable man had little to say on slavery. He owned many slaves, and being "a good father was a good master." There were, however, undercurrents which must have given him private concern. The French Revolution unloosed passionate violence, which in 1791 was reflected in the San Domingo slave uprising with its slaughter of the white planter families. Denmark Vesey's slave conspiracy at Charleston was a child of the Haitian revolt.

But farming North Carolina was in its Rip Van Winkle slumber and these outside reports brought only ripples of trepidation. More affected by fears of slave uprisings was the governing planter class, those in John Spencer Bassett's words "who touched the outside world, went to summer resorts, and to Congress, and to political conventions . . ." The farmer class as a class, he says, "came closer into touch with the slave and in a hundred ways softened the harshness of the institution which no one knew how to modify in law."

It was the Tar Heel farmers who at the turn of the nineteenth century came under the spell of the revivalist preachers, and by religious emotionalism brought the slaves and free Negroes into the same fold. It started in the Reverend Mr. Caldwell's parlor where Mrs. Caldwell and other ladies prayed for a visitation of apostolic zeal and had their prayers answered in the Great Revival. Aside from the speaking in tongues, jerks, and other hypnotic aspects of the camp meetings, the Great Revival permanently increased the numbers of Negroes attending white churches. It brought Sunday schools where Negroes were taught to read, it saw resolutions not to separate Negro slave families. The singing at camp meetings developed impromptu spirituals by both races. Many of the Negro voices were raised in praise and hopes of salvation; others sang chants of freedom: *Go down, Moses, way down in Egypt land: Tell ol' Pharaoh, Let my People go.*

Potential violence, particularly in the coastal counties where blacks outnumbered whites, was a bass note in the chorus of camp meeting hallelujahs. In 1802 the report of a slave conspiracy in Duplin County ended in two executions of Negroes. Yet at Wilmington, Methodist Bishop Francis Asbury preached to a congregation of "876 Africans and a few whites in fellowship." Preceding this meeting, a Negro preacher, John Charles, had held a sunrise service. Bishop Asbury summed it up as "a high day in Zion."

Relaxations of slavery's protocol lasted through the first three decades of the nineteenth century. In Fayetteville, a free Negro shoemaker, Henry Evans, openly preached to his people on Sundays until the Town Council ordered him to stop. He continued secret meetings in the Sand Hills. Some white ladies of Fayetteville who noticed a reformation in their servants' manners and morals, tied it to Henry Evans' influence and backed construction of a frame church for him within town limits. Evans had two at-

tributes: a pulpit eloquence to attract whites to the seats reserved
for them; a deference toward white people which let them accept
the word of God from an ex-slave. Eventually all seats were taken
by whites and sheds built on the sides of the building where the
blacks were now seated. It was an accommodation which both
races accepted.

The Presbyterian Church, in this period, went even further in
honoring a Negro who became preacher and schoolmaster to
white children. They sent John Chavis to Princeton College "to
see if a Negro would take a college education." Princeton's With-
erspoon made him his private pupil. In 1809 he was received as a
licentiate by the Orange Presbytery. The Nutbush Congregation,
which forty years before had launched the first Regulator broad-
side, now heard a "full-blooded Negro of dark brown color preach
sermons abounding in illustrations . . . in remarkably pure English."

Chavis dined with the white patrons who sent their children to
him to school. He taught the sons of Chief Justice Henderson; one
of his pupils became United States Senator, another Governor of
North Carolina. In that dividing year of 1831, when acceptance of
gifted Negroes ended, the career of John Chavis was closed by the
interdict of the Legislature that no Negro might preach or teach.

•

There is a speculation inherent in those improving racial relations
of the nineteenth century's first decades. Could they have progressed into a transition between ownership of slaves and the
hire of freedmen? Already there were Free Negroes with skills as
craftsmen. Masters frequently let their slaves earn a living away
from the plantation, with $150 income for the master and the
slave's share saved to buy his freedom. In homes where kindness
prevailed, the slave cook ruled as tyrant over both her kitchen and
the discipline of the white children. The church had resolved that
Negro souls were salvageable. Even in the law, the eighteenth

century harshness of punishment was relieved in these decades.

What compensation might an owner have for a slave condemned and executed for a crime? The legal mind decided the owner should be paid two thirds of the slave's value, provided only that he had been well fed and well clothed—a left-handed acknowledgment that cruelty to the slave was contributory to the crime for which he suffered death.

In 1823 the Supreme Court declared that the killing of a slave might be tried as murder at common law. Justice Hall dissented on the ground that the slave was a chattel, but Justice Henderson for the majority declared "the laws of ancient Rome or modern Turkey are not the laws of our country, nor the mode from which they were taken. It is abhorrent to the hearts of all those who have felt the influence of the mild precepts of Christianity."

Judge William Gaston, who later ruled that malice could not be proved in the case of a slave defending his life from his master's attack, said in an address at Chapel Hill: "Disguise the truth as we may, and throw the blame where we will, it is slavery which, more than another cause, keeps us back in the career of improvement."

In the 1820s this same Judge Gaston, a Roman Catholic, was legal adviser to the Quakers in their project of acquiring slaves for the sole purpose of freeing them. His suggested device was a Manumission Society which might own slaves in common and dispose of them as it saw fit. Through it hundreds of slaves were sent into free-soil Northern states, to Liberia and Haiti. The Legislature finally closed it down, but it was the genesis of the later Underground Railroad.

Quakers were not the only people of the region to attempt the transition to emancipation. There were probably as many church and other groups working toward an end to slavery in North Carolina as there were in Massachusetts. None of them bore the onus of what was becoming a flaming word in the South, abolition.

•

A young Quaker, Levi Coffin, in 1821 changed the intentions of his patriarch neighbor, the Reverend David Caldwell, concerning the gift of Ede, a female Caldwell slave, to his son the Reverend Samuel Caldwell.

The elder Caldwell, who was ninety-five, had always kept slaves. They had been necessary to the running of his famous Academy; they now maintained his 200-acre Guilford farm. He thought it would be no hardship for Ede to exchange his benign rule for that of his son Sam. Except that this meant the separation of Ede from her husband and three children. A fourth, an infant in arms, she was to be allowed to take with her.

The Reverend Mr. Caldwell's neighbors, the Coffins, were orthodox Friends from Nantucket Island. Levi's grandfather died in 1781 of the smallpox, caught from British officers hospitalized in his home after the Battle of Guilford Courthouse. He left twelve children, the farm, and five shillings sevenpence in ready money. None of the Coffins ever kept slaves.

Levi was born in 1799. Once in his boyhood he watched a coffle of handcuffed and chained slaves trudinging under armed guard on their way to the Alabama slave markets. While they were resting beside the road, Levi sat beside a slave and heard from him that he was a Free Negro kidnaped in Pennsylvania and again sold into slavery.

Kidnaping a Free Negro was indictable. Accused kidnapers could be forced into court, and frequently were. The Coffin family had a code of its own. Slave law forbade aiding a slave to escape. This the Coffins obeyed. But the loophole in the law, which made it a citizen's duty to act against kidnaping, left the Coffin conscience free to shelter fugitive Negroes they believed escaped from the kidnaper's coffle. Levi absorbed the family doctrine.

At fifteen he was frequenting the Caldwell farm for two purposes. When a cornhusking frolic was on in the Caldwell barn, Levi was one of the white party happily shucking at one end of the heap while the slaves husked and sang and laughed at the other end. Levi's secretive invasions of Caldwell property began with a bag over his shoulder; ostensibly bound to feed hogs strayed into swamps and copses, he was in fact carrying bacon and meal to fugitive slaves. The boy and the Negroes had an arrangement by which General Hamilton's man Sol secretly queried the coffle and, when the guard and the patrollers were careless, occasionally brought a kidnaped slave to a woods rendezvous. There would be a long wait until affidavits confirming the Negro's free status could be returned and a writ against the kidnaper filed in the sheriff's office at Hillsboro.

By the time he was twenty-two, Levi, like his brother Vestal, was knowledgeable in marking out this first roadbed for an underground railroad headed north toward free soil. When in 1821 the Reverend Mr. Caldwell presented Ede and her infant to his son Sam, and Ede ran away into the woods with her child, the Coffins took her in. The minister had broken no law. The Coffins had.

By sheltering Caldwell's property they were liable to a prohibitively high fine. Ede had been in the woods for three days; the baby was sick. Mrs. Coffin nursed it most of the night, and in the morning Levi put on his good clothes and marched over to what he calls in his memoirs "the mansion of the aristocratic gentleman of the old school." The ancient divine received him cordially and made kindly jokes about Quaker lay preachers. Levi edged in the subject of the missing Ede. Caldwell spoke sternly:

"She needs a good flogging for her foolishness. She would have a good home at my son's house. Do you know where she is hiding?"

Levi was risking his family's arrest for sheltering fugitive slaves. But he also remembered that the rival Sandy Creek Baptist Association had resolved against separating slave families. He faced out the state's leading Presbyterian and told the whole story, with one eye to the engaged sympathies of Mrs. Caldwell.

"Thank your mother for taking care of the sick child," Mrs. Caldwell said.

Ede wished to come back, Levi put in. Dr. Caldwell broke his silence:

"Your father has done right. I shall not trouble him. As for you, you have done your part very well. Why, Mr. Coffin, you would make a pretty good preacher. I will give you theology lessons without charge. You may tell Ede to come home and I will not send her away."

Levi was too busy to accept free theology lessons. He found himself engaged in the affairs of Jack and Sam, both fugitive slaves but for different reasons. Jack had been house servant to a coastal planter, a bachelor whose will gave Jack his freedom and left him property. Relatives broke the will and seized the property. If the property clauses were null, so was the one which granted the slave freedom. Jack fled and the relatives put out reward notices. The Quakers were a known refuge, and the Coffins found themselves with Jack on their hands. The other slave, Sam, had no legal pretext for being a fugitive; but he did have a master, one Osborne, known for his cruelty. So Sam and Jack both became Levi's concern. There followed a chase into the Blue Ridge—made merry by flasks of whisky and jugs of apple brandy, but grim underneath.

Uncle Bethnel Coffin and his wife were about to leave North Carolina for Indiana. Their two-horse wagon was loaded with provisions and utensils for camping on the way. The Negro Jack had been working openly for the Coffins during the period after the court's ruling, but before a reward was put on his head. A family conference decided that Jack should go with Uncle Bethnel to Indiana. That still left Sam in hiding from Osborne. After Uncle Bethnel's departure, the rumor spread that a Negro man was with him. Osborne concluded it was his Sam, and rode in pursuit. Levi was provided with a good horse and instructions to overtake the wagon party and warn them that Osborne, disappointed in not finding Sam, could still seize Jack and bring him back for the reward.

Levi's horse caught up with Osborne. Now riding in company with the pursuer, Levi must somehow shake him off in order to alert the pursued. Osborne, pleased with Levi's company, passed a whisky flask back and forth until it tilted up empty. A strong streak of benign Quaker guile may have flawed Levi's character, but drinking whiskey was not among his habits. He had held Osborne's flask to innocently unopened lips. When they arrived for the night at Squire Howell's tavern, Levi bought the next flask for Osborne, and, on pretext of feeding his horse, drew Squire Howell outside and whispered his dilemma. From previous cattle-buying trips in Virginia, Levi knew the tavernkeeper would not aid Osborne's bounty hunters. He told the story of the slave who had inherited property and freedom and had lost both. Squire Howell produced a plan of action. He had some neighbors who would help.

Levi returned to Osborne with the good news that their host and some of his friends would join them in the slave hunt. If the Negro should prove to be Sam, Osborne suggested Levi would share the reward.

Next morning their party of eight caught up with Uncle Bethnel. Levi held them out of sight, warning that a posse of eight might frighten the slave into the bush, and that he would go in alone and make the capture. The others agreed and outvoted Osborne. He found his uncle and Jack, told them that Squire Howell's party was on their side, and persuaded Jack to remain in open sight. With a disappointed air he returned to tell Osborne that their quarry was not Sam. It was, he said, a Negro named Jack who had worked for his father. The party broke in on Uncle Bethnel, who produced a jug of old peach brandy.

"He looks a damned sight like that rascal Sam," Osborne protested, but with the aid of the peach brandy and in the presence of five armed men, who thought otherwise, Osborne was persuaded to let Jack go. Levi considered that "the hand of God was in it." He rode home with Osborne on the best of terms. Arrived at Guilford, it appeared that Osborne's Sam was still missing. To Levi's certain knowledge Sam was now weaving baskets in a deep thicket between the Coffin and Caldwell houses. When Osborne rode up to invite Levi to a second hunt for Sam, this time on family home grounds, Levi agreed. They spent the day in the deer and turkey runs, a mile south of Sam's thicket. Although Osborne found no trace of his slave, he was high in his praise of Levi's co-operation: "There wasn't a man in that neighborhood worth a damn to help me except young Levi Coffin."

•

In the early 1820s it was possible to argue slavery in public. Levi and Vestal Coffin taught a Negro Sunday school in a Deep River community. The North Carolina Manumission Society had thirty-three branches and a thousand members. Then the climate subtly changed. The Quakers of the New Garden Meeting began to follow Uncle Bethnel's trail into Indiana. Levi himself left permanently in 1826, settling in Newport, Indiana. There he prospered both in business and the extracurricular activity of helping slaves into free territory.

For a century, among the expanding population of the Cape Fear basin there had been adjustments to slavery—the teaching of Negro children, the saving of Negro souls, extending privileges to Free Negroes. These were the buffers against slave insurrections. King Roger Moore had needed no "proslavery party" to keep order in the Orton rice fields. But by now the long process of accommodation—from the whip and branding iron to fines against erring Free Negroes, from confinement in slave quarters to mixing on the Saturday afternoon sidewalks—had opened up prospects of complete freedom which some local white people encouraged and some Northern people began to demand.

Proslavery factions began to coalesce in the Legislature. Bills were introduced to prevent conversation between mulattoes and Free Negroes on the subject of freedom, to prevent the education of slaves, to forbid emancipation societies. The bills were defeated by close votes. In 1826 the Vermont Legislature petitioned North Carolina for the abolition of slavery, a piece of agitation which Governor Iredell thought "demanded from us a sleepless vigilance." Two years later Governor Owen sent to the Assembly a copy of an inflammatory circular found in slave hands. While the reaction to this was no more than resolutions deploring the circular, when William Lloyd Garrison reprinted it a few years later in the *Liberator,* the North Carolina Senate passed a bill to prevent slaves being taught to read and write. It was not difficult thereafter to get a majority favoring restrictive slave laws, and that majority was not solely reflecting the views of rice and cotton planters. A tide of insurrections was rising along the Southern seaboard; no owner could watch his slaves without some speculation of what thoughts might be hiding behind bland servile faces.

The critical year was 1831, when tremors of fright influenced the Tar Heel lawmakers, and when the bloody massacre of fifty white people in one night, in Southampton County, Virginia, gave all Southern states an excuse for harsh slave codes.

Nat Turner, leader of the insurrection, had seen visions, in the skies, on the ground. The blood of Jesus was seen by him on the corn. He met at night in the woods with five other slaves. After barbecuing a pig they dispersed to pick up weapons, recruited other slaves, and just before dawn went the rounds of all slave-owning farms, slaughtering everyone. The white retaliation was as fierce. In two days the organized man hunt indiscriminately killed 120 Negro men, women, and children. Twenty of the plotters were later formally tried and executed.

This mutual barbarity fixed a white determination that it would not happen to their families. Yet in the Cape Fear region the passage of preventive bills went on simultaneously with court cases which refined barbarisms out of the law, or at least tried.

John M. Morehead, on the issue of teaching Negroes to read, opposed a legislative bill intended "to keep unfortunate human beings in a state of utter ignorance, and to deprive them of an opportunity of reading the Word on which the hopes of the world depend."

Chief Justice Thomas Ruffin supported the right of Negroes to earn money for themselves. Judge William Gaston at the Constitutional Convention of 1835 spoke against the proposed denial of

: THE CAPE FEAR

the Free Negro's right to vote: "Let them know that they are part
of the body politic, and they will feel an attachment to the forms
of government." One of Gaston's opponents met this categori-
cally: "I do not acknowledge any equality between the white man
and the free negro in the enjoyment of political rights." Neither
did the majority of the Court Convention.

•

Levi Coffin at Newport, Indiana, became a leader of the Underground Railroad, eventually its president. The running of slaves
across the border had a secret language—which probably deceived no one—taken from the admired new steam railroads. A
"station" on the "principal line" of the U.G.R.R. was a house
whose owner sheltered runaways on the route North. Wrote Levi
reminiscently:

> The roads were always in running order, and there was no lack of
> passengers . . . the locomotive did not whistle, nor make any un-
> necessary noise.

A Negro slave, Eliza Harris, and her infant made the ice-floe
Ohio River crossing to find shelter with Levi and his wife Kathy.
Harriet Beecher Stowe put Eliza's crossing, complete with fic-
tional bloodhounds, into her *Uncle Tom's Cabin,* and made Levi
and his wife into the Quaker couple, Simeon and Rachel Halliday.
The Coffins moved to Cincinnati where their home became the
Grand Central of U.G.R.R. stations. The boy who had convinced
the Reverend David Caldwell, and had outwitted the harsh Osborne, wound up as a minor hero of a successful cause, complete
with a European lecture tour.

•

Frederick Law Olmsted during 1854-1855 spent fourteen months
in the South, that he might decide for himself between the horrors
of slavery as described by the Abolitionists and slave conditions as

they might actually exist. In 1856 he published in New York *A Journey in the Seaboard Slave States*. In his preface he confesses to too much faultfinding, and invites the reader "to travel in the company of an honest growler."

To the Southerners of that decade he was a Yankee snooper come among them to spread more lies. Actually, Olmsted was neither snooper nor agitator. He was a New York State gentleman farmer who sought out Southern planters for long talks on the relative merits of guano, bone, and manure. He was America's leading landscape architect, later to replace shanties and goats with the lakes and wooded rises of New York's Central Park. In the South his good manners earned him courtesy and hospitality.

His first North Carolina stop, Raleigh, he found a pleasant town of white houses and shaded streets. The Capitol he greatly admired, yet, since "architects should always begin their work upon the ground," he regretted that this noble building should be set in a field used as a hog pasture.

Used to the spanking pace of Eastern coaches, the "honest growler" had hard things to say about travel on the Raleigh-Fayetteville road, the old Kings Highway. The coach was late in starting, so Olmsted set out walking. In the piney woods his curiosity led him up paths to log cabins where listless clay eaters sat stolidly by their hearths. One woman had energy to smoke a pipe and rock a cradle; another . . . "once about a minute would suddenly throw up her chin and spit with perfect precision across the ten feet range into the hottest embers of the fire." Marksmanship among the males of the piney woods was perhaps as accurate, since the men occupied most of their time hunting with rifle and dogs.

The Yankee traveler inveighed against a stage driver who beat his underfed horse to the ground with a fence rail, yet he highly praised the smooth, fast travel over the plank road beginning ten miles outside Fayetteville. He cursed the bad service of a stagecoach inn, yet bestowed verbal blessings on Mrs. Barclay's tavern near Fayetteville:

It was right cheerful and comforting to open the door, from the dark, damp chilly night, into a large room filled with blazing light from a great fire of turpentine pine . . . and a nice, stout, kindly-looking, Quaker-like old lady coming forward to welcome me.

For dinner Mrs. Barclay served "seven preparations of swine's flesh, two of maize, wheat cakes, broiled quails, cold roast turkey, coffee and tea." Olmstead was housed for the night in a separate building where he found open fire, an easy chair and a tub of hot water to bathe feet weary from exploring the piney woods.

A steamboat carried Olmsted from Fayetteville to Wilmington. The course was crooked, the current very rapid, trees overhanging the banks made navigation hazardous. Olmstead queried the master on the river's fickle changes of depth. They were running in eighteen feet of water, a moderate summer stage. Once the master had left the boat aground overnight and found it floating in twenty-five feet of water. The extremes of low water and flood were as much as seventy feet. The stern-wheel craft drew only fourteen inches, yet at lowest summer stage the clearance over some bars was but four inches, so that freight carrying was abandoned and the steamer used to tow flats. The bulk of their present freight was turpentine, stowed disturbingly close to the boiler fires.

At eighty miles below Fayetteville, the banks became lower, the standing timber very large, and many of the trees were hung with the long waving drapery of Spanish moss and a thick network of flowering vines. When darkness fell, they passed many boats and rafts, blazing with great fires made upon a bed of clay, and their crews singing at their sweeps.

The steamer docked at Wilmington at 9:30 P.M. A carriage tour to three hotels found them booked up, but at the third Olmsted saw a notice of a new railroad line to Charleston. He shouldered his luggage and ran for the wharves, where he boarded a small steamboat and was landed at a downriver wharf. There stood a locomotive and train. In darkness he passed southward out of North Carolina.

Olmsted had more to say about North Carolina travel, farming, and scenery than he did about slavery conditions. That aspect, he concluded, was in some respects less lamentable than that of Virginia:

> There is not only less bigotry upon the subject, and more freedom of conversation, but I saw here, in the institution, more of patriarchal character than in any other State. The slave more frequently appears as a family servant—a member of his master's family, interested with him in his fortune, good or bad . . . Slavery thus loses much of its inhumanity. It is still questionable, however, if, as the subject race approaches civilization, the dominant race is not proportionately detained in its onward progress.

Rowan is the westernmost of that tier of piedmont counties which produced the insurgent Regulators. In Rowan the "Black Boys of Cabarrus" burned General Waddell's supply train and held up his juncture with Governor Tryon. Rowan farmers opposed Cornwallis and fought David Fanning's Tories. It was natural enough that the region should produce a contentious native son, but surprising that he should turn out to be the South's only Abolitionist author.

Hinton Rowan Helper was born in 1830, that dividing line in time between the relaxing and tightening of slave controls. During his boyhood, slaves were forbidden to learn their ABC's, roll dice or play cards, carry guns for hunting, be out at night, or foregather without permission. It was not sympathy for the slaves which stirred Hinton Helper. His book would dismiss Negroes as "an undesirable population," and propose their removal to Liberia or South America. The object of his open hatred were the slaveholders, "chevaliers of the lash," a "precious junto of flatterers and conjolers," "truth-murdering champions of slavery."

Helper wrote his book in Baltimore, at a safe remove from Rowan County. The preface to *The Impending Crisis in the South: How to Meet It* called upon "my fellow Southrons" to respect his Southern birth, then riled Southern abomination of *Uncle Tom's Cabin* by asserting that "Yankee wives have written the most popular anti-slavery literature of the day." No Northern pen outdid his diatribes against slavery and his huzzahs for freedom. His book, dedicated to *Non-Slave-holding Whites of the South,* came to a climax in his suggestions how slavery could be abolished in one day, if only nonslaveholders would unite on a plan containing, *inter alia,* these points: Disenfranchise all slaveholders; boycott slaveholders in politics, religion and society; boycott slaveholding doctors and merchants; "No Recognition of Proslavery men, except as Ruffians, Outlaws and Criminals;" a $60 tax on every slave to pay the cost of their transportation abroad or "to their comfortable settlement within the boundaries of the United States."

Helper had to publish the *Impending Crisis* in New York rather than Baltimore, because of an 1831 Maryland law which forbade printing "inflammatory matter to stir up insurrection among colored people." That law reflected the year when Nat Turner's rebellion and abolitionist literature combined to destroy the hope of a peaceful solution. The *Impending Crisis* sold 14,000 copies in its first year. The Republican Party bought 100,000 copies for propaganda in the 1860 Presidential election. Helper's concluding sentence read: "The first battle between freedom and slavery will be fought at home, and may God defend the right."

•

The saga of Negro slavery runs from the landing of the first African trader to Emancipation, yet no one generation along the Cape Fear knew at the time what it was adding to the development of the story. Roger Moore wanted his land cleared and worked. There was nothing to warn his generation—fighters and enslavers

of Indians—what this African trade might portend. David Caldwell was taught at Princeton to labor in the vineyard of white
souls. The Christian salvage of a friendly and useful black servant
was no more than an additional act of Grace. Levi Coffin accepted
the Quaker concept of the Godhead residing in every human being; and to separate God's people by color was unthinkable.
Frederick Law Olmsted was a humanist whose creed held that
pointing out breaches in the retaining wall of the rights of man
would rally forces to plug the breach. Hinton Rowan Helper was
a terrified man, who managed to convey his terror to a people
already overstrained by agitation.

Each of these five men had only his moment to speak his lines
in the long drama of Negro slavery. Yet each took a step toward
the climax of the Civil War. That closed all dispute on the ethics,
the economics, the religious concern with slavery. A fight for survival united all states from Virginia to Florida, and patched up
truces between coastal planters and piedmont farmers.

The decision to secede came hard for Tar Heels. In the 1860
election North Carolina had voted by a large majority for a Legislature which was committed to remaining in the Union. In February 1861 the State sent delegates to Montgomery, Alabama, to
plead with the newly forming Confederate government for a settlement of the North-South issues; other delegates went to the
peace conference which Virginia had called at Washington. Both
missions failed. On April 12 the firing on Fort Sumter opened the
war. North Carolina hesitated for another five weeks after Lincoln's call for 75,000 troops to suppress the Southern "insurrection." On May 20 North Carolina seceded, next to Tennessee the
last to enter the Confederacy.

Zebulon B. Vance, born in the valley below Mt. Mitchell, was
one of the Unionist leaders who held out to the last. He would
become a Confederate colonel, and then be governor for the last
two war years, and again governor during Reconstruction. Of his
agonized decision in the spring of 1861 he later wrote: "I was

pleading for the Union with hand upraised when news came of Fort Sumter and Lincoln's call for troops. When my hand came down from that impassioned gesticulation, it fell slowly and sadly by the side of a Secessionist."

# 6 : *Lee's Life Line*

Wilmington in the early nineteenth century came as near as any Tar Heel town to being that cosmopolitan center which Archibald Debow Murphey thought essential for jogging a dormant state out of its rural isolation. Wilmington wharves were lined with coastal and transatlantic ships. On the hills above the river were the ample homes of the Ashes, Waddells, Moores, De Rossetts, Sprunts, and McNeills, veterans and inheritors of the Revolution.

They were tolerant of Bishop Asbury when he led their Negroes "and a few whites" into an excited Methodism. They had a special fondness for the theater, dating back to the times of Royal Governor Tryon when that patron of the arts, in forwarding to the Bishop of London a young actor's petition for ordination in holy orders, did so with the reluctant sigh: "If your Lordship grants Mr. Gifford this petition, you will take off the best player on the American stage."

In the Thalian Association Hall professional companies held winter seasons. A young player, Elizabeth Hopkins, a girl of "great wide open mysterious eyes, high waist, the face of an elf, an Undine," appeared in an entr'acte, *Lisette and Annette or the*

*Bird Catcher*. She would later marry a fellow member of the company, David Poe, and become the mother of Edgar Allan Poe. She died in the year following her son's birth, aged twenty.

Another mother of an American genius had a longer association with Wilmington, being born of the clan McNeill, a descendant of one of the first McNeills to settle in the Brown Marsh section of Bladen County. Anna Mathilda McNeill spent her girlhood in Wilmington and Bladen County, then was moved by her doctor father to New York where she grew up to marry a young West Pointer, Lieutenant George Washington Whistler.

The Whistler family became European-minded when the United States Engineer Corps father was invited by the Czar of Russia to build a railroad. A glimpse of Anna Mathilda as a young woman visiting her half sister in England shows her dressed for a ball with "her hair piled high and adorned with puffs and curls . . . a fresh complexion, beautifully kept hands and high shapely arches."

Her husband died in Russia. The widow returned to America, and to an eventual strange adventure. In the year 1863 her son William Gibbs Whistler was a Confederate Army surgeon stationed in Richmond; her son James was painting in London. She managed to cross the Confederate lines into Virginia. She was nearing sixty, and having seen her surgeon son she determined to visit James. A way to do it was to board a blockade-runner out of Wilmington to Bermuda or Nassau, and thence an English ship to Liverpool.

Governor Zeb Vance took pride in the blockade-running operations of the Lower Cape Fear. Their success in supplying the Army of Northern Virginia with arms, medicines, and clothing was both an official and a personal satisfaction to the Governor. It lent him stature in his public quarrel with Jefferson Davis over conduct of the war. It was a risk for him to make a cutter available to Mrs. Whistler from Fayetteville to Wilmington and to arrange her passage to England, but Vance took risks, and Mrs. Whistler was a determined lady.

She reached a wartime Wilmington where the streets bore familiar names, but the people who walked them were strangers. Foreign sailors, gamblers, out-and-out toughs, well-dressed young Englishmen shared the streets with men of her own people, now in Confederate gray. Lady shoppers from the houses up on the hill had disappeared. It was a man's town engaged in the single purpose of running sleek gray ships through the Federal fleet lying off New Inlet and the Frying Pan Shoals. The speculators bought shares in ships and cargoes. The riffraff got drunk in the dockside taverns and staggered out to rob and murder in the dark of the shaded streets on the hill. The homeowner merchants and professional men stayed on; most of their women were on upcountry plantations to which they had fled from the yellow fever plague of the previous year.

The steamer *Kate* brought yellow fever from Nassau. No one had ever seen a case in Wilmington. Among the first fifteen stricken there were no recoveries. It was thought that burning tar might sweeten the air, and its black pall hung over the town. The garrison was sent away. Whoever had friends outside went to them. The editor of the *Journal* reported: "We have gone all over town in broad daylight without meeting a vehicle, save a doctor's buggy or a hearse." Another man encountered no one except an old Negro woman gathering wood, and a dog. There were 447 deaths before cold weather succeeded where burning tar and heroic doctors and clergymen had failed. It was a sad town which that autumn checked what neighbors had died of the plague and what sons had fallen at Sharpsburg.

By '63 the adventure and profits of blockade-running more than made up for population which had fled the plague. Shipbuilders and sailormen alike had grown wise in the ways of running three-cents-a-pound cotton to Liverpool where it fetched forty-five cents a pound in gold. Few wharves have ever changed character as Wilmington's did in the first two years of the war. In '61 the steamer from New York and small steamers on the Smithville run jostled for place among three tiers of masts. Neither side had foreseen the importance of steam in sea warfare. The Union Navy had four ships in home waters; the infant Confederate Navy had none. The race for sea power began when Lincoln announced a total blockade of the South's 189 harbors and more than thirty-five hundred miles of coast. The first comer to this fantastic assignment was a Federal armed tug named the *Uncle Ben.* The Confederates seized it and rechristened it the *Retribution.* On a tug of their own, the *Mariner,* they put one twenty-four-pounder foreward and two nine-pounders aft. The fight was on to starve the South of supplies, of munitions, of scalpels and opiates. The Confederacy issued letters of marque both to the great open-sea raiders, such as the *Alabama,* and to whatever craft could slip past blockaders. The latter were at first sailboats. One small craft manned by boys and carrying three bales of cotton had the humiliation of being overhauled and hoisted—boat, cargo and crew—to its captor's deck.

The first Confederate sailing ship from Wilmington might have been a mouse sneaking from its hole, but the Union cat was itself an odd creature. Off the coast lay a Federal fleet of double-ended ferryboats, pleasure steamers, tugs, sloops, and yawls.

English mills needed cotton. Idle Clydeside yards needed to build ships. The Scotch designers began to launch ships which the Lower Cape Fear pilots told them would suit the purpose. For forty miles north of New Inlet the beach shelved evenly to deep water. It was possible for a 200-foot paddle-wheeler of eight foot draft to scoot along outside the breakers, the noise of her engines muffled by the surf, her gray sides blending with the shoreline. When English and Southern capital put in orders for these gray ghosts, and eager crews were recruited for love of glory and a share of fantastic profits, the cat and mouse game began in earnest.

There came to be three Federal blockade lines. The conformity of Cape Fear forced the blockaders into a forty-mile arc to patrol New Inlet, the Frying Pan and the main bar south of Smithville. A second Federal line lay in wait along the Gulf Stream for runners blacked out at night and vulnerable in the first dawn. A third line guarded the waters off Nassau and the Bermudas.

It was a better than two-thirds chance that a fourteen-knot blockade-runner would reach Nassau. One night in 1863 saw Anna Mathilda McNeill Whistler off to her son "Jamie." That hot-tempered and handsome artist took his mother into his pleasant house in Chelsea. He gratified her by attending divine service with her every Sunday, and horrified her by keeping his mistress under the same roof. There were breaks between them, and reconciliations. The cool perfectionist side of his nature led him to label a portrait which he did of her "Arrangement in Gray and Black," yet something of his tenderness pervaded it. The public drew it to its heart as "Whistler's Mother."

•

The blockade-runners had their guardian angels in Fort Fisher and the man who conceived and commanded it, Colonel William Lamb. He had been assigned July 4, 1862, to strengthen a small fort of palmetto logs and railroad iron which had been thrown up north of New Inlet. This hurricane-created channel from ocean to river would admit a blockade-runner at any tide. Below it was Bald Head, the jutting spit of Cape Fear, and southward out to sea the Frying Pan. The main bar of the river was guarded by Fort Caswell, on the land side of the estuary. To have alternate entrances, so widely spaced, made the Lower Cape Fear the South's most easily defended harbor. The favored run was out New Inlet, then hard-a-port along the breakers and north beyond the watching Federal cruisers.

Colonel Lamb buried the palmetto fort in sand. He put shovels into the hands of his garrison and five hundred Negroes. Sand would absorb the shells from sea bombardment. He needed no moat since the beach shelved to the base of a twenty-foot-high face sodded with marsh grass. His work force could toss a million shovelfuls of sand a day. The world's largest earthen fortification reached 1,898 yards along the sea front and angled across the narrow spit from ocean to river another 682 yards. The parapet was twenty-five feet thick. The guns were mounted in barbette on Columbia carriages. Tunnels led through the traverses to shelters and powder storage rooms. The land face of the L shape was guarded by a palisade of sharpened logs, from the sea to the soggy marsh on the river side. Torpedoes, which could be fired electrically, were buried outside the palisade.

Lamb finished this off with a sixty-foot Mound Battery at the southern end, and a complete redoubt, Battery Buchanan, on the Cape Fear. Deepwater wharves here provided for Wilmington steamboat traffic.

By the time Fort Fisher was completed the Federal blockade had discarded ferryboats for powerful gunboats, and the fast, shallow-draft Confederate runners were in operation. Colonel Lamb defied the blockaders and protected their quarry. His cavalry and artillery were ready for runs up the hard-packed beach to salvage the cargoes of stranded blockade-runners and to fight off Federal landing parties bent on the same loot. One of the first of these duels was over the stranded *Modern Greece*, Wilmington-bound with 1,000 tons of powder and a battery of five Whitworth guns.

On June 27, 1862, the *Modern Greece* was pelted by the *Cambridge* and the *Stars and Stripes*, and forced to beach three miles north of Fort Fisher. A Confederate detail boarded her while the fort's guns held off the blockaders. Aside from clothing and barrels of spirits (later consumed "to the scandal of the fort and its defenders"), the Confederates rescued the five English-made Whitworth guns, a very great prize. The Whitworth had a range of five miles, causing the Federal fleet to double the distance it had been cruising off the fort. The gun was mobile and could be horse-drawn up the beach to defend stranded runners. The loss of one Whitworth in a fight over the beached *Hebe* was a cause of mourning at the fort.

The fourteen-knot *Hebe*, with a cargo of drugs, coffee, clothing, and provisions, was making her run down the coast when the U.S.S. *Niphon* forced her onto the beach nine miles above Fort Fisher. In a heavy sea, small boats from the *Niphon* attempted a landing. A detachment of Confederate cavalry watched them tumble through the surf and took them prisoner. By now Captain Daniel Munn, with a gun crew to man one Whitworth and two smaller guns, had arrived from the fort to do shore-to-ship battle with the *Niphon*. Munn drove her away from the *Hebe,* and won two days' grace for salvage work. Then the Federal steam frigate *Minnesota* and the *Shokoken,* in command of Lieutenant W. B. Cushing, joined the *Niphon* to bombard and set the *Hebe* on fire. Captain Munn serviced his guns from behind a dune until marines from the *Minnesota,* who had landed two miles up the beach, forced him to fall back, his last shot fired, a gunner killed and four of his squad wounded. The Whitworth fell into Federal hands.

Major General W. H. C. Whiting, District Commander for the Lower Cape Fear, informed the Confederate Secretary of War of the "heavy loss of that Whitworth, a gun that in the hands of the indefatigable Lamb has saved dozens of vessels and millions of money to the Confederate States."

General Whiting's comment on the beach attack on Captain Munn gave Richmond a warning it would have been well to heed: "This is the first time they have landed, but what they have done once they can do again, and doubtless will." Fort Fisher's Achilles' heel was the land approach.

•

Duty aboard the blockading fleet was painfully boring to the Union sailors. Occasionally a steamer left station to refuel at Federal-held Beaufort. That trip itself consumed coal. Back off Fort Fisher, the fires under the boilers were kept economically low, and full steam put on only when the lookout had spotted a Confederate ship. Then the Rebel as like as not would fire up its boilers with fat Nassau bacon or cotton dipped in turpentine, and slip out of sight before the Federal boilers could reach peak power.

It was likewise frustrating to be lying in flotilla when a blockade-runner, surprised by daylight or off course, made straight through the Federal ships, near enough to see faces and hear orders. To fire on the Confederate might be to "shoot at the cow and kill the calf." In the hesitation over hitting one of your own, the speedy Rebel could maneuver into the safe cover of Colonel Lamb's Whitworths.

Lieutenant Cushing of the U.S.S. *Shokoken*, weary of routine duty, decided to use his craft as a landing stage for small boat raids up the Cape Fear. If the Rebels could slip a 200-foot steamer out to sea, guided only by the fires of the many saltworks along the river, why could not he do blockade-running in reverse?

His first foray was aimed at kidnaping the Confederate commander at Smithville, General Hébert. Cushing's oarsmen carried him under the guns of Fort Caswell to a landing below the town. At Headquarters he was disappointed that General Hébert had spent the night elsewhere. As second prize, he spirited away the sleepy and flabbergasted adjutant.

Next Cushing's crew took him on a night raid to the east side of the estuary, landing him a mile below Wilmington. He made daylight observations of the town's defenses. He intercepted a Confederate courier from Fort Fisher and confiscated some interesting dispatches. Left to his own resources to get back to his ship, he did it.

On the strength of his Cape Fear exploits, Cushing was given permission to present to the Secretary of War at Washington his plans for blowing up the Confederate ironclad *Albemarle*, which in a fight with eight Federal cruisers in Albemarle Sound had sunk the U.S.S. *Southfield*, crippled the *Sassacus*, and driven off the others. This impregnable ram, now at Plymouth on the Roanoke River, Cushing proposed to blow up with a torpedo. The device had a fourteen-foot boom hinged at the near end to the bow, and holding the torpedo at the far end. The operator with one hand might lower the boom to the proper angle and with the other pull a lanyard to explode the charge. The *Albemarle* was lording it over the entire Federal fleet in the waters back of Beaufort. Washington gave the wild venture its approval.

Cushing recruited seven volunteers and made himself deft with the two-handed manipulation of the boom. He chose a moonless night to edge his launch along the wooded shore toward the *Albemarle*'s berth. He sighted her silhouette by the glare from a shore fire, which also revealed the shocking fact that a floating barricade of cedar logs surrounded the ironclad. The launch was seen and challenged. In reply to "What ship is that?", Cushing's men "gave comical answers," while he himself in a lightning decision determined that the top log might be slimy enough to grease the launch's keel over it. He ordered a top speed run at the log. The launch teetered and slipped inside. With rifles and a howitzer now peppering the launch, it made slow headway to the point where Cushing's right hand guided the torpedo to the vulnerable underside. His left hand yanked the exploding lanyard. In the falling wall of water and debris, Cushing climbed over the logs and swam for his life.

Twelve hours later, after crawling on his stomach through a swamp to steal a Confederate rowboat, and, after rowing for eleven hours, he reached the Federal fleet, the one which had been knocked about by the *Albemarle*. Cushing was restored by a brandy and the firing of rockets as the news passed from ship to ship that their enemy was sunk forever at her Plymouth mooring. Captain A. F. Warley, C.S.N., commander of the *Albemarle* during her first and last engagement with a launch, said of Cushing's feat: "A more gallant thing was not done during the war."

•

Sixty-six first class blockade-runners were built in Scotland and England; forty were destroyed. But the numbers of successful runs each ship made, plus the runs of ships other than those

British-built, brought tens of millions in gold into Wilmington. The U.S. Consul at Nassau, Seth C. Hawley, reported to Secretary Seward on one Confederate vessel, the *Ella and Annie*. She made four successful runs and was lost on the fifth. Deducting the $200,000 destroyed value of the ship and her cargo, the profits from her first four trips was $276,000.

Wilmington's new adventuresome population lived high on the hog. Bachelors jointly rented the big homes of owners gone up-country. One establishment of young Britishers made the nights merry with their songs and the minstrelsy of Negro entertainers. The town that had suffered under the occupation of Major Craig's redcoats in 1781 now had a distinct British flair. The young light-hearted Britishers were forgiven their riotous night noises by serious-minded Wilmingtonians, who were simultaneously saying their prayers that England would join the Confederacy and end this agony. It was a well-grounded hope, for England had to have Cape Fear cotton; the steam cotton press on the shore opposite Wilmington operated night and day to shape the bales, and British bottoms carried them across the Atlantic.

"Captain Roberts" of the blockade-runner *Don* was in fact the Honorable Augustus Charles Hobart-Hampden, son of the Earl of Buckinghamshire, on leave from the Royal Navy. He skippered five runs of the *Don* before returning to England. For a time he commanded the Queen's yacht, the *Victoria and Albert,* but tiring of steaming in and out of Cowes, he found more congenial employment fighting the Russians as Admiral-in-Chief of the Turkish Navy.

A younger British loan to the Confederacy was Thomas E. Taylor, put in charge at the age of twenty-one of a Liverpool company's fleet of fifteen blockade-runners. One of them, the *Banshee,* was the first steel vessel to cross the Atlantic. Tom Taylor made this first (and nearly last) trip. On the Nassau to Wilmington leg the *Banshee* sprang a leak, her coal was low, and her arrival off Fort Fisher at daylight put her in full view of the Federal blockaders. Captain Capper proposed going to sea again. Taylor decided the lesser risk was to run for it. The captain consented, with the accurate prophecy that "you'll get damned well peppered."

Taylor climbed the masthead to pick out what seemed the widest space between approaching blockaders. But two of them converged on the *Banshee*. A first shot carried away its flagstaff. The second went through the forehold and bulged out a plate on the opposite side. Bedding and blankets were applied to the new leak. With a full head of steam, the *Banshee*'s speed carried her between her tormentors. Taylor, standing on the paddle box, looked into muzzles of hostile guns firing at 150 yards range. Then from the fort, Lamb's more accurate Whitworths found the range of the blockaders and cleared the way to the bar, on which the excited pilot grounded the *Banshee* at full speed. Under shelter of the fort, she was hauled off.

•

As a schoolboy in Wilmington, James Sprunt had "delighted to wander along the wharves and watch the strangers from foreign lands, whose uncouth cries and unknown tongues inspired me with a longing for the sea." By the time blockade-running had shaken down to a grim game between Confederate ships and three lines of Federal cruisers stretched across the 700-mile seaway to the islands, Sprunt was old enough, seventeen, to ship as a purser. It was through being stranded in Bermuda by a spell of illness that he came upon the great love of his blockade-running career, the *Lillian*. She was Clyde-built, with two raked funnels and a turtleback deck forward to shoulder through rough seas. She was rated officially at 500 tons and fifteen knots, and by Sprunt as "a thing of beauty and a joy forever."

As purser he found it his first duty to bend over a keg of silver dollars and count out forty to each crew member as a sailing bounty. Loaded to the hatch coamings with gunpowder for Lee's army, the *Lillian* slipped out of the dark harbor—no lights, no smoking, and only a peephole through cloth at the binnacle. She made an afternoon landfall near Cape Lookout and set a close offshore course southward. At three o'clock the U.S.S. *Shenandoah* sighted her and gave chase. Eleven-inch shells from the big ship's Parrott guns tumbled end over end around the *Lillian*, yet by six o'clock there were still no hits. Three passengers, officers from the Confederate ship *Georgia*, tranquilly ticked off the number of seconds between the gun flashes and the passages of shells overhead. They had thrown their small arms overboard; Sprunt at the captain's orders had burned the Confederate mail. No one supposed that the black hull now abeam would not destroy or beach the *Lillian*.

The roll of the *Shenandoah*'s deck in a high sea spoiled the Parrott guns' aim at the bobbing target. But the saving grace was the bursting of one of the *Lillian*'s boilers. It slowed her down so that—in the growing dark and against the gray dunes—the *Shenandoah* failed to realize her absence, and kept course while flinging shells at the still visible line of surf. The *Lillian* headed out to sea across her pursuer's wake.

The gantlet of the Federal ships off Fort Fisher still had to be run. At first dawn the thick haze made ghosts of the blockaders, and served the same purpose for the *Lillian*. She was taken for a Federal ship returning to her station among them, until the brightening morning showed her lines and gray sides. At a hail: "Heave to, or I'll sink you!" the *Lillian*'s captain replied: "Aye, aye, sir, we will stop the engines." The bar was close and there was no intention to reverse engines. While the blockader slowed down to lower boats, the *Lillian* put on speed and came under Colonel Lamb's iron shield.

On August 24, 1864, the *Lillian* made her last successful run through the offshore line of blockaders. At daybreak of the second day out, the spars and hulls of three Gulf Stream Squadron blockaders appeared out of the mists and surrounded the unarmed *Lillian*. James Sprunt went North as prisoner of war on the U.S.S. *Keystone State*.

•

The odds against escaping the blockaders grew less during the last months of 1864. In this period the North was gaining in strength and momentum to bear on the shrinking periphery of Confederate-held territory. While young James Sprunt was being carried away from the Cape Fear on the *Keystone State,* news had just arrived that the Confederate raider *Alabama* had been sunk off Cherbourg by the U.S.S. *Kearsarge;* Sheridan was driving Early from the Shenandoah Valley; Grant was besieging Petersburg; Sherman was approaching Atlanta. When Sherman should reach Savannah and Charleston, the only open Southern port to receive supplies in support of the Army of Northern Virginia would be Wilmington. The blockade-runners of the Cape Fear had become Lee's life line.

A year before, the State of North Carolina itself had gone into blockade-running by buying the *Lord Clyde,* a twenty-knot sidewheeler on the Glasgow-Dublin run. They renamed her the *Ad-Vance.* Seven successful trips were made to Bermuda—cotton out, salt pork in—before the inferior quality of Deep River coal betrayed her. The mine at Egypt on the Deep was itself a jinx. An explosion had snuffed the lives of fifty miners, the collapsed shaft being left as their joint headstone. The digging went on; for in 1864 Egypt was one of three remaining Confederate coal mines.

Blockade-running skippers avoided Egypt coal as one of the seven plagues. But on her September '64 outbound trip the *Ad-Vance* bunkers held only Egypt coal. The raider *Tallahassee,* coaling up to prey on Federal commerce, had been allotted all available clean-burning Welsh coal. So it was that the *Ad-Vance* trailed a plume of black Egypt coal smoke across the horizon; and the U.S.S. *Santiago de Cuba* was guided to her defenseless side. Governor Vance had nippy words to say to Navy Secretary Stephen Mallory over this needless loss.

•

Tom Taylor had a knack for being present during crises. In late September '64 he took passage through the blockade to Bermuda so that he might make the return on his company's newest runner, the *Night Hawk*. The green skipper and the nonprofessional pilot were not to Taylor's liking. They bumped a coral reef off Hamilton on their way out. On the critical night run through the ring of Federal ships off Cape Fear the *Night Hawk* was seen, and the usual hullabaloo of shot and shell, rockets and flares followed them in to the approach to New Inlet.

Two armed Federal launches were lurking in the dark below the depression limit of Lamb's guns. They now joined their larger brothers outside in the general firing and illumination. They were very close to the *Night Hawk*. The captain disregarded Taylor's advice to wait awhile for high tide. The *Night Hawk* stuck fast on a sand bar. The crews of the launches boarded her, waved pistols at their captives, and set the *Night Hawk* afire fore and aft. An excited (and false) cry that the ship was loaded with gunpowder created enough confusion for Taylor and four others to escape through the surf to the beach immediately in front of the fort. On the rising tide the *Night Hawk* bumped over the bar and beached. Lamb's volunteers put out her fires.

Next day Taylor's agent in Wilmington sent three hundred Negroes to help in bailing and lightening the *Night Hawk*. But attempts to haul her off failed. Her anchors would not hold. There was no solid object to which chains might be fixed. That night the desired object appeared in the shape of the blockade-runner *Condor* which mistook the silhouette of the beached *Night Hawk* for a Federal ship, veered to port and stuck on the same bar which had held the *Night Hawk* fast. On it the *Condor* broke in two.

In the morning, October 2, Taylor walked on the beach to inspect this new mishap. Bodies from a capsized *Condor* lifeboat lay at the edge of the surf, one of them that of a beautiful woman. Attached to her waist was a bag heavy with gold sovereigns. Taylor identified her as the Confederate spy, Rose O'Neal Greenhow.

He had the body sent to Wilmington where, with full honors, Mrs. Greenhow was buried in Oakdale Cemetery.

Her death did not affect Confederate fortunes. It was too late. Her efforts in England and on the Continent to win official status for the South had been politely evaded. Her high tide of success had been during the first year of the war when she was in Washington, a rich and handsome young widow, friend of President Buchanan, dinner hostess to Secretary Seward as she had been to eminent Southerners before the war. With Colonel Thomas Jordan, before he left Washington to become Adjutant General of the Confederate Army, she had arranged to be a secret agent for the new Southern Government. Through a code message she gave General Beauregard information on the Federal plans to invade Virginia. The Union rout at Bull Run was credited to the accuracy of Mrs. Greenhow's reporting of conversations around her dinner table. Six months later Allan Pinkerton accused Mrs. Greenhow of "alienating the hearts of Federal officers from their sympathy with their country" and of possessing memoranda and maps supposedly known only to Federal officials.

They put Mrs. Greenhow under house arrest. When that did not stop the leaks, she and her small daughter were locked in a prison cell. Finally, to rid Washington of this irrepressible font, she was passed across the lines. Richmond sent her overseas as its unofficial emissary. She was given a private audience by Napoleon III. In England she published a book, *My Imprisonment, or the First Year of Abolition Rule in Washington*. Whatever message it was she was bringing back from London to Richmond was filed forever on the sands where Tom Taylor found her.

That resourceful young Britisher returned from Mrs. Greenhow's funeral to get on with the business of hauling the *Night Hawk* off the beach. He now had the wreck of the *Condor* as his fixed point to attach chains from the *Night Hawk*. For seven days, at each full tide, his work gang inched the *Night Hawk* toward deep water. At last she floated, and limped up to Wilmington, a scarecrow of a vessel with sides corrugated from the fires and her deck awry. Yet they patched her up and sent her back into blockade-running, a symbol of battered hopes soon coming to a close.

General Lee in November sent a message to Richmond that his food supply could last but thirty days. The seat of war now encompassed only Virginia and North Carolina. Tom Taylor, called to Richmond, was told to put his best ship in the service of feeding the Army of Northern Virginia. The *Banshee II* was at Wilmington. Within three days Taylor was on board and headed for Nassau.

At 6 P.M. on Christmas Eve, Taylor ordered the Nassau Negro pilot to take out the loaded *Banshee,* but was told the ship could not turn in the small harbor until high tide.

"Back her out," ordered Taylor.

"Perhaps do plenty damage," the pilot grinned.

"Never mind. Try it."

The "plenty damage" was to a British man-of-war into which the *Banshee* backed, grinding along the Britisher's side and smashing two of her boats. British officers, on deck ready to go below for Christmas dinner, gaped at this seamanship.

"Good-by," Taylor shouted. "A merry Christmas. Send the bill in for the boats."

At the moment Taylor was making his rude escape from Nassau, Fort Fisher was being bombarded by the entire Federal fleet under Admiral Porter. General Butler's army had landed and was probing the strength of that face of the fort which stretched across the peninsula. This Butler found to be impregnable, and to the disgust of Porter and Grant, Butler's force re-embarked and sailed north.

By December 28 Admiral Porter had also withdrawn. There were still the regular blockaders to be avoided, and few of Colonel Lamb's guns were left in commission after the bombardment. Yet the *Banshee* and her full cargo of Nassau pork and supplies for Lee's Army ran through New Inlet. They were cheered by

Lamb and his garrison, the more wildly in proportion that the defender of Fort Fisher supposed they had successfully driven off Butler and Porter.

So they had, for a week, until the Federal fleet returned and the Union land forces had been put in command of a man less easily discouraged than General Butler.

# 7 : *Amphibious Assault*

On August 23, 1864, Admiral Farragut captured Fort Morgan, the last Mobile Bay stronghold. The United States Navy had swept Confederate ships from the western rivers and Gulf ports. As Lincoln put it:

> The Father of Waters goes unvexed to the sea . . . Nor must Uncle Sam's web feet be forgotten. At all the watery margins they have been present. Not only on the deep sea, the broad bay, the rapid river, but also up the narrow muddy bayou, and wherever the ground was a little damp, they have made their tracks.

This rhetoric ignored the Port of Wilmington. Excepting the small boat raids of Lieutenant Cushing, Uncle Sam's webfeet had not paddled the Lower Cape Fear. By protecting the blockade-runners, the sand bastion of Fort Fisher was keeping the armies of Lee and Joe Johnston in the field.

One week after Mobile Bay, Secretary of the Navy Gideon Welles proposed that the now idle Federal fleet, with transports carrying a strong landing force, be sent to destroy that gadfly Colonel Lamb and his Whitworth guns. But Grant had several armies engaged in campaigns of movement, and had no men to release for the silencing of Fort Fisher. It was not until late fall that Grant penned up the Army of Northern Virginia behind Petersburg, and was ready to supply troops for the amphibious Cape Fear mission.

Under Admiral David D. Porter, foster brother of Farragut and a seasoned commander in the western naval fighting, the greatest flotilla in American history was assembled in Hampton Roads. More than six hundred guns (to Fort Fisher's forty-four) were mounted on five ironclads, three frigates and forty-two cruisers. This fire power could be counted on to silence the fort; a force of 6,500 troops would then land to take possession.

Grant reluctantly gave command of the landing force to General Benjamin F. Butler. This politician turned military man had the pendulant jowls and red face of one who had lost a lifelong fight with fried chicken and chocolate éclairs. Butler disliked his West Point associates, feeling that they were trying to discredit him. Perhaps they were. When Butler, seven months before, had been in command of the Army of the James, his West Point aides advised him to bridge the Appomattox River as the shortest route to his objective. Butler rejected this with the jibe that he "was not going to build a bridge for West Point men to retreat over." Instead he took up a position in a loop between the James and the Appomattox, where he became "a cork in a bottle," unable to advance and eventually defeated by Beauregard. Grant had sent Butler back to administrative duties at Fortress Monroe where, unhappily for Grant, Butler had the rank entitling him to command the expeditionary force on Porter's fleet. So it was that General Butler and Admiral Porter became incompatible mates in a partnership which demanded the closest co-operation of sea and land commands.

The fleet sailed south to the Cape Fear, only slightly delayed by a project by which Butler thought the bloody business of fighting their way into the fort could be avoided. A month before, an explosion in London had flattened many city blocks. This impressed

Butler. He conceived that a ship filled with gunpowder and exploded close to Fort Fisher would tumble the guns from their carriages, collapse Wilmington, and allow an easy entrance through windfalls of stunned defenders. Even the doubters were interested. Grant supposed Butler "activated by a desire to witness the effect of the explosion," and added a dour order for him to get on with the fight, explosion or no.

The obsolete vessel *Louisiana* was stuffed with 235 tons of gunpowder and warped in the darkness to within 300 yards of Fort Fisher. Admiral Porter moved his fleet twelve miles out, just to be sure. An intrepid crew laid slow fuses over the side, lit them and scuttled away from the holocaust.

The *Louisiana* obediently blew up, with attendant pillar of fire and a very loud noise, somewhat lost, however, in the Atlantic wastes, so that sleepers in Fort Fisher awakened, wondered whether a Yankee boiler had burst, and returned to slumber. Admiral Porter brought the fleet back to stations and next day, December 24, began the bombardment.

•

Both sides expected that a landing of Federal troops would follow the crippling by the Federal fleet of Fort Fisher's fire power. The only logical landing place was on the beach north of the fort. Here the terrain was broken by ridges and tree clumps. Colonel Lamb knew that the face of his bastion across the narrow peninsula was vulnerable. His buried torpedoes and sharpened-log palisade might deter Federal troops; the elevation of the ramparts would give Confederate guns and riflemen an advantage, but Lamb had only 1,400 men, and most of these would be servicing the sea face guns against the enemy fleet. The only assurance that he could hold out against simultaneous sea and land attack lay in reinforcement of troops and ammunition from the outside. Provision of both seemed well prepared.

General Braxton Bragg held the over-all Confederate command. He was in position at Sugar Loaf, the hill seven miles north where King Roger Moore had whipped the Indians 140 years before. Bragg had Major General Robert F. Hoke's division of 6,000 veterans of the Army of Northern Virginia, sent there by Lee out of his concern that his supply life line should not be broken. Lamb supposed that Hoke could take care of a Federal landing. Moreover, Lamb had his own open supply line in the enemy-free Cape Fear River, from Battery Buchanan to Wilmington.

Lamb spent Christmas Eve walking the traverses and talking with his gun crews. The Federal shots were coming from five ironclads arrogantly lined up close offshore. In the dark they were not very accurate. But at dawn, when the enemy's 627 guns let loose, a shell every second, stray drops of the iron rain fell directly on Fisher's gun emplacements. The fort's return fire was neither heavy nor damaging. Lamb was already beginning to ration his ammunition. An occasional hit on a Federal vessel was shaken off lightly by the great fiery sea monsters.

At one forty on Christmas afternoon General Butler's troops landed in small boats above the fort. General Godfrey Weitzel, field commander for Butler, sent skirmishers to within seventy-five yards of the fort's land face. They found the works substantially uninjured by the explosion of the powder ship. Weitzel reported to Butler that the fort could not be carried by assault. Butler ordered his force to re-embark, and, with the loss of one man drowned in the surf, the holiday outing returned to its transports.

Admiral Porter stormed in his cabin. The news was wired to Grant who as stormily relieved Butler of his command. Richmond papers rejoiced. The Northern press pilloried Butler who, aside from his ready acceptance of Fort Fisher's impregnability, could not resist making a speech to his men:

> I have refused to order the useless sacrifice of the lives of such soldiers, and I am relieved of your command. The wasted blood of my men does not stain my garments.

Porter had no other alternative than to head his fleet back to Hampton Roads, which he did on December 27. Next day Tom

Taylor brought the *Banshee* in through a seaway greatly depleted of Federal men-of-war.

•

There was celebration at the fort. Governor Vance came down from Raleigh to offer congratulations. The steamer brought a party of the ladies who had organized a society to nurse the wounded during Wilmington train stopovers. Colonel Lamb and Tom Taylor swapped adventures. From the *Ella*, last of the blockade-runners to be beached, cases of "London Dock" gin had been salvaged, which occasioned the chaplain to render a rather unusual grace at headquarters mess.

The *Banshee* proceeded to Wilmington for the unloading of Nassau bacon, fat back, and hams destined for Lee and Johnston. Colonel Lamb set the garrison to work replacing knocked-about guns. Braxton Bragg, in celebration of the Federal discomfiture, marched his troops several miles north of Wilmington and there held a grand review.

Lamb took dawn walks on the parapet, and on January 13 saw what he had expected, the masts of Admiral Porter's armada rising above the horizon.

•

In the second assault on Fort Fisher, Admiral Porter was fortunate in having replaced Butler with the seasoned Major General A. H. Terry. Before leaving Hampton Roads the two commanders had worked out a co-ordinated sea bombardment and land attack. The most extraordinary human factor was Porter's agreement that Terry, once landed and engaged against the fort, would assume the direction of tactics. If unorthodox, the arrangement was logical. The fleet's part was to soften up the fort to the point where the land attack could be confidently launched. There would come a time when the fleet must cease fire or else rake its advancing land forces. Porter in effect promised to use his entire fleet as one battery, to lay down a barrage when Terry called for it, to cease fire at Terry's order. To achieve this concerted action, Signal Corps men were at hand to send Terry's orders to Porter and from him through semaphore to each ship.

From interrogation of Confederate prisoners, from maps and landing reconnaissance parties, the positions of the enemy ashore would be ascertained. These three elements—command, communication, and intelligence—would be combined for the first planned amphibious assault in modern warfare.

The Federal fleet's transports carried some 6,500 men who had landed with Butler, plus 2,000 Negro troops. The Confederate defenders were not far outnumbered. Hoke had 6,000 at Sugar Loaf, Lamb 1,200 within the fort. Yet within the Confederate command was a personal distrust worth thousands of men to the enemy. Braxton Bragg, in command of Southern Virginia and North Carolina, supposed that he had reason to suspect the courage of his subordinate, Major General W. H. C. Whiting, in command of the Wilmington District. The rift had begun seven months before during the Battle of Drewry's Bluff. Whiting, under conflicting orders from Bragg and Beauregard, had failed to bring his 4,000 men into the Drewry's Bluff action. On the day after the battle, Whiting appeared with lowered eyes before Beauregard. He offered no excuses, confessed his fault, and requested that he be removed from duty in the field. Beauregard returned him to his former command at Wilmington. There seven months later, Braxton Bragg, now put in command of Southern Virginia and North Carolina, became Whiting's immediate superior.

Whiting had been graduated first cadet in the West Point class of 1845. The incident at Drewry's Bluff put him under a shadow with his fellow officers. Braxton Bragg, during the terrible three days of Federal land and sea assault on the fort, would disregard Whiting's telegraphed pleas for help. Why Bragg sat it out at Sugar Loaf, and let the fort fall, was to remain as unfathomable as Whiting's idle two days below Drewry's Bluff.

•

Colonel William Lamb was one of those amateur soldiers whose nature and abilities clothed him with the romance frequently authentic to the Lost Cause of the Confederacy. A native of Norfolk, Lamb graduated in law at the College of William and Mary. Literature being a second string to the bow of a Virginia lawyer, he was trying his hand at publishing when the war broke. By July 1862 he had progressed in military science to the point of being made colonel in charge of Fort Fisher. This assignment he performed with zest and brilliance. The twelve hundred North Carolina soldiers of his garrison had helped him build this earthenwork titan whose guns kept the pack of Federal cruisers at bay whenever a sleek gray blockade-runner had reached sanctuary within range of Lamb's Whitworths. The Colonel, whom the blockade-running skippers and pilots drank with in celebration of their escape, was still in his twenties, owning a face darkly handsome against the long hair and clipped chin beard then in the military mode. To his District Commander, General Whiting, Lamb was deeply attached, needing to have no concern with the rumor that Whiting had let down his fellow West Pointers at the Battle of Drewry's Bluff. Lamb (with a strong assist from Union General Butler) had blocked the first Federal attack on Fort Fisher. On the eve of the next sure-to-occur assault, morale at the fort was high.

On January 13 the Federal ironclads moved into a line twelve hundred yards offshore and opened the fight by bowling shells along the parapet, with the objective that some would roll into gun chambers and there explode. By 2:00 P.M. the main fleet had wheeled into line behind the ironclads and opened fire. The frigates *Minnesota* and *Wabash* each had fire power superior to all the guns on the fort's sea face. Lamb's appeal to Bragg for ammunition had not been answered. He had less than twenty-four hundred shot and shell left, and so he continued his order that gun crews limit their fire to one shot every half hour, a matter of some puzzlement to the ammunition-rich Federal fleet.

By 3:00 P.M. 200 small boats had beached above the Fort, each of the Union's 8,000 men carrying nine days' rations and 100 rounds of ammunition. During the afternoon 700 Confederate reinforcements disembarked at Battery Buchanan. General Whiting and his staff had also arrived, not in any official role, since Bragg had taken away Whiting's command of the harbor. He found Lamb at the works, grasped his hand and said, "Lamb, my boy, I have come to share your fate. You and your garrison are to be sacrificed."

"Don't say so, General," Lamb replied. "We shall certainly whip them again."

Bragg, Whiting told him, was removing stores and ammunition and looking for a place to fall back on if Fort Fisher fell. Lamb offered Whiting command of the fort. He refused, but offered to stand by and give what counsel he could on the defense.

Lamb had watched the Federal landing party disappear into the thickets. Now his glasses picked out a Confederate steam transport approaching a landing already in enemy hands. Lamb had a warning shot fired across her bows, but what he called "the stupid craft" continued and was captured. The C.S.N. *Chickamauga*, stationed on the Cape Fear, fired upon and sank the transport, destroying one of her own rather than let it fall to the enemy. Had the transport waited until dark, her sorely needed supplies could have been safely landed at Battery Buchanan.

Whiting telegraphed Sugar Loaf a plan for a simultaneous attack by Bragg and himself on the Federal landing party now hemmed into the five-mile strip of the peninsula between Bragg's line and the Fort. Although no reply came, Lamb readied ten companies and at dark sent out skirmishers. They drew Federal fire, and held their ground awaiting shots signifying Bragg was in action on the Federal far side. No shots came. At dawn the advance party returned to the fort. This was the night of the fourteenth. After thirty-six hours of bombardment, Lamb had lost 200 men, leaving his effectives at 1,200. Damage done to the fleet was trifling.

Terry and Porter had agreed that a full bombardment would

begin at nine o'clock on the morning of the fifteenth, and that at three o'clock the fleet's guns would cease and the assault begin on the fort's land face. Porter had an additional plan. A force of 1,600 sailors and 400 marines would attack the land face as a diversion to divide the Confederate defenders.

So at noon boats from thirty-five ships shoved off with Porter's force, flags flying line abreast toward the beach, a more formidable-looking array than they really were. They were units from different outfits, had been aboard ship for months, and never been drilled together. Porter, in true sea-dog tradition, had armed them with cutlasses and pistols, these to rout riflemen on ramparts above. The 2,000 lay down on the slope of the beach out of rifle range, waiting the signal for assault.

Over at Battery Buchanan a steamer from Bragg was landing reinforcements. Federal fire drove the vessel away after 350 South Carolina troops had gotten ashore. These went on the double-quick across the mile of sand to the fort where they arrived so exhausted that Lamb put them in shelters to recover.

A lookout sighted the Federal force advancing from the shore line, and called: "Colonel, the enemy are about to charge." Lamb ordered his men to the parapet. Whiting disappeared to send another telegram to Bragg at Sugar Loaf:

> The enemy are about to assault; they outnumber us heavily. We are just manning our parapets. Fleet have extended down the sea-front outside and are firing very heavily. Enemy on the beach in front of us in very heavy force, not more than seven hundred yards from us. Nearly all our guns disabled. Attack! Attack! It is all I can say and all you can do.

Whiting returned to the parapet just as the guns of the fleet ceased fire. To besieged and besiegers alike this silence could mean only one thing. General Terry had signaled Admiral Porter that Fort Fisher was sufficiently softened up. Cease the artillery coverage so that the infantry might take over the attack. The signal for that came at 3:25 P.M. from the wide-open steam whistles on every ship in the fleet.

The Union sailors and marines advanced toward the angle where the land face and sea face met. The odds were all against them. With many losses from rifle fire above, a first wave reached the angle and mistakenly waited for the next wave instead of taking better shelter along the face. The rest caught up, filling the sands like sheep packed in a pen. The Confederate riflemen on the parapet—themselves the victims of thirty-six hours of relentless shelling by the fleet from which this hapless foray had come—fired savagely into the blue-clad mass. With an unscalable wall in front of them, their pistols of no use, the invaders did the sensible thing. They scrambled back to the slope of the beach, leaving 300 dead or wounded on the sand below the angle. If this was a diversion to distract attention from Terry's column creeping up to the land face, it was successful.

Lamb turned away from watching the slaughter of the sailors to see three Federal battle flags on the ramparts near his Number 4 gun chamber. To his further dismay, the Stars and Stripes had also been sighted from Battery Buchanan which turned its guns on the invader insignia and reaped a harvest of both friend and foe before the Battery command realized its error.

Whiting, in formal command or not, reverted to field leader. Sword high and shouting encouragement, he was running to the new crisis when two bullets felled him. Men carried him below to a hospital shelter. Lamb stood apart, a momentary spectator of the fight going on at the gun chamber, at such close quarters that it was impossible to load and fire, and muskets were being used as clubs. The wires to the land torpedoes had been cut by the fleet's fire. The enemy had found a weak spot. Lamb dispatched an orderly with another telegram begging Bragg to come to their rescue, then began ordering up gun crews to concentrate on this breach in their ramparts. The massed defense might have held off the attack, except for the remorseless and accurate barrage from the fleet. The ironclads and heavy frigates exploded shells in the interior of the sally port and drove the Confederates back before their advancing assailants. Yet the attack was the point of a wedge, and there were many defenders. If he could hold out until dark, and then have Bragg's reinforcements . . .

A blue column appeared coming around the bastion where it ended at the river. Lamb ordered guns turned on it, and himself ran the length of the fort, on his return trip putting his head into the galleries and begging the sick and wounded to make one supreme effort to dislodge the enemy now holding three of his gun chambers. The scene, as he described it later, was one of horror. Great cannon were broken in two, with the dead lying over them partly buried in graves dug by the shells which had killed them. Lamb herded his volunteers to the point where an attack could be launched on the Federal column. He had given the order: "Charge bayonets!" and was advancing, when a rifle ball in his left hip dropped him and his guidon sword. He turned the command over to Captain Munn, promising to bind his wound and be back shortly. He was too sanguine. The wound was more serious than that. There was no bayonet charge. Another Federal brigade entered the sally port and began cleaning up the gun chambers one by one until reaching the last of them at Mound Battery. Lamb and Whiting were carried on stretchers across the mile of sand to Battery Buchanan.

There Lamb could well believe Whiting's dour remark that the garrison had been sacrificed. Battery Buchanan's guns had been spiked and all Confederate boats were gone. One incoming vessel, however, docked at the wharf, bringing General Colquitt and three staff officers. This was at 9:45 P.M. Many of the fort's garrison who had retreated down the traverses and reached Battery Buchanan had sampled hospital whisky on the way down. General Colquitt announced that he had been sent to take command of Fort Fisher. The wounded Lamb attempted to explain how little there was left to command. A Confederate soldier, doubtless one of the medical whisky samplers, raised his pistol at the breast of one of General Colquitt's staff members. A more sober hand struck the pistol arm down. A soldier broke in to report Federal officers at the door. General Colquitt and staff retired to the wharf and boarded their boat for Wilmington.

The surrender took place a few minutes later, at 10 P.M.

•

The Lower Cape Fear for the first time in four years was open to United States ships. The continuing defense of the estuary was stiff. The high embankment of Fort Anderson had been thrown up across the site of old Brunswick Town, which had seen its last military invasion when Cornwallis had set fire to the place in 1776. Now, during the short Federal siege of Fort Anderson, Confederate dead and wounded were laid out within the roofless walls of St. Philips Church. It was foregone that Federal strength on sea and land would roll up the Lower Cape Fear, obliterating Fort Anderson on the way. Wilmington was entered on February 23. Blockade-running days were ended. The edge of hunger bit into the armies of Lee and Joe Johnston.

•

The United States recovered a thousand tons of iron from Fort Fisher, remnants of the fifty thousand shot and shell it had expended to occupy the site. General Whiting died from his wounds in a Yankee prison in New York harbor. To his West Point comrades his fight beyond the call of duty at Fort Fisher had expiated that strange indecision to move against Butler at Drewry's Bluff.

Former Colonel William Lamb, C.S.A., survived into a peaceful old age. But he never forgave Braxton Bragg.

•

The Federal officer in command of the mopping up of the Lower Cape Fear was General Schofield. One of his first acts after occupying Wilmington was to send an army tug, with the Stars and Stripes flying at the masthead, to bear news of the fall of Fort Fisher up the Cape Fear to Fayetteville. There the tug docked to the cheers of men in blue uniforms lining the bank—the recently arrived troops of William Tecumseh Sherman.

# 8 : The March Through Fayetteville

Two armies invaded the Cape Fear Valley, Cornwallis in 1781, Sherman in 1865. Each struggle was between kinsmen, Englishmen against Englishmen, then Americans against Americans, leaving deeper moral wounds than any foreign army could have inflicted. Cornwallis left behind him that hatred between Loyalists and Patriots which sank the people into the decades of poverty and isolation of the "Rip Van Winkle State." Sherman's fifty-mile swath of destruction across the valley swept away all means of industry and caused many a once prosperous farmer to begin the long Reconstruction period with a heifer-drawn plow, a tight belt, and a bitter heart.

The grandsons of the Loyalist Scots and the Patriot planters had made their own peace. The 1850s had brought public schools, the Plank Road, the Iron Horse. Tar Heels had become one people, just in time for Secession to divide them again. Sherman, like Cornwallis before him, supposed that, once the nettle of South Carolina was grasped, there would be the balm of North Carolina sympathy for his cause. It is extraordinary how these able commanders deceived themselves.

Each paused below the North Carolina border to issue declarations of amity. Cornwallis banned all harassment of civilians, and —declaring North Carolinians entitled to the rights of Englishmen—bade them join his forces. Sherman noted how reluctantly North Carolina had left the Union and counted on Union sympathizers to see to it that his army would not be bedeviled on its march across the State to Virginia. If there would be no hostilities and no bridge burnings, Sherman promised to hold a leash on his foragers and "bummers."

Granted the self-interested sincerity of both men in wanting to avoid harassment of their marching columns, each had let loose uncontrollable dogs of war. Cornwallis had countenanced the bands of Tory guerrillas ranging his flanks to pillage and murder. Sherman on the long march through Georgia and South Carolina had subsisted 60,000 men and 13,000 animals on what his foragers could steal from pastures, barns, pantries, and smokehouses—or could discover by probing bayonets in any suspiciously new-turned earth. This living on the countryside, Sherman held, was as old as war. Foragers under officer command were forbidden to enter households, and sometimes they did so refrain. "Sherman's bummers" were something else.

The bummers deserted the line of march to form marauding bands, illicitly; yet who would report a man with hams and turkeys swung over a stolen mule? If he contributed to the stewpan, the loot in his bulging pockets might be overlooked.

At the South Carolina town of Cheraw, Sherman's staff, mellowed by fine old wines (mistakenly sent there from Charleston for safekeeping), heard from Sherman the new softer policy toward civilians to be put into effect at the North Carolina border. General Slocum, in field command, issued the order:

All officers and soldiers of this command are reminded that North Carolina was one of the last states that passed the ordinance of secession . . . The act never met the approval of the great mass of the people. It should not be assumed that the inhabitants are enemies of our Government . . . you must prevent any wanton destruction of property, or any unkind treatment of citizens.

It was far too late. The march from Atlanta to the sea had begun the looting and burnings. Sherman's feeling against South Carolina as the mother of Secession—conjoined with his conviction that total war was the short cut to peace—had slackened his reins on foragers and bummers alike.

But now the dreadful crossing of South Carolina swamps was behind them. Along the high ridges facing no immediate enemy, a schoolboy hilarity broke out. One band of foragers, while awaiting the main column, dressed themselves in antiquated uniforms filched from plantation attic trunks. Their leader, sporting Revolutionary attire, rode his mule in review, waving a plumed hat at the head of his command—consisting of one cow, one mule and two horses—ridden postillion and hauling a family carriage heaped with hams, bacon, and sweet potatoes.

Foragers were the darlings of the troops. They left camp at dawn and ranged seven miles ahead, spread out with an eye for both barnyards and enemy patrols. Confederate officers acknowledged their usefulness to Sherman as an advance cavalry screen.

The bummers were no one's favorites. Their gifts of stolen food sat heavily on the conscience. The Confederate cavalry caught them occasionally and left them with slit throats by the side of the road for Federal columns to come upon. Notes were passed between Sherman and Wade Hampton in the style of: You kill one of my men taken prisoner and I'll kill two of yours.

There it stood when Sherman crossed the Pee Dee and entered the piney woods between Rockingham and Fayetteville. By that time, if a Union sympathizer had waved the Star Spangled Banner from his veranda, it is likely that bummers would have been behind the house stealing his chickens.

•

To shorten the strung-out line, the roads were given over to the wheels of artillery, ambulances, and wagons. Cavalry rode on the flanks; infantry slogged along the road verges. On caissons stood tethered gamecocks, victors in the pit over opponents now gone to the stewpans. Ahead, the bummers, finding no farms to loot in the North Carolina piney woods, touched matches to the turpentine sap caught in cavities cut in the longleaf pine. At once the blaze swept up the scarified trunks. Smoke in the ceiling of branches formed a black canopy shot with perpendicular flames. At one creek a thousand resin barrels melted into a lavalike flow which burned away all bridges below. The Lumber River, in spate from days of torrential rain, silenced the quips of the regimental wits in favor of the grunts of the engineers laying down corduroy roads. By the light of fat-pine fires the army passed waist-deep to solid ground and the plank road to Fayetteville.

•

The day Sherman took Fayetteville, March 10, 1865, was one month before Lee surrendered to Grant at Appomattox Courthouse. Only the last moves remained to be played on the checkerboard, which by now had shrunk from the width of half a continent to the central areas of Virginia and North Carolina. Grant before Richmond was the anvil and Sherman the descending hammer. The only military question left was whether Lee could evade Grant and join the Confederacy's only remaining army in movement, that of Lieutenant General Joseph E. Johnston, in order that their combined forces might have strength to attack Sherman.

As in the last phase of the Revolution, when Cornwallis exhausted his strength by fighting up and down the length of the Cape Fear, the last two battles of Sherman's campaign were to be fought in that same territory. The difference was that the opponent of Cornwallis, Nathanael Greene, had fresh Continental reserves at his bidding; Cornwallis none. The Confederacy in those final weeks was in the plight of Cornwallis.

Joe Johnston, put in command a month before, had the survivors of his Army of the Tennessee, the Corps of Lieutenant General

William J. Hardee, the divisions of Beauregard and Bragg, and his cavalry under Lieutenant General Wade Hampton, a total effective force of 30,000. This would diminish in the coming weeks. But the 60,000 Union invaders who crossed into North Carolina during the first week in March would, by the time of Appomattox, total 88,000.

Joe Johnston's hope was to catch one of Sherman's advancing columns, defeat it and turn against another one. Sherman's habit of advancing on parallel roads lent some color to the hope. So Johnston summoned Bragg and Hoke from the coast, waited with his Army of the Tennessee, and assigned to Hardee the task of impeding Sherman by falling back slowly before him.

Sherman's ambition was to sweep through North Carolina and join Grant in time for what now loomed as Lee's inevitable surrender. Parched corn had replaced bacon in Lee's fry pans. There were desertions, many by soldiers frantic at the thought of their families caught in Sherman's line of march. But that skilled reader of people's fears was to be delayed by the unusual rainfall (known on the Cape Fear as "Sherman's fresh") and by noncooperative Tar Heels.

"The city of Fayetteville," one of his officers was to complain, "was offensively rebellious."

●

Horse-borne troops are now one with the ages. No more will the centaur-cavalryman answer the bugle call to stables, currycomb by the numbers, get bitten in the rear while examining a hoof, curse the stubborn brutes at drill and love them at full-gallop eyes-right to the guidon. No more will the descending saber strike the foe or, as likely, sever the rider's own horse's head. That particular form of human joy in madness has gone, and with it the gay blade who assumed that his being a cavalryman gave an advantage in affairs of the heart.

Cornwallis had his rakehell cavalry arm in Banastre Tarleton. Sherman's horse-borne brigadier, Judson Kilpatrick, was known to his troopers as "Don Juan," or, in less envious mood, as "Little Kil." It was he whose cavalry rode advance to Sherman, he whose troopers chased the last Confederates out of Fayetteville and in the process almost captured Lieutenant General Wade Hampton himself.

Confusion reigned in the streets of Fayetteville that day. A cavalry engagement in the town's streets became that obvious show of Tar Heel hostility which canceled Sherman's promise not to harass civilians. On one road running north a Confederate cavalry column found itself joined for the moment by horsemen in blue.

Little Kil took solace for these rigors by using the twilight moments before the night's encampment to ride in the carriage of a beautiful woman who had shared his dangers all the way from South Carolina. A Confederate prisoner, detailed to walk alongside her carriage, had the opportunity to share vicariously in this twilight moment, but was shooed away when the couple entered their night's bivouac, the Charles Monroe farmhouse.

Wade Hampton learned of Kilpatrick's hideaway. He laid plans for a dawn capture, placing Wheeler's cavalrymen in the woods, dismounted and with reins in hand. A swamp in back of the Monroe house was to be crossed by Confederates in force. Little Kil, confident in the presence of his own troopers, came out onto the veranda at next morning's first light, in slippers and underwear, with a yawn for the new day and a slapping of arms against the March chill. Next moment the quiet was shattered by pounding hooves and Rebel yells. The Union cavalry general beat a dismounted retreat into the swamp.

The Confederate attack went askew. The riders in the rear could not find their way through the swamp. Yankee troopers sprang into action. The detail assigned to capture Kilpatrick had for second prize the lady herself, come out in her nightdress in alarm at bullets whizzing through her bedroom. A Confederate cavalier dismounted and led her to the safety of a ditch.

Kilpatrick, restored to the semblance of a general, joined in the rally which drove Wheeler's force from the field. Men on both

sides were killed or wounded in what, on the records, was known
as the engagement at Monroe's Cross-Roads but which among the
troopers was celebrated as "Kilpatrick's Shirt-tail Skeedaddle."
Don Juan himself, in the fraternizing days after the war, told a
Confederate opponent that duty had brought him out on the veranda to see that his horses—at one hundred yards distance—
were being properly fed. The Reb laughed.

•

Four years before Miss Alice Campbell had watched the honored
old Fayetteville Independent Light Infantry march off to the
War. She shed tears of joy when, after their first battle, they returned to parade under a banner spelling out in jets of gas:
WELCOME HEROES OF BETHEL. She observed the forming of new
companies: Plow Boys, Scotch Tigers, Starr's Battery. She and
other ladies untrimmed their own bonnets to decorate the soldiers'
brimmed hats with a gold band and two black plumes. For four
years she had woven socks and gloves, cut up carpets for soldiers'
blankets, prepared boxes of eatables, written letters, and waited.
Then: "on the 11th of March, Sherman, with his hordes of de-
praved and lawless men, came upon us like swarms of bees, bringing sorrow and desolation in their pathway."
Wrote Miss Alice:

> Every yard and every house was teeming with the bummers, who
> went into our homes—no place was sacred; they even went into
> our trunks and bureau drawers, stealing everything they could find.
> . . . One of my friends had a hen setting, and she took her watch
> and other valued jewels and hid them in the nest, under the hen—
> they did not remain long concealed, for they soon found them and
> enjoyed the joke. They pulled elegant pianos into the yard with
> valuable furniture, china, cut glass, and everything that was dear
> to the heart, even old family portraits, and chopped them up with
> axes—rolled barrels of flour and molasses into the parlors, and
> poured out their contents on beautiful velvet carpets. . . . The
> crowning point to this terrible nightmare of destruction was the

burning and battering down of our beautiful and grandly magnificent Arsenal, which was our pride, and the showplace of our town.

The advance guard of pillaging bummers was held in check when Sherman placed Major General Absolom Baird in command of the town. Baird put dwellings under the guard of young Yankee officers who in most cases sympathized with the victims of bummer outrages, and in some cases won the families' gratitude. But destruction of shops, factories, tanneries and blacksmithies was army policy. The Arsenal itself was a military objective. Sherman had chosen the Fayetteville route so that he might destroy this supplier of Lee's munitions.

In antebellum years the Arsenal walks and drives through evergreens and oak groves had been Fayetteville's family outing grounds. The cream-colored brick residences were sinecures for superannuated bachelor officers, who entertained pleasantly and had few duties other than guard mounts. After John Brown's raid, the Harpers Ferry machinery and guns were sent to Fayetteville and a Federal detachment placed in the Arsenal. The ladies of the town called on the officers' wives. Picnics continued on the Arsenal grounds.

In the Spring of '61, some weeks before formal Secession, a squirrel-rifle regiment of Fayetteville men, boys, and grandfathers took over the Arsenal from its commanding officer, Lieutenant De Lagnal. He put up a fine show of surrender in the face of overwhelming odds, and, as soon as he could, resigned to accept a Confederate Army commission.

During all the war years, Deep River coal and iron had been fused by a large work force into a highly important supply of Confederate arms. Sherman's engineers now stripped off the woodwork and battered the cream-colored walls with railroad rails swung from an X framework. A cheer went up for each collapsing roof. A final conflagration lighted the whole town. What remained were millions of bricks which Uncle Sam later sold at bargain rates for the rebuilding of Fayetteville.

•

On the Sunday morning of Sherman's four-day stay at Fayetteville, the army tug *Davidson*, sent by General Schofield from Wilmington, blew a triumphant whistle at the Cape Fear landing.
The army and its general alike roared a welcome. Said Sherman:
"The effect was electric, and no one can realize the feeling unless
like us he had been cut off from all communications with friends."

Of the eight steamers lying at Fayetteville wharves only two
were in commission, the rickety *North Carolina* and the fine new
paddle-wheeler *Hurt*. Sherman sent them downriver with Union
refugees.

At Monroe's Cross-Roads, history had dropped the curtain on
the scene of Little Kil's light-o'-love, in her own peculiar battle
dress, taking shelter in a ditch under the protective custody of the
gallant Confederate cavalryman. Speculation, with some flavor of
fact, has it that she rejoined the Union and was one of those sent
by Sherman to Wilmington on the *Hurt*, doubtless with an outside
cabin.

A more serious refugee problem was the host of slaves following in Sherman's train. The Negro grapevine had spread the word
that Lincoln's liberty was passing by. For days slave families had
crossed fields and come out of woods, old and young, carrying
their goods, on foot, in farm wagons and creaking old carriages,
mounted on mules and horses, and trailed by hounds and yard-
dogs. The patriarch of one family had swung four small grandchildren, two to a side, in bags attached to his mule's saddle
blanket. This happy invention took on. Tent flies permitted multiple papoose suspensions. General Slocum observed one mule of
which nothing could be seen except head, tail and feet: "all else
being covered by the black woolly heads and bright shining eyes
of the little darkies. Occasionally a cow served, furnishing rations
as well as transportation for the babies."

They were a military burden to Sherman. In this month of
heavy rains it was imperative to move pontoons forward as soon

as the army had crossed, yet, after every river and swamp was passed, there were the thousands of blacks crowding for their turn over the pontoons. And they were hungry. At Fayetteville Sherman reckoned he had twenty thousand extra mouths to feed. He detailed two hundred troopers to escort them to Wilmington. In high spirits, with shouts and songs, the straggling train disappeared down the river road to anticipated freedom.

On his retreat from Fayetteville, Joe Johnston had burned the old Clarendon Bridge over the Cape Fear. It was a military act, yet Sherman had said in advance, "If the bridge is destroyed we will deal heavily with the town." It meant for Sherman at least two more days of delay in joining Grant. During those two days his destruction crews ranged below Rockfish Creek and above Lower Little River. The plank roads were torn up to feed their campfires. No village smithy or foundry escaped, so that iron tools, without which farming stops, would be lacking for years to come. In town, his officers rocked on a hotel veranda, sipping Madeira from the cellar of the Rebel editor Edward Jones Hale, watching flames destroy his *Fayetteville Observer* across the street. Major George W. Nichols, U.S.A., must have missed this scene while busy jotting down his impression that the Federal forces were "painfully disappointed in looking for the Union sentiment in North Carolina about which so much has been said."

# 9 : *End of Sherman's March*

Three hundred thousand Yankees lie dead in Southern dust;
We got three hundred thousand before they conquered us.
They died of Southern fever, of Southern shell and shot;
And I wish it was three million instead of what we got.
——Unreconstructed Rebel

On March 15, 1865, Sherman's army crossed the Cape Fear at
Fayetteville on two pontoon bridges. To hide his intention, he led
one force up the King's Highway toward Raleigh and sent another
on the northeasterly road to Goldsboro. Anything which split
Sherman's juggernaut was a boon to Joe Johnston. He ordered
Hardee's Corps to confront Sherman's column, while he himself
made rendezvous with Beauregard and Bragg to face the Union
wing marching toward Goldsboro.

Kilpatrick's cavalry, riding in advance of Sherman, came on
Hardee entrenched across the flat land between the Cape Fear
and the Black rivers, four miles below the town of Averasboro.
Sherman ordered an attack for the next day, the sixteenth.

The Battle of Averasboro receives scant mention in the record
of Sherman's engagements. It was a delaying action by Hardee's
6,000 men, the outcome certain to be a Confederate retreat. After
the day's fighting there were 108 Confederate and 77 Federal
dead on the field. Hardee retired during the night. Sherman, ending his feint toward Raleigh, was free to reunite his columns to

confront Joe Johnston at the hamlet of Bentonville, thirty miles east.

The fighting at Averasboro produced the curious phenomenon of a commanding general lolling in his tent, almost beyond range of spent Minié balls, receiving an occasional dispatch from the scene of fighting yet content to let his officers conduct the affair while he sat in cross-legged contemplation. It bothered his Headquarters Guard officer, Lieutenant James Cox of the Ohio Sharp-Shooters. It was Cox's conviction that his general should be in there giving orders. Sherman remained imperturbably inactive.

His phlegm was counterbalanced by the passionate reaction of a civilian caught under fire in a ravine two miles north of Sherman's tent. Janie Smith was watching her family's plantation and mansion house being desecrated by the hated Yankees. She had eight brothers in Confederate uniform.

●

Twelve years before, Frederick Law Olmstead had passed the Smith plantations on his coach trip from Raleigh to Fayetteville. He must have missed the Smith houses in the dark. Had he, during that part of the journey when he went afoot, passed by some of the turpentine workers' sorry log cabins and knocked on the door of one of the three Smith houses, he would have been welcomed into a prosperous planter home, three stories of heart-of-pine beams and stringers, longleaf siding, a ballroom the width of the house, hams in the smokehouse, hospitality at the door. Had he hit upon the first of the three Smith houses, Janie, aged six, would have curtsied to him.

But in 1865 Janie had graduated from the young ladies' seminary at Charlotte, and had grown from a child to a woman during the Confederacy. There is a wartime photographic montage of Janie and her eight brothers. She is in the center, small toque sitting on her dark curls, eyes of a dove but a straight-line mouth. The brothers encircle her, five of the older ones with reflective stern eyes above beards ranging from Walt Whitman to Napoleon

III. The top three smooth-cheeked teen-agers glare defiantly at camera and the absentee Yankee foe, the very top boy with bayonet at the ready and his eyes under the black plumed hat those of a hawk.

On March 15 skirmishing began in the rain. From Janie's Uncle John's house farthest downriver of the Smith plantations, the family were ordered into the trenches. There they remained until afternoon when they retreated, wet, muddy, and hungry, to Janie's home. In the dreary drizzle of the next dawn the battle began with a Yankee charge which captured the first line of Hardee's trenches. Janie's house was taken over as a Confederate hospital.

In a letter written afterward on pieces of wallpaper and old envelopes, Janie described her part in the battle to her friend Jane Robeson of Bladen County:

One half of the house was prepared for the soldiers . . . Every barn was full and under every shed and trees the tables were carried for amputating the limbs. I just felt like my heart would break when I would see our brave men rushing into the battle and then coming back so mangled . . . the blood lay in puddles in the grove, the groans of the dying and complaints of those undergoing amputation was horrible. The painful impression has scarred my heart . . . We were kept busy making and rolling bandages when orders came to leave home . . . imagine us all and Uncle John's family trudging through the rain and mud down to a ravine near the river; each one with a shawl, blanket and basket of provisions . . . the firing was right over us. We could hear the commands of the officers and the groans and shrieks of the wounded. A line of battle was formed in front of us . . . one of the vedettes saw my white flag (my handkerchief on a pole) and came to us. I accosted him: "Are you one of our men or a Yankee?" "I'm a Reb, Mam." "Can't you go and report to the commanding officer that the hillside is lined with women and children he sent here for protection, and the line of battle over there will destroy us?" "I'll do all I can for you," was the gallant reply and in a short time we were ordered home.

Her experiences turned the gently bred Janie into a spitfire. Her uncle's house she described as "ruined with the blood of the Yankee wounded . . . The scamps left our piano, used Aunt Mary's as an amputation table . . . They took a special delight in burying the stinking carcasses right at everybody's door. I wish every foot of Cumberland County were used in that way."

●

William Tecumseh Sherman's passing left that kind of language in his train. He had ridden out of Columbia, South Carolina, through a lane of hisses. Southern editors called him ravisher, incendiary, thief with hyena's soul lurking in a foul mass of corruption. He never apologized for his conduct of total war. To Halleck at Savannah he had explained: "We are not only fighting hostile armies, but a hostile people, and must make old and young, rich and poor, feel the hard hand of war, as well as their organized armies." Sherman at the time had South Carolinians in mind. His attempt to exempt Tar Heels brought no surcease of hostility.

The man in the tent behind the battle lines at Averasboro—while Janie Smith was learning a new depth of hatred toward him—must have been using his reverie to plan ahead. That is what generals do, and Sherman was on the verge of momentous action. Joe Johnston's remnants of three Confederate armies would not be able to withstand him. His long march was coming to an end in certain victory. There would be terms of peace to decide . . . Was Sherman reviewing the things he had done to arouse Southern hate, and what his own attitude should be toward Southerners in defeat?

Janie Smith and Uncle John and all those under fire on the hillside would have no difficulty in answering: a victorious Sherman would remain the ravaging hyena. And yet within the month Sherman would be offering Joe Johnston terms of surrender which, had Washington let them stand, might have saved the South from the terrible Reconstruction times ahead, from political anarchy, from Federal armies of occupation.

There are markers along the course of Sherman's career which help explain this paradox. His early adult associations were all Southern. Among those who graduated with him in the West Point Class of 1840 were Jubal Early, Braxton Bragg, and Pierre Gustave Toutant Beauregard. His first six years of service were spent at Southern posts. An officer's uniform was a passport to society. In Saint Augustine his praise of the beauty of Spanish ladies led his fiancée, Ellen Ewing, to advise him to leave the army and enter a religious career. In Wilmington he spent three days at parties celebrating the marriage of Governor Dudley's daughter.

He married his Northern Ellen, resigned his commission, and spent a dozen years in feckless attempts at a fortune. In 1859 army friends got him the presidency of the Louisiana Seminary of Learning and Military Academy (now Louisiana State University) where he expressed a longing for his wife and himself to "drive our tent pins and pick out a magnolia under which to sleep the long sleep." The firing on Fort Sumter broke into this fantasy. He said good-by to his faculty and students, with whom he was on terms of respect and affection, and turned his back on the South.

He disliked Abolitionists: "I would not if I could abolish or modify slavery." What troubled him deeply was the breakup of the Union. He paced the floor, telling a Seminary professor friend how tragic Secession would be: "I will do no act, breathe no word, think no thought hostile to the Government of the United States."

So he left, torn between Southern friendships and hatred of Secession. The inward struggle gave him a bad start as a Union officer, smote him with unmilitary self-doubts and hesitation. Then at Shiloh he distinguished himself, and there he resolved the dichotomy by a decision that a dragged-out war between armies was crueler in the long run; that total war—in which enemy morale and supply would suffer through devastation of their homeland—would end the agony more quickly, and so be more humane.

When Sherman was a day's march west of Atlanta, about to attack, he received a letter from a girl he had known in his bachelor days at Charleston. Now Mrs. Annie Gilman Bower of Baltimore, she appealed to his former friendship with herself and her family, unwilling to believe that he would ravage the country of those he had once loved. Sherman wrote her a thoughtful reply:

> . . . little did I dream when I knew you . . . that I should control a vast army pointing, like a swarm of Alaric, towards the plains of the South.
>
> Why, oh, why is this? If I know my own heart, it beats as warmly as ever toward those kind and generous families that greeted us with such warm hospitality in days long past but still present in memory; and today were any or all of our cherished circle, their children, or even their children's children, to come to me as of old, the stern feeling of duty and conviction would melt as snow before the genial sun . . . And yet they call me barbarian, vandal and a monster and all the epithets that language can invent that are significant of malignity and hate. All I pretend to say, on earth as in heaven, man must submit to an arbiter. He must not throw off his allegiance to his Government or his God without just cause and reason . . . Had we declined battle America would have sunk . . . I would not subjugate the South in the sense so offensively assumed, but I would make every citizen of the land obey the law, submit to the same that we do—no more, no less—our equals and not our superiors . . . I hope when the clouds of anger and passion are dispersed, and truth emerges bright and clear, you and all who knew me in the early years, will not blush that we were once close friends.

He did nothing, however, to dispel the clouds of anger and passion by relaxing his policy of total war. One of his own chaplains described the bummers as "wild young men amongst the drafted people . . . deserters from the Confederate Army, refugees from the South, bounty jumpers, shirks, butternuts and substitutes, many of whom are the scrapings of society. The 300 added to this

Regiment, together with the whiskey rations, have demoralized
this command to a shameful extent."

When he entered North Carolina, Sherman himself thought
there should be an end to this. He issued an order that foragers
were "to be regulated and systematized, so as not to degenerate
into common robbers." That they already were and would remain,
to the eternal damnation of Sherman in the South.

The markers in Sherman's career pointing toward his generous
terms of surrender offered Joe Johnston are discoverable, lying in
the rubble of his ruined cities. To the City Council of Atlanta he
said:

> But, my dear sirs, when peace does come, you may call upon me
> for everything. Then I will share with you the last cracker, and
> watch with you to shield your houses and families against dangers
> from any quarter.

In Savannah he issued an order to shoot down on the spot anyone caught "in unsoldier like deeds." It was he who suggested that
50,000 bushels of captured rice be sold in the North and the
money be used to buy more necessary food for the city. A fore-
shadowing of his political thinking was his abortive move to take
Georgia out of the war, have it elect members to the national
Congress and resume its functions in the Union.

The man on horseback did not make public his private emo-
tions. To his wife he wrote in 1863: "Indeed do I wish I had been
killed long since." And to her a year later he said he had begun "to
regard the death and mangling of a couple of thousand men as a
small affair, a kind of morning dash—and it may well be that we
become so hardened."

•

One month after the Battle of Averasboro the 700-mile march
ended. At Bentonville, March 19-21, Sherman faced Joe Johnston,
Bragg, and Beauregard for the last time. The fighting was as cruel

as that in the Wilderness. Johnston, without the reserves to carry it through, broke off the fight.

President Lincoln called Grant and Sherman to meet with him on the steamer *River Queen,* at anchor off City Point on the James. Aside from assurances given Lincoln by his generals that victory was at hand on both fronts, no discussion of surrender terms was held on the *River Queen.* Sherman on April 5 was back at Goldsboro. Here he learned that Richmond had fallen. He ordered a march to Raleigh, still hoping to join Grant: but on April 12 the news came of surrender at Appomattox. He set off after Johnston, now retreated toward the Haw River, and ordered no further destruction of private property or railroads.

On April 14 he received from Johnston a request for a cessation of hostilities and a meeting between them on the seventeenth. On his way out of camp on the day of the meeting, a soldier handed him a telegram that Lincoln had been assassinated. He withheld the news during his first talk with Joe Johnston, held at Mrs. Bennett's farmhouse on the road between Durham and Hillsboro. As commander of the largest Confederate force now in the field, General Johnston offered to surrender his own and all other Confederate forces, providing the terms were acceptable.

Sherman took two days to draw up the terms. His draft contained the usual military requirements, then went on to make concessions which in Sherman's mind conformed in spirit to his promise to the Atlanta City Council—a sharing of bread once peace was restored.

These clauses appeared:

> Recognition by the Executive of the United States of Southern States on their taking the oath prescribed by the Constitution.
>
> Re-establishment of the Federal Courts.
>
> Restoration of personal property and political rights.
>
> No disturbance of any of the people by reason of the late war.

Both Johnston and Sherman signed the document, with the saving paragraph that, if their respective principals would fulfill the terms, they would promptly carry them out.

The political lid blew off in Washington. Admit Rebels back into the Union without punishment? Five days after Mr. Lincoln's murder? Secretary of War Stanton repudiated Sherman's terms and ordered him to make the same arrangements as Grant's with Lee at Appomattox. Grant, fond of Sherman, came to Raleigh to break the news in person that he himself had had orders from Lincoln not to touch on politics in any surrender document. Crestfallen, Sherman informed Joe Johnston of his error. On April 26 Johnston surrendered, was given the Army of Northern Virginia's rights for officers to retain side arms and all officers and men to ride their mounts home for a late spring plowing.

Johnston had a store of minted silver intended for aiding the escape of high officers, President Davis included, in case of defeat. But Davis was well on his way to Georgia. Johnston ordered that $38,000 be counted out to his men. Each one got a silver dollar and fifteen cents. At Averasboro, on his way home, one of Johnston's veterans died, in his pocket a silver dollar on which an awl and hammer had pounded out his name and his home, a small town in Mississippi.

# 10 : Decline and Fall of Averasboro

A river is more than water flowing between two banks. It is the basin which it drains, the rain seeping through forest humus to join in subterranean runnels and bubble up from under a rock or on the slope of a meadow. It is the waterfall and the pool below, the frog on the bank and the brown snake that swallows him. It is the surface rain eroding the dirt to stain the flowing river and sink in slack water into mud flats. The river is a changeling with the seasons. A February ribbon boils into a March spate, destruction bound.

Any river owning a wide basin has great antiquity, having been born of the mists of the earth's first atmosphere and forever after being subject to the power of gravity drawing it like a whiplash over the width of the basin, carving rock obstructions, churning through mud and sand in an insensate drive to find that lowest place, to go by the shortest route to its mother the sea. When a river is very old it remains in its fixed course, owning only variations of dappled sunshine or moon quiet, edged with the light green reflections of spring or laced under the banks with darkly mirrored winter limbs. It is hard to conceive it as young whirling water carving its way through primordial earth miles away from its present mapped and accepted bed.

The drainage system which came to be named the Cape Fear in its youth molded the slopes which sustain the hardwood timber reserve; deposited the alluvial soil where the wheat and tobacco and collards grow. The milk of departed cows was transmuted out of river meadow grass to nourish the ancestors of the old farmer leaning on the fence to observe with pride a new calf. The people of the basin were creatures of the river, originally, even if the stream is now hidden and forgotten behind its high hedge of willow, gums, and sycamores.

The Cape Fear changed men, but men failed to change the river to fit their needs. It served the first arrivals as the highway to lands of their own, the earthly paradise flamboyantly praised in Scotch and English broadsides. Then, staying the same, it became too small for use. It remained a periauger and raft stream, while schooners were penetrating the Hudson's inland empire. When ships in the transatlantic trade grew beyond 300-ton registry, their skippers preferred Northern harbors to the Frying Pan Shoals.

Three generations tried different devices to bypass the mere sixty-seven-foot drop to Fayetteville from the forks of the Haw and Deep. Each saw the river contemptuously hit one telling blow before returning to its course. After these disasters many of the losers abandoned their farms and headed west or south. The 1860 census showed 300,000 born Tar Heels living in other States. Those who remained to fight the Civil War learned from it that living solely off the products of the soil left them at a sad disadvantage in conflict with the farming and industrial North.

The flood called "Sherman's Fresh"—in mockery of the human disaster which arrived simultaneously on the Cape Fear—marked both an end of an era and the end of the Cape Fear as a vital force in the life of the valley. In that spring of 1865 all the rivers of the Southern coastal plain were swollen with unrelenting rains. The Haw and the Deep gathered to themselves the piedmont rains and brought them clashing together at Mermaid Point. Here on the high ground between the meeting streams was Haygood, in its first state as a ghost town. The last of her river steamers was grounded, her cabin for a while to be a shoemaker's shop until summer people no longer returned to the houses they had built during Haygood's brief boom. The land speculators had absorbed their losses. The veranda sagged on Ambrose Ramsey's old tavern where Cornwallis had stayed until a bridge could be built over the Deep for his retreating army. The 200 acres of Mermaid's Point itself, piously reserved "for orphans" but actually devoted to a race track and cockfighting pits, had already sprouted the saplings which would eventually return it to wilderness.

Sherman's Fresh boiled mightily over Buckhorn Falls, smoothing out all trace of canals, locks and dams. The brown water swept in a long S bend around Lillington, the new county seat of a new Harnett County. At Averasboro, Sherman's Fresh rolled past its namesake, an Achilles moping in his tent as Janie Smith, Uncle John, and the rest of the family sat on their rainy hillside, not much comforted by blankets and picnic baskets while the whine of Yankee bullets and shouts to charge their position rang in their ears.

A mile below, the flood was joined by Little River at whose mouth the growth of a century covered the foundations of Choeffenington, another victim of the river's inability to support the hopes of its founders. Whether or not the tongue-twisting name contributed to its demise, Choeffenington in the decade before the Revolution had the gristmill, frame houses, log courthouse, and jail signifying its dignity as county seat of Cumberland County. The trading post of Cross Creek—being below the last of the river rifts—captured the courthouse in 1765 and left Choeffenington to rot.

At Fayetteville the Fresh lapped up Person Street, dousing the last embers of riverside farmhouses fired by Sherman's bummers. It cleared away the wreckage of the Clarendon Bridge, flowed a mile wide across the low-lying east shore and, on the hillocks which dot it, isolated small communities of barnyard fowl, refugee possums and racoons, and all the humans of the submerged neighborhoods.

The plantation homes on the high west bank, from Fayetteville to Wilmington, were safe enough, what very few were left of them. And at Wilmington, Sherman's Fresh met its match in the wide salt waters of the estuary. It still had the power, by depositing the silt from the hillsides of a score of counties, to seal further the doom of two more ghost towns, Charles Town at the mouth of Old Town Creek and Old Brunswick Town. Politics had a share in the destruction of both. Charles Town had died nearly two centuries before when the Lords Proprietors vacillated in their support of rival colonizing groups. Brunswick Town was destroyed in prestige by Governor Burrington, physically by Lord Cornwallis. Yet, had both towns escaped politics and war, both eventually would have been strangled by the river's inexorable deposit of silt on the Flats. Ships of the eighteenth century had anchored within voice call of their waterfronts. By the nineteenth century their former harbors were shallow extensions of their rice-field bottomlands.

•

Averasboro survived Sherman's Fresh. Next to Wilmington and Fayetteville it was the Cape Fear's largest town. Once it had advanced not unreasonable claims to be the capital of the colony. Before the Revolution it had been a crossroads of highway and river travel. A first gristmill had attracted settlers weary of pounding corn in a hollowed tree trunk. Wherever a gristmill brings gossipers together, a tavern is sure to follow. John Martinlear's ferry across the Cape Fear opened up the west bank farm trade to Averasboro. Poleboatmen ended their hard upriver journey at Averasboro, and were ready for fun and frolic.

Averasboro developed two social strata, the rough and tough boatmen and the church folk. Unhappily it is not the decorous but the violators of decorum whose deeds are remembered. George Miller's fame, outlasting the town itself, rested on his ability to

butt the heads out of rosin barrels in practice for ramlike on-
slaughts on the midriffs of human opponents. One casualty of the
town's love of fighting was the Reverend William Byrd. An argument with a parishioner over interpretation of the Word degener-
ated into a brawl in which the tip of the parson's nose was bitten
off. Brought before the Association for conduct unbefitting the
cloth, he was exonerated on the ground that anyone with a record
of only one fight in three years of Averasboro residence was to be
commended for his pious restraint.

The river dominated the town. Profits from its trade built the
churches and the Academy, laid out squares of residences and
stores. At Stewart's Tavern local and outside investors speculated
in river-frontage land. The destroying freshet of 1859 was followed too quickly by the Civil War for Averasboro to realize that
its river trade was ended. The young men volunteered or were
drafted. The fighting was in Virginia or the far West. Averasboro
scraped through the four years, and to those who came back in '65
the shaded streets seemed about the same. But both Joe Wheeler's
cavalrymen and Sherman's bummers had swept across the town's
trading area. There were no cash crops or horses to draw wagons
to Averasboro stores. Their agility had saved the long-snouted
woods hogs from foragers and left a little stringy bacon for
Averasboro. But the forges were destroyed and the iron was missing to shape the anvil on which to beat out the plowshares.

Rural North Carolina had returned to the isolation and poverty
which had marked the Rip Van Winkle State after the Revolution.
Averasboro, half its young men dead or missing, fended for itself
without much heed to the forces contending at Raleigh and at
Washington between readmission of the South to the Union or
punishing the South for her defection.

What brought this home to Averasboro was Federal Military
Occupation and the Ku Klux Klan, organized by General Ned
Forrest in Tennessee and spread South-wide. This ghoulish notice
was tacked on a tree:

K  K  K
Attention! First hour! In the Mist!
At the Flash! Come. Come. Come!!!
Retribution is impatient! The grave yawns!
The spectre bones rattle!
Let the doomed quake!

The barn burnings and murders of the Klan years were an echo
of the hatred between Tories and Patriots during the birth pangs
of the Republic. As in the times of Lord Cornwallis and David
Fanning, an outside army was in occupation under a policy of
restoring the loyalty of the people to the old regime. This time the
split was not only between whites; a part of the ex-slaves joined
with the Northerners of the Union League. It was these Negroes
whom the night riders meant to terrify back into obedience, they
and the whites who abetted them.

Averasboro was one of the two Klan centers of Harnett County.
Hooded and cowled "deer" stalked the night woods. One of them
forced the door of a Negro cabin and had his head split with an
ax. This was near the end of the formal Klan organization, when
General Forrest decided "Ride, Redeem and Restore Order" had
begun to slip over into violence for its own sake, the use of terror
in revenge on personal enemies.

The honorable Ned Forrest had let loose a power as irresponsi-
ble as Sherman's bummers. No order of his could halt it. At
Averasboro the necessity to hide Klan activity and membership
from Federal marshals added a fillip of danger to the night rides.

One Federal agent managed to join the Averasboro Klan. He
had gathered a list of its members, but his hooded brothers discovered what he was up to. A meeting was held in the Academy
building, with wives present. During it the informer was shot
dead in the street outside. Federal marshals surrounded the
Academy. The distance to the dead man meant a shot from a rifle.
The women were allowed to leave before the marshals ransacked

the Academy in search of the rifle, finding none. It had gone out the door under the sweeping coat of a woman, walking, if the marshals had noticed, in a stiff-legged way.

The men went straight from the meeting to saddle up and put distance between them and the informer's list. Texas was then the favorite of men who wished to lose themselves, and to Texas this particular emigration went. Many of their wives followed them. The dead and the departed outnumbered those who held on at Averasboro. These over the next few years began to move four miles east to the crossroads of Lucknow. When that town should change its name to Dunn, and the railroad was built through it, Averasboro was left to those who needed old boards for henhouses. The Academy, the churches, the tavern disappeared. Salt Mill Street was plowed up for pole beans. The fields in time became as vacant as a rug when the cardboard houses are put away after Christmas. The name Averasboro was left off the maps and survives only in connection with a Civil War engagement.

As with Haywood, Choeffenington, Charles Town, and Old Brunswick, the original rooftrees raised at Averasboro became indistinguishably mixed in the alluvial soil of the betraying river, which now flows smoothly over the stubs of the spikes which once supported the wharves where the periaugers landed.

# 11 : *The Power and the Glory Move Upstream*

Beneath these crystal waters
A maiden once did lie,
The fairest of earth's daughters,
A gem to deck the sky.

In caves of pearled enamel,
We weave a maiden's shroud
For all the foolish damsels
That dare to stray abroad.

———Anonymous Deep River ballad

During the Reconstruction years the mills of New England spun Tar Heel cotton into cloth and manufactured shoes from the hides of piedmont cattle, transmuting these raw materials into Victorian mansions, electrically lighted streets, college endowments, and oysters on the half shell. Cape Fear people stuck to hog and hominy. With the spinning mills left as blackened, roofless walls, the women returned to the treadle and bobbin of their mothers' hand looms.

One hope for industry lay in the coal and iron ore deposits along the Deep River. During the war the Fayetteville Arsenal had been supplied with iron pigs produced at a Buckhorn blast furnace by Ironmaster John Colvin. Coal from the mine at Egypt had fired the boilers of blockade-runners. Skippers of the Confederate gray ghosts, trying to steal along the beach unseen by the Federal fleet, hated the revealing black plumes of Egypt coal. But the gunmakers at Fayetteville were proud indeed of the quality of the Buckhorn iron pigs.

In 1870 a railroad car wheel from a captured Confederate train fell into the hands of George G. Lobdell, head of a Delaware plant which specialized in chilled-tread car wheels. At a time of frequent railroad wrecks caused by defective wheels, Lobdell was breaking up hundreds of flawed car wheels rather than run the risk of sending one bad one out of his plant. The quality of this Rebel car wheel began a search for its origin, which proved to be John Colvin's rude blast furnace.

Lobdell visited the red hills of Buckhorn, riding along that twenty-mile stretch where the Deep River runs east-west to join the Haw at Mermaid's Point. The land was like a stormy sea checked into immobility—too difficult for timbering, too steep for farming. Underneath it the geologic ages had churned, faulted and been shot through with fiery infusions, now cooled into deposits luring the geologist to follow their meanderings. How much of this rare iron was hidden under the hills?

Fred Genth, consulting chemist and geologist, reported to the Franklin Institute: "At Buckhorn on the Cape Fear there is a large bed of granular magnetite from which about 6,000 tons of very superior iron have been produced. The bed is between twenty and thirty feet thick. . . ."

Granular magnetite melts at a comparatively low temperature into pea-sized nodules, in effect already steel. John Colvin had proved the practicality of turning out his pigs solely by use of local materials. Wide-tired Conestoga wagons brought charcoal from kilns scattered in the woods. His lime was boated up the Cape Fear from the oystershell deposits of Tertiary Bluff below Fayetteville. When he built his blast furnace of Harnett County stone, he left apertures for the air blasts which he provided by rigging a waterwheel to operate compressed air cylinders. It was a triumph of Colvin's Scotch ingenuity, but some credit must be given the defeated men who had dug the old sluice around Buckhorn Falls. It was this sanded-up channel which Colvin and Big Henry, his man Friday, had cleared, dammed, and used to drive the air compresser.

The freshet of 1859 had ruined the lock and dam system below Buckhorn Falls, but the Deep was still navigable from a point above the blast furnace twenty miles west to McIver's Station on the railroad to Fayetteville.

George Lobdell acquired all the necessary rights and formed the Cape Fear Iron & Steel Company. Buckhorn was to be a second Pittsburgh. Turbines replaced water wheels. A cable railway took ore downhill and brought back the finished pigs for loading onto the steamer *George G. Lobdell* bound upriver for McIver's Station.

When three weeks of operations had produced 383 tons of iron, the mine boss came to Lobdell with appalling news. The ore vein had come up against the face of faulted rock. The furnace cooled. Test borings were made in all directions from the vein's end. Lobdell tramped the woods, unwilling to concede. In the end he had to, when Professor A. E. Verrill of Yale reported: "The great mass of ore at Buckhorn seems to be entirely worked out . . . abruptly cut off by two faults of the rocks . . . The Buckhorn mine may now be regarded as exhausted."

George Lobdell joined a gallant company—the eighteenth century canal builders, the diggers of locks and builders of dams, the gunpowder blasters of Smilie's Falls, the steamboat companies and the town builders—who had broken themselves against the willful strength of the Cape Fear.

The miners and the charcoal burners, the crew of the *George G. Lobdell,* and the furnace workers went back to their farms.

•

At Raleigh, Reconstruction politics threw Governor Zebulon Baird Vance out of office and replaced him with William H. Holden, who was impeached and succeeded by Zeb Vance. At Washington President Ulysses S. Grant relied too much on his friends. All this was important to North Carolina lawyers, merchants, planters, and Chapel Hill professors. The majority of Tar Heels still ran cattle and hogs, bouted with the Devil at the crossroads tavern on Saturday nights and conceded defeat at church on Sunday morning. They still square-danced to the fiddle's "Weevily Wheat" . . .

> Charlie he's the fancy man:
> Charlie he's your dandy;
> Charlie he's the very lad
> Who drank up Grover's brandy.

At school recess a line of little girls ducked under the outstretched arms and clasped hands of two players ready to descend and capture a victim:

> The needle's eye it doth supply
> The thread that runs so truly;
> Many a beau have I let go
> Because I wanted *Julie!*

Become, Julie, half of the needle's eye and catch your own victim from the living thread.

The songs Negroes had made for themselves at camp meetings and on slave quarter evenings survived into freedom, but there were also banjo-pickin' lighthearted songs:

> Me and my wife and a stump-tailed dog
> Crossed Cane River on a hickory log;
> The log did break and she fell in;
> Lost my wife and a bottle of gin.

One favorite could be taken two ways: the prattle of a flirt; an offer of innocence:

> Here I stand both fresh and fair,
> Dark brown eyes and curly hair,
> Rosy cheeks and dimpled chin,
> One little heart that beats within.

The words changed as the singer forgot his father's phrasing, or a visitor took it back home not remembering it rightly, or the song went West. One Deep River ballad, "Poor Naomi," was sung across Tennessee into Arkansas:

> Come all you good people, I'd have you draw near,
> A sorrowful story you quickly shall hear:
> A story I'll tell you about N'omi Wise
> How she was deluded by Lewis's lies.
>
> He promised to marry and use me quite well;
> But conduct contrary I sadly must tell,
> He promised to wed me at Adams's Springs,
> He promised me marriage and many fine things.
>
> I got up behind him and straightway did go
> To the banks of Deep River, where the water did flow.
> He says, "Now, Naomi, I'll tell you my mind,
> I intend here to drown you, and leave you behind."
>
> O! pity your infant and spare me my life;
> Let me go rejected and not be your wife.
> "No pity, no pity," this monster did cry,
> "In Deep River's bottom your body shall lie."

In April, 1875, the *Greensboro Patriot* published the prose version of *Poor Naomi*. The by-line credited "Charlie Vernon," pen name of the President of Trinity College, Braxton Craven. The scene of Naomi's drowning was at a waterfall on the Deep River due south of Greensboro. The murder and subsequent man hunt had been far enough back to become folk legend. Braxton Craven, hearing it at cabin hearths from old-timers, let himself as "Charlie Vernon" pull out all the stops of Victorian melodrama. But the scholar side of President Craven drew a picture of what life had been like in Naomi's Deep River neighborhood:

> A few families of nature's noblest quality lived in the vicinity
> . . . what our people call good livers, honest, hospitable and kind.
> Their farms supplied enough for their own tables, and surplus sufficient for a brisk trade with Fayetteville. The wild forest hills and immense glades afforded bountiful quantities of game, whilst Deep

River abounded with the finest fish . . . trading as a regular business was unknown, except for a few merchants. The people were somewhat rude, still, however, hospitable and kind.

Most of the settlers migrated from Pennsylvania and Virginia. Physical force was frequently necessary for self-defense. The Lewis family were tall, broad, muscular. In the manner of fighting very common at that time, viz: to lay aside all clothing but pantaloons, and then try for victory by striking with the fist, scratching, gouging and biting, a Lewis was not to be vanquished. The family were the lions of the country. Nearly all of them drank to intoxication.

Naomi Wise had early been thrown upon the cold charity of the world. Though serving as cook and sometimes as out-door hand, she was the light of the Adams's family. Her size was medium; her figure beautifully formed; her eye keen yet mild; her words soft and winning. Jonathan Lewis of Polecat Creek saw Naomi Wise and loved her . . .

The tendrils of woman's affection despise the shrubs of order and beauty to entwine closely and eternally around the high forest trees that are exposed to howling storms and the thunders of Jove. The trees may be *rough* and *crooked* but then they are *trees* . . . Naomi's young and guileless heart beat with a new and higher life . . .

Instead of going to the piano, to the dance and other such latter day inventions, youngsters then went with the ladies to milk the cows, and display their gallantry by holding away the calves while the operation was performed; they then accompanied the damsels to the spring to put away the milk, and brought back a pail of water . . .

Braxton Craven leads us to understand that Jonathan's courting of Naomi was not all that innocent. We find her pleading with tears and prayers for marriage to protect her unborn child. But Jonathan's mother thought that he might obtain the hand of Hettie Elliot, his employer's sister. Thus, writes the moralist Craven: "Money, name and station were the influences that clouded the fair prospects of innocence, opened the floodgates of evil and involved all the parties concerned in ruin."

Hoofprints from a stump by the Adams spring fitted those of Lewis's horse. Horse hairs upon the skirt in which Naomi rode were found to fit in color. A small piece torn from Lewis's coat fitted both the rent and the texture. Screams from the middle of the ford over the Deep had brought a party with lanterns. A horseman was seen riding up the opposite bank. The body of Naomi, not swept over the falls, was found next morning, caught in the willow roots of a turf island.

Lewis was jailed at Asheboro. He used his great strength in a jail break and made his way to Kentucky. It was years before it was known that he had settled at the falls of the Ohio. A Deep River posse followed him there. Through strategy and numbers they captured the giant and brought him back to Guilford for trial. Witnesses had died or moved away. Lewis was set free. When a few years later he lay dying, to his father (Craven's version) he confessed that "his sleep was broken by her cries for mercy, and in the dim twilight her shadowy form was ever before him."

•

At the time of the appearance of this narrative, 1875, the cascade on the Deep had long been known as Naomi Falls. Four years later it was harnessed to the first textile mill at the new town of Randleman. There M. Penny published an early example of that astute American use of romance to lead the reader into a sympathetic mood to hear about a commercial enterprise. The booklet contained *Naomi Wise, or the Wrongs of a Beautiful Girl* (pirated from Braxton Craven), and *Randolf's Manufacturing*. There was no transition between Naomi and the new mill. First her lament:

> We live in rolling billows;
> We float upon the mist,
> We sing on foaming pillows:
> "Poor Naomi of the past."

Then the proud announcement:

On July 7th, 1879, Mr. J. B. Randleman and the present Naomi Falls Company commenced building a cotton factory, which today stands as a monument of their energy and enterprise. There is now a beautiful town of about 500 inhabitants, and the hum of 500 spindles and the clash of 164 looms and the voices of 225 employees is heard within less than 200 yards of the ford where the tragedy referred to in this book was enacted . . . The spring where Naomi met Lewis and mounted his horse on that fatal night is now used to supply water for the New Salem Steam Mill and Tannery Company . . .

The trial at Guilford of Jonathan Lewis for the murder of Naomi Wise had taken place early in the nineteenth century. It may have had some influence on young Archibald Debow Murphey who at the time was living on his family's plantation, Hawfields, a short morning's ride east of the Deep River falls. His father, a colonel in the Revolution, was a prosperous planter who traded with Fayetteville and Petersburg and for his amusement raised blooded horses. Colonel Murphey's was one of the neighboring "few families of nature's noblest quality" cited by Braxton Craven in his early version of *An American Tragedy*. Whether the younger Murphey understood what lay between Lewis and Naomi, or merely enjoyed the plaintive ballad, it was the eye gougings, scratching and biting, the bare-breasted fighters in pantaloons, the ignorance and the poor lives of his neighbors that set the course of his adult career in attempts to get schooling for them, to build roads for their produce, and to create somewhere along the Cape Fear a shining, civilized city.

When Murphey died in 1832 he still had faith in the Cape Fear River as the grand water highway from the piedmont to Wilmington and on beyond to the highways of the sea where there is no littleness of water. The "Murphey Plan" survived him—in the public schools founded in 1840, in the minds of the Chapel Hill students he had harangued, and in the purposes of their successors.

Sherman interrupted the Murphey Plan. Carpetbaggers bought

up railroads, sold bonds to extend them, and put the money in their pockets. George Lobdell dreamed of a Southern Pittsburgh and ended wandering the red hills of Buckhorn. With his eyes to the ground looking for outcroppings of coal or iron ore, he missed the source of power in the drop of the Deep River over Naomi Falls. In a decade there were three mills at Randleman—"the industrial monument to the memory of the beautiful but unfortunate Naomi Wise." The piedmont had outgrown the times when beautiful orphans worked in the fields "as objects of the world's cold charity"; as witness M. Penny's tribute to that modern girl of 1888: "Miss Mamie Pomeroy than whom there is perhaps no more accurate accountant in this land of flowers and fair women . . ."

The mills were working twenty-five hundred bales of cotton a year and producing a million pounds of warp. The annual payroll was $50,000—an unimpressive $200 annual millhand income; yet it was seed money to grow a world textile center.

•

It had taken two centuries for the power and glory of the Throne of Charles II to move up the Cape Fear from tidewater to the piedmont. Royal authority rested for a time at Brunswick and Wilmington . . . Governor William Tryon nudged it eighty miles up the coast to his palace at New Bern, but rebellion sent the new Patriot Congress flying inland away from the British fleet. Upon independence, the new State's Legislature drifted back as far as Fayetteville, long enough to ratify the United States Constitution and found the University of North Carolina.

The population center had gone upriver far enough to exert political power in the location of a permanent State Capital. To Fayetteville's great wrath the choice was a Wake County farm lying between the basin of the Cape Fear and Neuse rivers, and there the grid of surveyor's ink was called Raleigh.

None of this groping for a city to embody the power and the glory of the state would have been necessary had nature endowed the Cape Fear with as deep and capacious an Atlantic harbor as

Boston, New York, Philadelphia, or Norfolk. The Frying Pan's shoals and geysers, the estuary's silted channels, and the upper river's fickle floods or low water made a gullet too narrow for a giant's growth. It was at Naomi Falls that the giant took his first step into industry, that force in human affairs which had at length, in England and America, displaced the power and glory of kings.

Water power began it. Steam and electricity took over in the building of a piedmont crescent of textile, trade and tobacco cities strung across the Indian trail John Lawson had followed in 1708.

The river at Naomi Falls, as a final gift to those it had drawn to itself from across the Atlantic, at least had done that much for its people.

# III : The Twentieth Century
## *Longings for Lost Innocence*

*You're a river fair,*
*Brown in the Spring as a cinnamon bear,*
*Bred in the laurel as a crystal spring*
*Up high meadows where the red-birds sing,*
*You grew up and so did I,*
*Pickin' up dirt as you passed it by;*
*You and me has a wrastlin' match*
*To settle our score in the bottom patch.*

# 1 : *Taming the River*

An old road follows the stream up the mountain behind my cabin.
Wherever the steep pitch flattens out into a miniature meadow
there are signs that a family once lived there—an apple tree, the
cut stone of a chimney, a band of iron embedded in the bark of an
ancient maple. They left so long ago that the mountain has recovered. Beech, oak, maple, dogwood, and sweetgum have standing
room. The banks of the branch are covered in spring with blood-
root, lady's-slippers, and May apples. When you come on a cluster
of ghostly white Indian pipes, you may say with confidence that a
bulldozer has not been that way.

This is the springtime of the life of a river, kept cool by its
rhododendron cover, oxidized by its leaps down the ledges. It
leaves the mountain as trout water; in half a mile a catfish would
gasp in the dirt picked up from the gullies and sewage from the
town.

The Cape Fear shares the common lot of those Atlantic coast
rivers which rise in the highlands, slow down on the plains to a
muddy meander, and end in a final purification in salt water. Few
houses stand on the banks. There are few swimmers and fisher-

men. The water stirred by the oars of periaugers lies somnolent and disregarded.

It no longer matters to Cape Fear people that the fight was lost to blast the rock ribs of Smilie's Falls with hot vinegar and gunpowder. Ten-ton trucks make the grade there in the flicker of an eye. But the river still demands that men spend money and energy to deal with its eccentricities. The few pages of an 1856 report propose the expenditure of $185,000 to improve navigation from Fayetteville to Haywood, on the premise that through tapping the resources of "an immense and populous valley, North Carolina from the products of her own bosom . . . would no longer witness the diversion of her products to the building up of the Commercial Cities in the States on her North and South . . ."

Today North Carolina stands as tall as her sisters, Virginia and South Carolina, but small thanks to navigation on the Cape Fear. That stream's legacy from the past are the freshets which ruined the works of the nineteenth century engineers and still flood two hundred square miles of farm bottomland whenever the farmers grow too forgetful of past calamities. In 1964 the Congress of the United States voted twenty-five million dollars to build the first of a series of Cape Fear Basin flood-control dams, where the Haw and New Hope Rivers come together.

Thirty thousand acres of farm and forest land will be scrubbed clean and drowned. The bones of Scotch-Irish ancestors will be transplanted to cemeteries on high ground. Orchard and shade trees will join the funeral pyre of bulldozed frame homesteads. Government provision of houses on land above the new lake could not quite compensate for the wornout red soil Orange County people must leave. Their Congressman voiced their anguish, then bowed to the inevitable. An Orange County homesite will be flooded in order to tame the freshets and save young green sprouts of corn and tobacco in Cumberland County. The ancient quarrel of piedmont against coastal plain has been arbitrated by the compulsive hand of technology.

If a century and a half has produced such irresistible toys as earth-moving equipment and pre-tensed steel bars imbedded in concrete, it has also proliferated the deferential bows and courtesies among the agencies of government. The 1856 *Report Upon the Cape Fear and Deep Rivers* was presented for legislative action by a committee of three. In the current 220-page *Cape Fear Basin, North Carolina,* the Secretary of the Army presents the recommendations of the U.S. Engineer Corps to the Speaker of the House, who is assured that the Director of the Budget finds no objections; although Interior frets a bit about flooding archeological remains; Health Education and Welfare caution about the impounded water's oxygen content; the Coast and Geodetic Survey would like, please, to link in the national geodetic survey, and the Weather Bureau has a word on the evaporation rate at the new location.

The shade of Archibald Debow Murphey—ruined and jailed for debt in 1829 through his advocacy of river improvements—may well be in a state of bliss tinged with awe at this exaltation of his dream. Where his surveyors trudged through cypress swamps to limn an unrealized canal, the U.S. Corps of Engineers today draws a map of the Cape Fear Basin, from the Frying Pan almost to the Virginia border, complete with drawings of the harnessed rivers and lakes as they will be in the year 2065 A.D.

A perhaps more entranced ghost would be the pioneer John Lawson, parts of whose 1708 trail the Engineer Corps proposes to drown. By God's assistance, wrote John Lawson, "we got safe to the north side of the famous Hau-River . . . which is one of the main branches of the Cape Fair, there being rich land enough to contain some thousands of Families . . ."

Today along the arc of Lawson's route lie the cities of Winston-Salem, High Point, Greensboro, Burlington, Durham, and Raleigh. Few of their people are the independent farmerfolk whom Lawson envisaged. The region leads the United States in the manufacture of tobacco products, textiles and wooden furniture. The bloodlines of Scotch-Irish, English, German, Swiss, French, and Highlander Scot are no longer distinguishable in this concentration of the Cape Fear peoples. The entire population of the basin, now one million, will in 2010 A.D.—the Engineer Corps predicts—reach 2.6 million. The present average income will be quintupled in that affluent year.

And shall that be a triumph of civilization?—or, for the increased millions, will it be a life cribbed, cabined, and confined? The eighteenth century could not foresee an overpopulated wilderness, or the bear hunter imagine the stars blotted out by neon lights.

The sleepy Rip Van Winkle State picked its way through the debris of the Revolution and the Civil War, arriving in the twentieth century in comparative tatters. But the schoolmen had been at work. Along the piedmont crescent of explosive young cities are strung the Women's College at Old Salem, the State Women's College at Greensboro, Guilford College, Wake Forest, Duke, Chapel Hill, and North Carolina State. The latter three form a triangle—Duke at Durham, State at Raleigh, and the University of North Carolina at Chapel Hill. Within this "Research Triangle" are laboratories which draw on the pool of scientific skills of all three universities. A pot of state, industrial and Federal gold is at the end of these rainbow bands of academic disciplines. Atomic reactors and computers are its tools. Its research fructifies textiles, forestry products, and the worn and patient Tar Heel soil.

For some years in the region there has been hatching a plot to forestall the fate which too much progress imposes on cities. "Ribbon Effect" is the name of the monster which slyly places a filling station between two towns, then adds a store, a few dwellings, a hairdresser's, a pizza palace, a motel, some signboards, a souvenir shop, a highway cloverleaf, a supermarket, and on and on along the ribbon until countryside, cities and states lose identity to the neon-lighted honky-tonks of the mature dragon. The piedmont crescent—sweeping across the headwaters of the Cape Fear and down a dogleg to booming Charlotte—would like to escape the ribbon effect and leave its cities their own identity. By the year 2000 they mean to have green open spaces between population clusters, highways for through traffic, and secondary roads to get produce and workers to market and mill, and a sure supply of pure water.

Such is the immemorial stability of human wants that their satisfaction in the affluent age remains basically the same as when the buffalo hunter knelt to drink from the forest spring, hacked blazes on the Indian trails, and traded his furs for rum. Schooling he lacked, but did not need for survival. He carried his own government in his powder horn. But there were not four hundred of him to the square mile. It has been left to our own age of orange juice and two hundred-pound high school tackles to settle the problem of how to fish basic needs out of an overcrowded pool.

Midway on a prop-jet flight from Charlotte to Raleigh, I looked down on the living features of the maps I had been scanning to follow the fortunes of Upper Cape Fear generations. There at a glance was the great right-angle bend which sends the Deep River eastward to meet the line of the Haw, and to the south their waters joined in the Cape Fear, a silver ribbon diminishing to the horizon. The region is a palimpsest of past writings over which the bulldozer proposes to scrawl new lakes to wink in the sunshine at whatever air vehicles flash over them in the year 1975, 2010, 2065.

The falls where the despicable Lewis drowned Naomi will be damned to make a lake reaching to High Point. Below on the Deep at Howard's Mills the waters will be backed up to flood the meadow racecourse where Scaldhead Dave Fanning's brilliant mare, Bay Doe, won purses for her master. A finger of the planned New Hope Lake will creep up Morgan's Creek on the outskirts of Chapel Hill, but not far enough to frustrate Bill Hunt's life ambition to preserve the valley of the creek as it was when a gristmill ground the corn grown on its forty-acre bottomland. It is rumor that a professor once wooed and won the miller's daughter. It is certain that Chapel Hill students for a century past have been carving their names and their class numerals on the brown sandstone slabs near a picnic pool.

The valley is a meeting ground for high-altitude and sea-level plant adventurers. Rhododendron escaped from the Blue Ridge to grow on the hillside; coastal plain sparkleberry and yellow jasmine bloom in sunny openings along the creek. Bill Hunt led me through the valley, tossing off Latin names on the assumption that my botanical learning was a match for my interest. A year later the William Lanier Hunt Arboretum was dedicated as a perpetual wilderness for student field trips and faculty research. Bill Hunt had routed the picknicker and his pop bottle, and, when the power company had sought to cut a 200-foot swath across the valley, he had lowered his scholarly head and driven the kilowatt hosts away from his arbutus and fire pinks. Yet, much as I applaud research in the habitat of fothergilla, I prefer to think Bill Hunt was moved by a desire to see one patch of Tar Heel land preserved as the professor and the miller's daughter roamed it.

## The Purple Pod

Fred Koch, Jr., is the son of the late "Prof" Koch who started the Carolina Players at Chapel Hill, and, through being mentor to Paul Green, was spiritual grandfather of the pageant, *The Lost Colony*, and succeeding outdoor dramas re-enacting history on Carolina summer nights. Fred and I have stretches of the same Blue Ridge stream. Discussing one day the rainbow hues of his valley stretch of the stream, whenever the hosiery mill chooses red, brown, or blue dyes for that day's sock production, we covered stream pollution in general and the Cape Fear River in particular.

Upon their graduation from Chapel Hill, Fred and a classmate had launched their canoe, the *Purple Pod*, at Mermaid Point and paddled the length of the Upper River. Moreover, Fred had kept a diary.

"Let me see it?" I asked.

"My head was stuffed with Thoreau and Wordsworth, and no one sees my juvenile prose."

"Think of posterity!" I begged. "You knew the Cape Fear in its semi-innocence. You are one with the periauger voyagers, the rafters, the poleboatmen—a modern William Hilton!"

"The rain smeared my notebooks. Anyway, they're lost."

A year later I wangled a loan of the log of the *Purple Pod*.

There is enchantment in river travel. *The Wind in the Willows* would not so beguile the heart were the willows' feet on dry land. Mark Twain needed the Mississippi to log the conquest of a continent. The muddy polluted Cape Fear of the 1930s catches a reflection of virginal waters when seen through eyes recently raised from reading *Walden*.

The scribbling in Fred's splotched and yellowing notebooks, done by campfire light with paddle-cramped fingers, attains an economy of prepositions and connectives but is rich in English A-4 adjectives:

Easter morning—shooting our first rapids we whiz water over the bow, wring clothes, bail, sponge and shove off again . . . the brown water is mixed with sunlight & powder blue this morning, in spots a sparkling saphire stream, near the sheltered banks calm pools of brownish yellow . . . a feathered cypress dripping low with silver moss, a chalk-stemmed sycamore set like polished ivory in a sky of sunlit blue—from deep in the woods the rich, sad whistle of the mourning dove—camped in the mammoth oven of Raven Rocks—the brows of the river, immense grottoes carved from the rock, dry dirt floors, water dripping from festoons of moss—a scenery like that of an inland lagoon, still, bewitching . . .

Just as we had settled ourselves for a week of lazy drifting & paddling we heard a faint rustling ahead, like a wind in the woods, but the calm water gleaming like a glazed crock under the noon sun told us there was no wind—the murmur grew slowly to a roar and rounding a bend we sighted swift water. The smooth sheet squeezed narrowly between two rocky banks & pitched in turmoil of yellow froth over the rocky bed beneath—our hearts quickened

—the current sucked impatiently at our purple pod—with a sense of horror I realized we were drifting swiftly toward the maelstrom—the next thing I knew it was over and we were bobbing playfully on the choppy sea below . . .

Near sunset we came upon a rocky bluff high over our port bow . . . we slid the *Purple Pod* from its coffee colored stream into an inky branch where we chained her for the night—the ebony water coughed up bits of paper and refuse from time to time—the sewage of Erwin . . . the insects and the whippoorwills and rain and the rapids filled our ears with drowsy music. Next morning as the dishpan was being emptied—millhands with bamboo poles and worm cans plunged their lines into the ebony creek—the catfish loved sewage water, we were told, and they tasted none the worse for their questionable diet . . . stopped 3 m. below Fayetteville to fill our water cooler from a spout of clear mineral water gushing from the face of a white & pink sandstone cliff over a mossy green chute into the dun-colored water . . .

At Elizabethtown chained up beside a derelict river steamer, the *Thelma* . . . lying on the sand, looking up from the ruddy embers of our nite fire into the black I can see only trees dancing in the glare, but there's a lone star in the east—some nite creature beyond the cozy circle of our camp fire has just splashed softly into the water—the insects are tinkling their tiny glasses with silver mallets—well, I had sworn not to write any but the barest impressions —notebook entries becoming tedious so I'll close and go to bed—a hoot-owl applauds . . .

## The Damyankee

Frederick Law Olmsted's account of the antebellum South describes his overnight paddle-wheeler trip from Fayetteville to Wilmington. A century later, following his route on the oil company tug *Damyankee*, I amused myself with comparisons between his dashing white pleasure steamer and my short-coupled marine workhorse. His berth and seat at the captain's table must have outclassed my blanketless bunk (it was cold on the river that April night) and my dawn cup of coffee in which the spoon, instead of standing upright in thick Stygian essence, was all too visible in the cook's colored hot water. But the *Damyankee* beat Olmstead's time by five hours, and this with equal stops in the pits. The paddle-wheeler had to push her nose on the bank for several woodings-up, the tug halted three times to descend the locks—at Tolar's Landing, Elizabethtown, and King's Bluff. Olmsted's steamer carried 300 barrels of turpentine; the tug pushed a steel barge of 10,000 barrels capacity. Olmsted's steamer took the hairpin turns with a swing of the wheel and an even head of steam. At the same river bend the *Damyankee* pushed her barge up to the far bank, reversed propellers with a teeth-shaking shudder of the diesels, then by the skipper's manipulations on push buttons, used the loss of headway to warp the barge's prow into the new course. With trees on the port bank shedding leaves over tug and barge, there was full speed ahead for a straightaway of a few hundred yards, sufficient in the old days for a periauger to raise sail.

The river is a lonely highway between walls of trees no longer broken by plantation landings. The few houses are the shacks of outboard enthusiasts and shad fishermen. The captain admitted me to the bridge where his experience knew what flick of the wheel, what finger on button would keep the barge in channel. Ahead appeared a snowy crust on the water, bank to bank.

"Waste from the paper company," the captain said.

The *Damyankee* plowed a lane through the two-inch sulphurous layer. For some distance downriver the floes floated like bergs from a glacier. The sharp pinch in the nostrils lasted until the high banks flattened into the salt meadow stretch above Wilmington.

A pipeline snaking its way from the Southwest oil fields is due to make the *Damyankee* as obsolete as the derelict paddle-wheeler *Thelma* to which Fred Koch hitched the *Purple Pod* another river generation ago. What price boating and fishing and houses again on the high west bank? If forty engineers with forty maps should work for half a year, do you suppose the Washington Walrus could sweep the river clear?

## The Weekend Ghouls

In Harnett County the descendants of the Highlander Scots lead lives as individual as the conformity of the twentieth century permits. If you are running for sheriff next election it will help to have a Scotch name. Lillington, the county seat, has about the same population as it had when Sherman's bummers liberated the last razorback. That I became cousin to anybody in Harnett County is due to Lillington's son and the county historian, Malcolm Fowler. As a Reconstructed Rebel, Malcolm spent World War II in a submerged submarine doing sonar research. As a Son of the Old South he becomes Captain Fowler C.S.A. at Civil War battle re-enactments, once almost changing history by leading his company at Gettysburg into a field of thistles whose hostile bees had been brainwashed by Yankee agents.

Malcolm Fowler grew up in the countryside along Buie's Creek. So did Paul Green. Malcolm's great-grandfather did not return from the Civil War. Paul's Confederate grandfather hitched up the remaining bull-yearling to a rusty plow. Through Paul's father's lifetime and his own boyhood, Harnett was a poor county. Paul worked at a sawmill and read books at lunchtime. Once he raised a tobacco patch, sold his crop for nineteen dollars and bought a set of Shakespeare. Campbell College on Buie's Creek thought to enroll this gangling scholar, but he chose the (to Buie's Creek) godless University at Chapel Hill. To get there he first taught school for two years at fifty dollars a month. "Prof" Koch took on an adult and dedicated drama student who would in time project to Broadway audiences through *In Abraham's Bosom* the wrath against injustice toward Negroes with which his Buie's Creek boyhood had imbued him.

Malcolm Fowler is the Tar Heel who stayed at home, in Lillington's genteel lack of affluence. He and Paul Green and some weekend ghouls from Cumberland County haunt cemeteries to collect epitaphs and ascertain which McNeill was kin to Jennie

Bahn, and whether the two small graves really were those of
Flora MacDonald's children. They let me join a couple of their
safaris. It is true that I was the only born Yankee, but the rest
were a mixed geneological lot. Jack Crane, christened Vance
Hampton Crane, still has that Yankee author of *The Red Badge of
Courage* on his family tree. Dr. Albert Stewart headed a search
for the site of Flora MacDonald's Killiegrey, on whose foundation
stones Stewart forebears built their house. John McPhaul led us to
McPhaul's Mill, seat of his Scots Highlander Loyalist ancestors
who fought the forebears of fellow ghoul, Dr. Will Farmer. Yet
there was a marked lack of the ancient animosities among us.

It came up that the failure of Malcolm Fowler's great-grandfather to return from the Civil War was due to some tons of Egypt
mine rock which fell on his chest.

"It was beyond the call of duty," Malcolm explained. "Mining
at Egypt was much more dangerous than being shot at by Yankees."

We found ancestral graves in unfenced stands of oak, in family
burying grounds where the manse cellars had gone to briers. At
Bluff Church we read that Duncan McNeill of Kintyre died in
1791, "Leaving his children the legacy of an upright character."
We also invaded an area rich in old cemeteries and battle sites,
the Fort Bragg Reservation.

## Unconventional Warfare

Ten miles north of Fayetteville the Cape Fear becomes the eastern boundary of the Reservation, a vast reach of hilly land carved
out of Cumberland and Hoke counties. The 100-acre plots of Scottish settlers who harvested its longleaf pine and plowed its virgin
soil are now a military complex of barracks, headquarters, flying
fields, and tank parks. Parachutes and artillery salvoes blossom in
its western limits. Longstreet, once a country road, is a bulldozed
highway spanned by signal flags on wires to direct low-flying heli-
copter ambulances.

Old Longstreet Presbyterian Church is kept freshly white by trustees of a long-dispersed congregation. We found deer droppings under its high portico. Its graveyard has antebellum epitaphs in Gaelic. In their zeal to dig up Confederate buttons at old campsites, the weekend ghouls have had to outrace artillery fire on restricted roads, and were once picked up by Military Police who could not believe that copying epitaphs was not undercover work for a Foreign Power.

They took me to where they supposed the Piney Bottom Massacre had taken place. One sluggish stream looks like another, but it was somewhere near this place that partisan Tories clove the head of a twelve-year-old boy with a claymore and went on to murder his kinfolk and burn their wagon train. "Cunning John" McNeill and the rest of the Tories galloped back to their homes in time to appear innocently at breakfast.

The civilian slaughter and arson of 1781 did not yet have the name of guerrilla warfare. That came with Spanish peasant tactics against Napoleon. Marion the Swamp Fox and John Singleton Moseby perfected the partisan art. The Commandos of World War II put it in modern dress. But what made Fort Bragg the headquarters for Special Forces was the adoption in Asia of infiltration and terror as the instruments of Communist take-over. The Western World perforce shifted to guerrilla tactics, although we give it the euphonious name of Unconventional Warfare. Counterinsurgency is a sort of doctorate-level course at Fort Bragg for our Special Forces and for their commando counterparts from those countries of five continents still comprising the free world.

I returned to visit Fort Bragg out of a conviction that Unconventional Warfare could not be a direct descendant of the senseless passion which let loose the Piney Bottom Massacre. By prearrangement I sat around a table with five Special Forces veterans of Laos and South Viet Nam. I already knew that those permitted to wear the Special Forces green beret were tough hombres, experts at judo, underwater demolition, jungle survival, and escape stratagems. Now it appeared that along with these attributes, every man must have a second language and master a special skill —medicine, communication, intelligence operations.

The ranking major, ringmaster at our talk, introduced a Laos veteran, a captain and leader of one of the twelve-man teams which include two each trained in the specialist skills. The tall, somber captain's soft speech described his team's life in a native village. They learned the Laotian language, ate rice, taught cleanliness and sanitation as well as small arms handling, and set up stations to treat the sick.

"You and the Peace Corps!" I said.

This raised a laugh, but led to admission of common aims. The millions who live on rice, the captain said, have no loyalties to rulers. A paddy and a family hut is the world. But an unsafe world once the strangers with guns and a gift for unrest trickle in from the bush.

"What must come," the captain said, "is the education of a class between the upper crust and the bottom layer."

"A Special Forces assignment?"

The captain smiled and passed the buck to a psychological warfare specialist, to a flying officer, to a sergeant and back to the major. The sergeant described home-grounds fun and games— how he and a squad avoided discovery on night sallies down the Cape Fear, and how in full-scale war maneuvers the counterintelligence scouts, dressed in civilian clothes, would try to seduce the minds of Fayetteville citizens into support of their side.

I left with respect for the green beret, and a chill down my spine at recollection that the Piney Bottom Massacre had been touched off by the theft of a piece of homespun from a servant girl; that partisan hatreds had set McPhauls against Fowlers, and that modern brush-fire wars are not easily extinguishable.

## Carolina Bays

Once on a flight south from Washington I looked down on scattered ellipses and circles dotting the unwinding ribbon of coastal plain. What geometrician drew those perfect lines? I asked the stewardess, who disappeared into the sanctum up forward and returned with the word: "Captain says it was an old meteor shower." It must have been a bright and shining morning when those stars began to fall.

A long while later, bouncing in a jeep over a coastal plantation, I received ground-level opinion on those "Carolina bays," locally known as pocosins. The superintendent of thirty thousand cultivated acres, John Rogers, was cutting across an open field near a fenced wood when he sounded his horn and was answered by a mighty brouhaha from thousands of turkey gobblers within the enclosure. The field was sandy soil, he told me, but the humus of the turkeys' pocosin was rich in the leached juices of the ages. It was once, he said, a depression in the sand plowed up by a meteor coming in at a slant from the northwest. That slight rise which our road had followed was the rim thrown up by the meteor's impact. The lines between original sand and meteor-treated soil were unmistakable. He could tell whether cotton had been grown on sandy or pocosin soil.

Where the pilot and the farmer had agreed, the scientists fall out. The origin of the Carolina bays is still a cosmic whodunit.

They were first noticed in 1895. Forty years passed before aerial photographs revealed an astounding pattern of ellipses from Virginia into Georgia, an estimated half million, ranging from a few feet to seven miles. Some, in marshy territory, are oval lakes. Many overlap. Whatever force created them, the elongation of every bay is from northwest to southeast.

The meteor-shower school takes comfort from W. F. Prouty of Chapel Hill, whose research ended only at his death and was carried on by his son. The Proutys fired rifles at a slant into a powdery layer on top of a bed of clay. The bullet, by shock and air waves, blew out an elliptical-shaped saucer in the soft upper layer and in the clay made a hole of its own diameter. The result was a scale model of what may have happened when a meteor out of the northwest splayed the coastal sand and buried itself in the hard core at the southeast end.

No, said other men of science, and proposed the birth of the bays attended by the action of wind and water, "submarine scour," melting icebergs, or the round-and-round underwater swishing of the tails of primordial fish.

In my lay ignorance I favored the Proutys. I could not swallow the tale of the fish cleverly carving out ellipses on the same axis. Big primordial fish for big bays? Small primordial fry for little bays?

As a check, I wrote to a famous institution and in reply received an endorsement of the researches of C. Wythe Cooke, U.S. Geological Survey, and in a final sentence a chilling word for falling-star aficionados: "I hope you agree that these craters are not due to the impact of a meteorite."

Cooke holds that the Carolina bays were originally hollows in the surface of marine terraces. Eddies of the interglacial seas carved them; wind and waves built their sandy rims. The gyroscopic effect of the earth's rotation gave an elliptical shape to the eddies, which, when the seas retreated, went through transitions from open water, to bog, to Carolina bay.

That shook me. The rotation of the earth, then, created the bays by sloshing water about in the sand as (I had already accepted) the earth's rotation over the aeons bent the Cape Fear's progress through glacial sand into a southeasterly parabola. Could rotation be responsible for the river effect and not for the bays? I reverted to the Prouty premise of a meteorite lying deep in the southeastern end of every pocosin. Either they are there, or they are not.

I learned of a nuclear scientist with a side-line interest in the meteor theory. After a reminder that his search for metal in the bays along the Cape Fear River was not a "professional study," he committed himself this far:

> I did make a rather detailed survey of one bay called Bandeau Bay located about ten miles SE from Elizabethtown. Here I surveyed out a grid running NW-SE along the axis of the bay and crossed at ten-foot intervals in the NE-SW direction. Measurements of topography to 0.1 foot with simultaneous "dip needle" readings appear to show the possibility of a magnetic mass under the southeasterly third of the bay. While this appears to support the meteor concept, it was not conclusive.

Near that Bandeau Bay surveyed by my correspondent lies White Lake. Its white sand bottom shelves from northwest to southeast. Sitting on its shore one summer day, I speculated whether far below the swimmers and outboard motors there might be a lump of heavenly debris flung at the empty sand reaches 10,000 years ago.

Come with your dip needles, scientists, and end this argument!

## End of the Longleaf Pines

Tar Heels take their name from the old days of treading in the pitch of the longleaf pines. The first money to build plantation houses came from the sale of turpentine, tar, and masts to the British Navy. The last of the longleafs to support Cape Fear people were cut down in 1935 in the lake region east of the river at Elizabethtown. When the Scots first settled there the timber was tall, the wild game, fish, and blueberries bounteous. But by the time of the Depression of the 1930s the longleafs were gone, the only farming patches were the flood-prone bottomlands along the Cape Fear. Half the people lived on Federal relief.

I had been told that since those doleful years the region had staged a comeback. Leaving the prosperous west bank country (cattle, peanuts, poultry, tobacco, and blueberries), I crossed the

River at Elizabethtown and sought out Graham Chamblee, head man of the Bladen Lakes State Forest. He brought out the 1935 records of a dying region. These are some of the family "net worths" of 1935:

John McIntyre owned livestock $4, personal property $34; Sarah Little owned livestock $12.25, personal property $22.25, owed $100, a minus net worth of $65. Some family incomes (from farming and day labor) for 1935 were: Jed Martin $85.50; Donald Duncan $138; George Cullen − $32; Clara Atkins $10.

In that same year the Resettlement Administration bought 35,-000 acres at $4.71 per acre. The objective was to grow trees, market forest products, give the marsh dwellers a chance. It worked. The State of North Carolina Forestry Division took it over. Graham Chamblee flipped over the pages of his records to thirty years later. Forest products (everything from timber to pine straw to Christmas trees) rose from a gross income of less than $200 to more than $200,000. Family incomes went from minus figures to Forest Service salaries sufficient to send the young ones to college.

Today's pay crop is loblolly and slash pine. But the Forest has planted 1,500 acres of longleaf seedlings out of consideration of twenty-first century needs. Had the nineteenth century left seedling plumes among the longleaf stumps, the great beams might still be rafted to Wilmington. Still, nature be thanked for the longleaf's lesser cousins. I drove back to Elizabethtown on a road hemmed on both sides by the fast-growth loblollies. Young Tar Heels walked along the verge, swinging book straps on the way back from a schooling their grandpappys never had.

## U.S.S. North Carolina (Retired)

The skipper of the *Damyankee* said that if I was headed for the U.S.S. *North Carolina*, he could land me right alongside her slip. Under reversed propellers the tug shuddered to a halt on the shore line opposite Wilmington. I shook hands all round and climbed down a ladder to slimy low-tide rocks below a seawall.

Dangling a suitcase in one hand and waving the *Damyankee* crew good-by with the other, I felt the fool I looked. I tossed the suitcase to the turf above. It was too high for a leap. I climbed up the seawall, recovered my luggage and marched—as seamanlike as a civilian can with a smudge of river muck across his nice seersucker jacket—to the slip where the U.S.S. *North Carolina* rests in her final berth. The torpedo and kamikaze wounds of forty months in the South Pacific are repaired and painted over. There is no crew aboard to tackle the pumpkin pie crust whose recipe (still hanging in the galley) calls for: shortening 100 lbs., salt 6 lbs., flour 200 lbs., water 35 qts.

For a few days I was the lone guest aboard of Hugh Morton, who headed the state committee which saved the ship from the scrap pile and berthed her as her own public monument.

The loneliness of a deserted ship comes out at night. Daytimes, small boys pounded their heels on the armor-plate ceiling of my cabin and cried their ack-ack-acks in the antiaircraft turret outside my porthole. Nights, there were too many echoes along the metallic maze of passageways and cabins where men had lived when the great ship was coursing the Pacific. But mornings were made cheerful by coffee with Bob Ellis who, as Rear Admiral Robert B. Ellis (U.S.N. Retired), spends his days managing the affairs of the retired battleship. Talk got around to that first amphibious landing mounted by Admiral Porter's fleet and General Terry's army at Fort Fisher on January 15, 1865. Eighty years later, on February 28, 1945, the *North Carolina* and the *Texas* threw their hundreds of tons of steel at the Japanese rock-face blockhouses on Iwo Jima. The liaison between sea and land (substituting radio for semaphore) was tactically the same. If fire power had increased in 1945, so had the impregnability of Iwo Jima caves compared to Fort Fisher sand bastions. For the fighting men there were no technological improvements that mattered. Squads landed from small boats. Men died from muskets at Fort Fisher, from machine guns at Iwo Jima. But they will never again die in just this manner of warfare. Nuclear fission was in the wings offstage from the last amphibious attack of the battleship era.

The *North Carolina* sailed home to be mothballed for fourteen years. Her turn to be made into razor blades was put off by Governor Terry Sanford's plea for Tar Heel possession. A smiling Jack Kennedy accepted the post of first Admiral of the North Carolina fleet, and thereafter the children's pennies and the adult's checks bought the *North Carolina*. She hove to one foggy fall night in 1961 off the same Frying Pan Shoals where fog was the Confederate blockade-runner's friend a century before.

On her precarious towing trip up the estuary to Wilmington, the ship's hundred-foot beam set the channel buoys awash. Captain B. M. Burriss, grandson of a blockade-runner pilot, guided the Coast Guard cutter and nudging tugs to the point where a 729-foot vessel had to be warped into a slip with less than 500-feet of maneuvering room. The *North Carolina*'s last encounter was with the concrete hull of a World War I vessel converted into a restaurant and made fast to a Wilmington wharf. The battleship's stern bumped it, occasioning the only recorded instance of "Abandon ship!" being sounded in a seafood palace. The tugs and a line to a bulldozer on shore swung the great ship into her last berth.

One night on the *North Carolina* the loneliness of my mighty hostel sent me to the aft rail where I watched the lights of Wilmington weaving patterns on the Cape Fear. That failed to fill up my empty evening. The river and the battleship appeared to my desolate mood as derelicts, each in its time of immense importance to people, both now obsolete. The public does pay a fee to board the *North Carolina*, but I doubt if anyone would pay to see the Cape Fear. The concrete bridges over its upper reaches are merely parts of the highways. Wilmington has turned its back on the estuary which nourished and amused its ancestors.

The power mowers that day had cut the lawn on the verge of the *North Carolina*'s slip. The fragrance of the mown lawn drifting on the night air set me to exploring a fantasy . . . The grass took on Walt Whitman's meaning of people—all people today yesterday and tomorrow—sending off an ineffable essence of themselves which penetrates the smudge of ill and foolish doings in an imperfect world. For an instant the grass fragrance dispelled the dank river smell, and on the same small breeze came an evocative sense of all the rowdy, cruel, heroic, and saintly living that had been done along the river. Their lives were the true Cape Fear, not the indignities of sulphurous fumes and sewage-fed catfish which the generations had imposed on it.

It was not hard in this setting to realize their presence . . . In the Confederate shipyard once located a hundred yards from where I stood, workers in 1862 had built another *North Carolina*. She was a small ironclad powered by an engine taken out of the first captured Federal blockader, the tug *Uncle Ben*. Under this weak propulsion the C.S.N. *North Carolina* waddled out of New Inlet one night to confront the whole Federal line. At dawn they chased her back under Fort Fisher's protection. It was her last sally. At anchor off Smithville, torredo sea worms engaged her soft underbelly and sank her.

There were other Confederate installations on the west bank. The cotton press stood here, and the wharf for loading bales on the blockade-runners. Here too was the station to fumigate outbound ships and drive stowaways out of hiding. One at least held his breath, for the young purser of the *Ella,* James Sprunt, reported the rescue of a stowaway slave from a rowboat in the open sea where another runner had marooned him.

Grass now covers the foundations of shipyard, cotton press, and fumigating station, but across the river I could make out the massive 1858 building housing that popular night-life rendezvous of Confederate sailors and soldiers, the Thalian Association Theatre. That afternoon I had been let in to admire its gilded charms, and had copied down some of its wartime playbills. On February 10, 1862, the presentation of *Confederate Minstrels* inspired the *Daily Journal* to a prissy editorial: "Surely the soldier or officer who spends his time laughing at our friend 'Bones' does better than if he spent his time and money in a barroom."

For three war years the theater prospered, with tickets reaching five dollars a seat when three-cent Wilmington cotton was selling for forty-three cents at Liverpool. The pickup cast of *Confederate Minstrels* had changed to professional presentations, such as:

MAJOR JONES COURTSHIP!

OR

*The Adventures of a Christmas Eve!*

AFTER WHICH

Grand Fancy Dance . . . . . Miss Selina Walker

To conclude with the Screaming Farce of

SKETCHES IN INDIA

There were performances through January 13, 1865, the night when Porter's fleet was aligned off Fort Fisher and Terry's landing force had gotten between Lamb's defenses and Bragg's army. After the fall of Fort Fisher the play went on until Wilmington itself fell to the Federal forces on February 22. A week later General Terry let the Thalian reopen. Ticket prices under Union occupation fell to $1.00 dress circle, 25¢ colored gallery. The traders in Liverpool cotton had disappeared. Wilmington was feeling the first chill wind of Reconstruction hard times.

## Gray Ghosts of Fort Fisher

Twenty miles south of Wilmington the spit of land dividing the Atlantic Ocean from the Lower Cape Fear narrows to less than a mile. Here was L-shaped Fort Fisher, the long leg rimming the Atlantic, the short one crossing from sea to river. Thirty years ago a natural sandstone shelf north of the fort was removed for road material. The released tides gnawed at the three-quarter-mile sand bastion, dissolving the L-angle where three hundred Union sailors died, leaving only the fort's land face.

The state's archeologist, Stanley South, walked me over the grass-grown mounds where the Columbiad emplacements had been. Here General Whiting and Colonel Lamb were hit by rifle bullets, small pellets, yet as crippling to the Confederate defense as the tons of shells hurled by Porter's offshore flotilla.

A lone Whitworth gun today guards the empty beach where the fort stood. It is the same Whitworth that Captain Munn ran up the beach to fight Federal landing parties away from a stranded blockade-runner. That ship, and forty more Confederate gray ghosts and Federal vessels, still lie offshore under ten to thirty feet of water. Many are aligned where they beached in 1863 and 1864, and where they were visible until the sea engulfed them and flattened Fort Fisher into shelving underwater sand.

In its destruction, the sea at least preserved the blockade-runners' cargoes for a hundred years, until our scuba era could salvage them. Navy divers in 1962 began bringing up Enfield rifles, Whitworth shells, scalpels, surgical saws, dinnerware and a sensational if banged-about commode. Stanley South took me through a laboratory where 32-pounders are in pickling baths and smaller relics are being cleaned, waxed, and otherwise receiving tender loving care. He let me handle an Enfield rifle which, had not a blockade-runner been chased onto the beach in 1864, would have been issued to an infantryman in the Army of Northern Virginia.

## Orton

The young Confederate who checked off the cases of Enfields on his purser's lading list, James Sprunt, survived blockade-running and a northern prison to become the historian of the Lower Cape Fear. He lived until 1924. His son, James Laurence Sprunt, is the present owner of Orton Plantation. In pursuit of this living projection into the past, I exchanged the feel of the Enfield's walnut stock for the cool of a tall glass in the Sprunts' pleasant garden.

Orton's bearded live oaks were old even when Roger Moore

first saw them. Its cypresses are reflected in black fresh-water pools. The first warm days of March touch fire to the banked azaleas and set both the birds and the garden tourists to chirping excitedly. But underneath the formal walks and boxwood mazes are the ribs of a working plantation. The flat tongue of land projecting into the Cape Fear was the rice field, flooded in season by flumes of fresh water from a six-mile pond back in the woods. Turpentine, tobacco, and cotton paid for the saddle horses and London finery. Plantation houses extended for miles along the river, but they were of wood. War, arson, and faulty flues destroyed them. Orton alone remains to explain the past.

The lightwood blaze on Orton's hearth has illumined the faces of Indian fighters, royal governors, Confederate officers, and the pale cheeks of Union soldiers hospitalized there after their army's capture of Fort Anderson. During twenty years of Reconstruction the hearth was cold, then rekindled in the warmth of Victorian hospitality. A nineteenth century visitor wrote his nostalgic memories of Orton:

> Here in the exhilaration of the hunter, the restful seclusion of the angler, the quiet quest of the naturalist, the peaceful contemplation of the student, is found surcease from the vanities and vexations of urban life . . . We sat upon a sheltered seat and heard the faint "Yo ho!" of the sailor outward bound . . . The spacious hall with its ample hearth and blazing logs, after the bountiful evening meal, the old songs sung and the old tales told, and fun and frolic to keep dull care beyond the threshold. . . .

James Sprunt bought Orton in 1904, and there assembled his *Chronicles of the Cape Fear*, a compendium of the lives of people committed in their fortunes and their frolics to the river. There is little left to show for it. Within sight of Orton there once was another tended lawn where Cornelius Harnett marched with 450 men to tell Governor Tryon that the tea ships must return to England. Russellboro now is rubble. At Old Brunswick Town beyond it, Stanley South's crew is uncovering ballast cobble foundations hidden by vines and brush since 1776.

Sitting with Laurence Sprunt and watching his seasoned face crinkle with pleasure in hospitable talk was recompense for the faint Yo Ho of the outward bound sailor. I could even momentarily forgive the bulldozer operator who leveled the ancient Dram Tree. Progress at a cost.

"What happened to make people turn their backs on the river?" I asked. "If they can't make a living on it any more, it still has flowing water and fish and birds."

"That freighter out there is still making a living," my host replied. "Not all backs are turned. Of course the ocean beaches lure the suntan set, but there are a lot of us embattled river folk. They come here in droves, and their admission fees maintain Orton as it was when rice and turpentine footed the bills. The garden tourists overrun us, and we love 'em. Mrs. Sprunt is my spy. She walks around making ladylike noises over the azaleas and eavesdrops on the enthusiasms of our vistors. The river still has its moments."

I told him how the weekend ghouls of Harnett and Cumberland waste good golfing weather running down epitaphs.

"Good for them!" he said. "They have a feeling that the river was flowing a long whiles back. They know who they are. We're not licked yet!"

"We?"

"Your friends upriver and the lady tourists and a whole stable of scientists, Parks people, university biologists—and a hard core of soft sentimentalists like myself. And I suspect you."

It appeared that the formidable alliance of river people is out to preserve Bald Head as it has been for the four hundred years since Allyón's ship was wrecked on the Frying Pan—Bald Head being the familiar local name for the Cape of Feare. A move to turn the wild reaches of Bald Head into a resort had rallied support for the rights of modern man to set aside for his contemplation a patch of sea and sand and ancient verdure in its wilderness innocence.

## Promontorium Tremendum

Governor John White on his 1585 voyage to Roanoke Island was swept so near to disaster on the Shoals that he named the headland *Promontorium Tremendum*. The Cape of Feare it so became, and so is, although the centuries dubbed in lesser titles. When the Lords Proprietors turned plain Thomas Smith of Charleston into Landgrave Smith, his land grant became Smith's Island. Sporadic attempts were made to exorcise the dragon of sand and spume by calling it Cape Fair. The currently familiar name, Bald Head, was invented by nineteenth century sailors to describe the sand bluff at the western rim of the Cape, a sort of humped Moby Dick rising from the green wave of live oak forest.

The Cape is a meeting place of violent forces. Atlantic rollers break on the exposed sand bars of the Frying Pan in fifty-foot spouts of water. Hurricanes close one sea-to-river inlet and create a new one. The interplay of ocean tide and river flow constantly edit charts of the channel.

The classic description of Promontorium Tremendum was written in 1879 by George Davis, former attorney general of the Confederacy. In it the malevolent partnership of the Cape and its Shoals received this judgment:

*Together they stand for warning and for woe . . .*
*Suggestive, not of repose and beauty, but of desolation and terror . . .*
*Bleak and threatening and pitiless . . .*
*As its nature, so its name, is now, always has been, and always will be, the Cape of Fear . . .*

George Davis was summing up three centuries of folk memory; the breaking up of Sir John Yeamans' supply sloop on the Shoals in 1663; the Indians' slaughter of shipwrecked passengers; the Confederate ironclad that broke her back on a sand bar; the long

roll of the drowned. The late nineteenth century continued to justify Davis' harsh opinion—in 1893 five ships were driven on shore
by one August storm; on September 28, 1894, the crew of a three-
masted schooner, fast on the Shoals five miles south of the Cape,
was rescued by the Life Saving Station dory a few minutes before
the ship broke up.

For all of this, revolutionary changes were at work to amend
the Davis indictment of the Cape. The causes of awe and terror
diminished when the steady thrust of propellers replaced the vari-
able force of wind on sail; when steam dredges canceled the Frying Pan's ability to silt up the channel; when radar and hurricane
warnings and powerful lighthouses remitted the charge of *standing for warning and for woe.*

Stronger still—for it affects not only sailormen but all the people of America—was the revolution in the attitude toward wilderness wastes, from ancient fears of the Cape to a need for a
relationship with nature in her unviolated innocence. William Bartram fell in love with Cape Fear during his naturalist visits there
from 1761 to 1772. He found an undisturbed community of sea,
forest, marsh, and tidal stream. Brown pelicans gathered at low
tide on the exposed Shoals, their stomachs replete with speckled
trout, bluefish and mackerel, their ancient eyes holding a digni-
fied disregard of the spectacular swoops of black skimmers and
shearwaters. On the beach were the tracks of female loggerheads,
leading surfward from the clutch of buried eggs left for the sun to
hatch. The domed canopy of live oaks reaching across the Cape
had a lively company of raccoon, fox, and squirrel. In the marshes
behind the forest the otter and the mink held dominion over the
golden mouse and other small proletarians of the community.

Bartram's clever drawing fingers caught the clapper rail in its
hungry investigation of a burrowing crustacean. He memorialized
the wading birds—egrets, heron, ibis—and so made himself
founding member of those who reverse George Davis by finding
Old Baldy suggestive not of desolation and terror but of repose
and beauty.

Some of those who came later to the Cape were involuntary converts to its enchantment. Captain David A. Buie (surely kin to Archie the bowlegged piper of Buie's Creek) was stationed there in 1864 at Fort Holmes, which General Whiting had built to defend the river's mouth against Federal raids by Lieutenant Cushing and his ilk. Having cut and sent some Bald Head palmetto fronds to his girl, Captain Buie wrote her:

> I will ask a favor of you, a pretty big one too. Will you grant it? It is this. To make a palmetto hat for me, number 7 (i.e., on a block 7 inches in diameter), the brim inclined to be wide, low crown and a broad band. The hat is not for my own head. I promised Captain Whiting six months ago to have him one made—a nice one, and forgot to tell you when I saw you. If you'll make it, I'll be your most obedient and do as much for you sometime when the war is over.

In another letter Captain Buie wrote: "Bald Head is one of the most beautiful places on the coast . . . It would be murder for me to attempt a description so I'll leave its beauties for you to picture in your imagination."

Both the Cape pilots and the Life-Saving Service established villages (complete with families) on Bald Head in the 1880s. The hunters of Southport (formerly Smithville) went there for "marsh-henning," their name for bagging clapper rail. Fishermen learned that the biggest channel bass could be caught by casting off islets of the Frying Pan, now christened "The Lumps." Drop-line anglers discovered that the submerged hulks of 1864 blockade-runners were superb fishing holes.

Lovers of Old Baldy they all became, yet tongue-tied regarding the varied charms of their mistress. Then in 1963, when death to the wilderness innocence was threatened by summer resort plans, very vocal spokesmen entered the lists as Bald Head's champions. The North Carolina Academy of Science and Wildlife Preserves came forward to defend the integrity of the Cape Fear community, showing why it is that the great white heron must be allowed

316 : THE CAPE FEAR

to take his toll of fingerlings; how the frog and the clapper rail, the owl and the mouse will strike a survival balance if man will withhold his devastating hand.

Dune, forest, and marsh have come to an understanding of their mutual roles.

On the southern rim the wind piles a barrier dune to protect twenty thousand live oaks from too great a salt spray—but just enough salty globules to give the forest canopy its rounded dome and let sunlight filter into the shadowland below. In the lee of the forest, the sabal-palmetto, peapod cactus, and laurel cherry thrive in this their northernmost limit.

For another ten miles up the Cape there are the forested ridges of two antecedent capes. In between them the salt-marsh meadows and tidal creeks function as a pair of nursing mothers to juvenile shrimps and gamefish, oysters, clams, mullet, and spot. Salt-marsh grasses have a fixation of 6.1 per cent of the solar energy falling on them, making them the most productive in the world. Into the grasses the tidal streams reach to withdraw nearly half of the organic detritus, and carry it as provender to the infant crustaceans, bivalves, and fish.

The shrimp boats and the big game fishermen would have no quarry should the salt-marsh streams be blocked by a seawall. The sand dunes protecting the live oaks would disappear should jetties and piers on the Atlantic beach meddle with the riparian rights of the southbound ocean currents. It takes a power saw five minutes to level a mature live oak, but it would require five centuries for a sapling live oak to replace it.

The embattled botanists, biologists, and marine scientists, with their universities and parks services, have researched enough to know that the Cape Fear complex is unique along the Atlantic coast, and very vulnerable. But their concern is matched by the philosophers who see this innocence of nature as a font for the spiritual cleansing of an urban generation. The wilderness has been a place for men to wrestle with their souls—St. John, Jesus

Christ, the anchorites, and on down to Walt Whitman and David Thoreau.

A scholar with a book to write, John Lewis Longley, Jr., brought his family to live one summer in an abandoned Cape Fear Lighthouse cottage.

"The most persistent memory," he wrote later, "is waking each morning at dawn, sipping fresh coffee, and sitting on the front steps of the cottage with my clipboard on my knee, ready to begin the day's writing. The wonder is that the book got drafted at all . . . The great massed cacophony of pink and salmon clouds would fill the sky overhead, and the restless gray of Frying Pan would extend as far as the eye could see . . . We began to settle into a rhythm of days untroubled by clocks or calendars, and learned to know what a different place the island is at night when the moon is full; the raccoons and foxes wander about and the great sea turtles come out of the ocean to lay their eggs. . . ."

Longley's is today's mood, which at times needs to replace the haze of gasoline fumes with the gray mists over the Frying Pan. George Davis had command of sonorous Victorian prose, conceiving Cape and Shoals as "the playground of billows and tempests, the kingdom of silence and awe, disturbed by no sound save the sea-gull's shriek and breakers' roar . . . Imagination cannot adorn it. Romance cannot hallow it. Local pride cannot soften it . . . And there it will stand, bleak and threatening and pitiless, until the earth and the sea shall give up their dead . . ."

George Davis was looking at the Cape from the sea, in a small shallop not designed to grapple such a maelstrom. It is a reading of the modern pulse when Longley could say eighty years later that those who have been exposed to Old Baldy acquire "a passionate love of the island of unsurpassed natural wonder and beauty, and the burning conviction that it must never be ruined, overwhelmed or destroyed."

# Acknowledgments

The first comers to a new region are the darlings of history. Governor Bradford of Plymouth and Captain John Smith of Jamestown were assigned their places in folklore generations before the first permanent settlers took up land along the Cape Fear. When the first general histories of the Republic came to be written, North Carolina remained a footnote to a New England text. Tar Heel ante-bellum writers were lawyers and preachers. It never occurred to them to launch North Carolina on the broad tide of American history.

I dwell on this the greater to show my debt to the amateur chroniclers who supposed local Cape Fear history worth the compilation. They shed a warm light on their times. Many of them were participants in their own tales, or kin to the founding fathers, or simply in love with their own locality. John Lawson, earliest chronicler, wrote with compassion about the Indians, and died of lighted splinters stuck into him by the Tuscaroras. Samuel A'Court Ashe was descended from that stout Member of The Family, John Baptista Ashe. Alfred Moore Waddell had the blood of both the original James Moore and of the Indian fighter Hugh Waddell. John Hill Wheeler and E. W. Carruthers wrote colorfully about colonial characters to whom they were not far distant in time.

If a Federal gun had knocked the purser of the Confederate blockade-runner *Ella* off his station on the paddle-wheel box, James Sprunt would not have survived to assemble the *Chronicles of the Cape Fear.* I am grateful to the bad aim of the Federal gunners.

The North Carolina Colonial Records, first published in the 1890s, inspired a flood of scholarly papers. I found invaluable the writings of John Spencer Bassett and Stephen Beauregard Weeks.

The flavor of local life and events appears in the writings of dedicated county historians. John Alexander Oates gathered Fayetteville and Cumberland County material. Louis T. Moore, a Wilmington stem of The Family, wrote of the Lower Cape Fear. The late Hector C. Clark celebrated his own Bladen County. In our times, Malcolm Fowler still haunts graveyards to read epitaphs into his tape recorder. Next to St. Peter's, his are the most complete Harnett County records.

Twentieth century disciplines in research and documentation produced such Tar Heel scholars as R. D. W. Connor, C. C. Crittenden, and Albert Ray Newsome. The latter, with Hugh Talmage Lefler, wrote the definitive *North Carolina: The History of a Southern State.*

To Dr. Lefler, Kenan Professor of History at the University of North Carolina, I am most particularly indebted. He guided my first research in Cape Fear materials; his several books have been within reach; he read the manuscript of this book. In addition, he supervised the doctorate work of two writers upon whom I have drawn liberally, Enoch Lawrence Lee, Jr., and Duane Meyer.

The University of North Carolina Press, under Lambert Davis, published Lee and Meyer and other Carolinians, including useful volumes on Sherman's March and the Civil War in North Carolina by John G. Barrett, North Carolina born and now professor at Virginia Military Institute.

Arthur W. Cooper, Sheafe Satterthwaite and F. Stuart Chapin, Jr., —and I include the U. S. Engineer Corps—are thanked for materials essential to Part III of this book.

The kindness and the enthusiasm met along the Cape Fear led me to dedicate this book to three of the Valley's sons. There were many others who helped. Four of us became fascinated by conflicting tales about Flora MacDonald. Her collateral kin, Archibald Donald Mac-Donald Strange-Boston, corresponded with authorities in Scotland. I found myself compiling a history of Flora MacDonald, and was obliged to confine her story to those incidents directly affecting her role in

Cape Fear history. For the pains they took to inform me, I hereby thank Miss M. F. Cameron, Hon. Secretary The '45 Association of Scotland; Lady Flora McLeod, Dunvegan Castle, Isle of Skye; Allan Douglas, editor *The Weekly Scotsman;* Donald B. MacCulloch, author, Glasgow; Carleton R. S. Malcolm, F.S.A., Lochgilphead.

Librarians hold the keys to the past. Fortunately for writers they are the kindest of human creatures. I cite William S. Powell, librarian of the North Carolina Collection, Chapel Hill; Mrs. Elizabeth B. Huey, State Librarian at Raleigh, and her associates, Mrs. Lois S. Neal and Miss Georgia H. Faison, now retired; Mrs. Dorothy Thomas, Yancey County librarian; and the staff of the Richter Library of the University of Miami.

The back files of both the Raleigh *News and Observer* and the Fayetteville *Observer* show a high editorial regard for covering the events and personalities of the region. For lack of space I can only extend blanket thanks for benefits received.

In their special fields of learning and friendship these people aided this book: Stanley South, archeologist for the North Carolina Department of Archives and History; Mrs. Louis T. Moore; J. Laurence Sprunt; Graham V. Chamblee; Gertrude S. Carraway, director of the Tryon Palace Restoration; Hugh Morton, Buddy Lynch, Rear Admiral Robert M. Ellis (Retired); many officers of Special Forces, Fort Bragg; Theodore Bolton, Carl Carmer, Jean Crawford; Marjory Stoneman Douglas, and my personal built-in *vox pop,* my wife Camille.

April 25, 1965
Burnsville, North Carolina

# Bibliography

Adams, W. J., *The House in the Horseshoe and Other Papers*. N.p.;
    n.p.; n.d.
Ashe, Samuel A'Court, *History of North Carolina*. 2 vols. Greensboro:
    Charles L. Van Noppen, 1925.
Bartram, William, *The Travels of William Bartram*, edited by Mark
    Van Doren. New York: Dover Publications, 1928.
Barrett, John G., *Sherman's March Through the Carolinas*. Chapel Hill:
    University of North Carolina Press, 1956.
———— *The Civil War in North Carolina*. Chapel Hill: University of
    North Carolina Press, 1963.
Bassett, John Spencer, *The Regulators of North Carolina* (1765-1771).
    American Historical Association. Washington, D.C.: Government
    Printing Office, 1895.
Battle, Kemp B., *Otway Burns, Privateer and Legislator*. North Caro-
    lina University Magazine, Vol. XXXII, 1901.
Black, R. C., *The Railroads of the Confederacy*. Chapel Hill: Univer-
    sity of North Carolina Press, 1952.
Brown, Frank C., *The Frank C. Brown Collection of North Carolina
    Folklore*. 5 vols. Durham: Duke University Press, 1952.
Burns, Francis, *Captain Otway Burns, Patriot, Privateer and Legisla-
    tor*. New York: Privately printed, 1905.

*Cape Fear Basin, North Carolina*. Report from the Chief of Engineers, Department of the Army, 87th Congress House Document No. 508. Washington, D.C.: Government Printing Office, 1962.

Cappon, L. C., *Iron-Making: A Forgotten Industry in North Carolina*. North Carolina Historical Review Vol. IX, 1932.

Caruthers, Rev. E. W., *Life and Character of the Rev. David Caldwell*. Greensboro: Swain and Sherwood, 1842.

Chapin, F. Stuart, Jr. (ed.), *Urban Growth Dynamics*. New York: John Wiley & Sons, Inc., 1962.

Coffin, Levi, *Reminiscences of Levi Coffin*. Cincinnati: Western Tract Society, 1876.

Connor, R. D. W., *History of North Carolina: The Colonial and Revolutionary Periods*. Chicago: 1919.

———— *North Carolina: Rebuilding an Ancient Commonwealth 1584-1925*. 4 vols. New York: The American Historical Society, Inc., 1929.

———— *Cornelius Harnett: an Essay in North Carolina History*. Raleigh: North Carolina Historical Review, 1909.

———— *The Genesis of Higher Education in North Carolina*. Raleigh: North Carolina Historical Review Vol. XXVIII, 1915.

Cooke, C. Wythe, *Carolina Bays and the Shapes of Eddies*. Washington, D.C.: Geological Survey Professional Paper 254-1, U. S. Government Printing Office, 1954.

Cooper, Arthur W. and Satterthwaite, Sheafe, *Smith Island and the Cape Fear Peninsula*. Raleigh: Wildlife Preserves, Inc., in cooperation with the North Carolina Academy of Science, 1964.

Crittenden, Charles Christopher, *Means of Communication in North Carolina, 1763-1789*. Raleigh: North Carolina Historical Review Vol. VIII, 1931.

———— *Inland Navigation in North Carolina, 1763-1789*. Raleigh: North Carolina Historical Review Vol. VIII, 1931.

———— *Ships and Shipping in North Carolina, 1763-1789*. Raleigh: North Carolina Historical Review Vol. VIII, 1931.

Eller, Admiral E. M., *Seapower's Decisive Influence in the Civil War*. Washington, D.C.: Naval History Division. U. S. Naval Department.

Fanning, David, *The Narrative of Colonel David Fanning*. Richmond: 1861.

Fowler, Malcolm, *They Passed This Way: A Personal Narrative of Har-*

*nett County History*. Lillington: Harnett County Centennial, Inc., 1955.

Fries, Adelaide L., *The Road to Salem*. Chapel Hill: University of North Carolina Press, 1944.

Gwynn, Colonel, *Report on the Cape Fear and Deep River Development*. Raleigh: North Carolina Public Document, 1856-1857.

Helper, Hinton Rowan, *The Impending Crisis of the South: How to Meet It*. New York: A. B. Burdick, 1859.

Hilton, William, *A Relation of a Discovery*. London: Printed by F. C. for Simon Miller, 1664.

Howell, Andrew Jackson, *The Book of Wilmington*. Wilmington: Privately printed, 1930.

Johnson, Guion G., *Ante-Bellum North Carolina: A Social History:* Chapel Hill: University of North Carolina Press, 1937.

Kerr, W. C., *Report of the Geological Survey of North Carolina*. Raleigh: Josiah Turner, State Printer, 1870.

King, Capt. Joseph E., U. S. Army (Ret.), *The Fort Fisher Campaign*. U. S. Naval Institute Proceedings, August 1951.

Lamb, William, *Defense of Fort Fisher, North Carolina*. Boston: Military Historical Society of Massachusetts Papers, 1912.

Lawson, John, *History of Carolina*. London: 1714.

Lee, Enoch Lawrence, Jr., *Old Brunswick: The Story of a Colonial Town*. Raleigh: North Carolina Historical Review Vol. XXIX, 1952.

────── *Lower Cape Fear in Colonial Days*. Chapel Hill: University of North Carolina Press, 1965.

Lefler, Hugh Talmage, *A Guide to the Study and Reading of North Carolina History*. Chapel Hill: University of North Carolina Press, 1935.

────── *Hinton Rowan Helper, Advocate of a "White America."* Charlottesville: The Historical Publishing Co., Inc., 1935.

────── (ed.) *History Told By Contemporaries*. Chapel Hill: University of North Carolina Press, 1948.

Lefler, Hugh Talmage and Albert Ray Newsome, *North Carolina: The History of a Southern State*. Chapel Hill: University of North Carolina Press, 1954.

Meyer, Duane, *The Highland Scots of North Carolina 1732-1776*. Chapel Hill: University of North Carolina Press, 1961.

Moore, Louis T., *Stories Old and New of the Cape Fear Region.* Wilmington: Privately published, 1956.

Murphey, Archibald Debow, *The Papers of Archibald Debow Murphey.* 2 vols. Edited by William Henry Hoyt. Raleigh: E. M. Uzzell & Co., State Printers, 1914.

*North Carolina Guide,* edited by Blackwell P. Robinson. Chapel Hill: University of North Carolina Press, 1955.

Oates, John A., *The Story of Fayetteville and the Upper Cape Fear.* Charlotte: The Dowd Press, Inc., 1950.

Olmsted, Frederick Law, *A Journey in the Seaboard Slave States, in the years 1853-1854.* New York: Dix & Edwards, 1856.

*Piedmont Industrial Crescent Studies.* Reports of the University of North Carolina Institute for Research in Social Science. New York: John Wiley & Sons, 1962.

Powell, William S., *The Proprietors of North Carolina.* Raleigh: The North Carolina Charter Tercentenary Commission, 1963.

Prouty, W. F., *Carolina Bays and Their Origin.* New York: Bulletin of the Geological Society of America. Vol. 63, 1953.

Raper, C. L., *Why North Carolina at First Refused to Ratify the Federal Constitution.* American Historical Association Annual Report, 1895.

*Report of the President and Directors of the Fayetteville and Western Plank Road Company.* Raleigh: North Carolina Legislature Documents, 1850.

Rulfs, Donald J., *The Professional Theatre in Wilmington, 1858-1930.* North Carolina Historical Review Vol. XXVIII, 1951.

Sitterton, J. C., *The Secession Movement of North Carolina.* James Sprunt Historical Papers, Vol. XXIII, 1939.

——— *Derelicts.* Baltimore: The Lord Baltimore Press, 1920.

——— *Tales and Traditions of the Lower Cape Fear, 1661-1896.* Wilmington: Le Gwyn Brothers, Printing, 1896.

Sprunt, James Laurence, *The Story of Orton Plantation.* Wilmington: 1958.

Starling, Robert B., *The Plank Road Movement in North Carolina.* Raleigh: North Carolina Historical Review, Vol. XVI, 1939.

Stinson, Mrs. Elizabeth Tillinghast, *Taking of the Arsenal* (in *War Days in Fayetteville*). Fayetteville: J.E.B. Stuart Chapter, United Daughters of the Confederacy, 1910.

Trevelyan, G. M., *A Shortened History of England.* London: Pelican Books, 1960.

Vernon, Charlie (pseud. Braxton Craven), *Naomi Wise.* Greensboro: Greensboro *Patriot,* April 1874.

Waddell, Alfred Moore, *A History of New Hanover County and the Lower Cape Fear Region, 1723-1800.* Wilmington: Privately printed, 1909.

*Water Resources of North Carolina, Cape Fear River Basin.* Raleigh: North Carolina Department of Conservation and Development, 1958.

*The Way to Appomattox: Battles and Leaders of the Civil War.* Vol. IV. Edited by Robert Underwood Johnson and Clarence Clough Buel. London and New York: Thomas Yoseloff, 1956.

Waynick, Capus, *North Carolina Roads and Their Builders.* Raleigh: Superior Stone Company, 1952.

Weeks, Stephen Beauregard, *Church and State in North Carolina.* Baltimore: Johns Hopkins University Studies, 1893.

—— *The Religious Development in the Province of North Carolina.* Baltimore: Johns Hopkins University Studies, 1892.

—— *Southern Quakers and Slavery.* Baltimore: Johns Hopkins University Studies, 1896.

Wheeler, John Hill, *Historical Sketches of North Carolina from 1584 to 1851.* Philadelphia: Lippincott, Grambo and Co., 1851.

Worth, Mrs. Josephine Bryan, *Sherman's Raid* (in *War Days in Fayetteville*). Fayetteville: J.E.B. Stuart Chapter, United Daughters of the Confederacy, 1910.

LETTERS

General Sir William Howe, letter of April 25, 1776, *A Narrative of the Proceedings of a Body of Loyalists in North Carolina.* English Records, 1776. Raleigh: Manuscript in Department of Archives and History.

Janet Smith, letter to Jane Robeson of Bladen County, dated: *Where Home Used To Be.* Averasboro, April 12, 1865.

# Index

Monroe, Charles, 256
Monroe's Crossroads, Battle of, 257, 259
Moore, George, 66
Moore, James, 21
Moore, James, Jr., 22, 25, 66
Moore, James (son of Maurice), 32, 101, 106, 107, 121
Moore, Maurice, 23, 25, 26, 30, 32, 66, 69, 77, 99
Moore, Nathaniel, 25
Moore, Reverend Joseph, 175
Moore, Roger ("King"), 30, 32, 68, 200, 202
Moore family, 21, 25, 31, 37, 201
Moravian settlement, 58, 60, 61, 82, 83, 162, 164
Morehead, Governor John M., 197, 213
Morgan, Dan, 138, 140
Morton, Hugh, 306
Moseley, Edward, 25, 31, 36, 57, 67
Munn, Captain Daniel, 227
Murphey, Archibald Debow, 180, 185, 186, 187
    Death, 284
    Interest in education, 186, 284
    Report on transportation, 179, 182, 291
Murray, James, 30
*My Imprisonment,* 235

Naomi Falls, 283
Naomi Falls Company, 284
*Narrative,* 152
Nation, Christopher, 88
Naval forces, 176
Naval stores, 4, 26, 29, 39, 65, 304
Navy, Confederate, 224, 229, 233, 245, 308
Navy, Union. *See* Blockade-running: Fort Fisher
Negroes, 200
    Education, 212, 213
    Integration, 205, 206
    Treatment of, 212
    Troops, 243

*See also* Charles, John; Evans, Henry; Chavis, John
Neill's Creek, 50
Neuse River, 22, 35
New Bern, 77, 130
    Governor's mansion, 77, 83, 84
    Indian massacre, 22
    Threatened by Regulators, 92
New Hanover County, 75, 118, 160
New Hope Chapel, 170
New Hope Lake, 293
New Inlet, 44, 160
New Liverpool, 38
New Providence Island, 23
New Salem Steam Mill and Tannery Company, 284
New Town, 38
Newspapers
    Daily Journal, 308
    Fayetteville Observer, 193, 260
    Greensboro Patriot, 281
    Journal, 223
    N.C. Gazette, 71
    North Carolinian, 192
    Tarboro Southerner, 193
Newton, 38, 39, 49
*Night Hawk,* 234, 235
Nonimportation Act, 106
*North Carolina,* U.S.S., 305
North Carolina Academy of Science and Wildlife Preserves, 315
North Carolina Railroad, 198
Nutbush congregation, 206

Oakland, 163
Ocracoke Inlet, 25, 176
O'Daniell, John, 146
Old Town Creek, 13, 66, 273
Olmstead, Frederick Law, 200, 214, 296
Onslow County, 177
Orange County, 63, 80, 84, 86, 88, 123, 146, 166, 179, 290
Orton (plantation), 32, 34, 132, 310
Owen, Governor John, 212

DATE DUE